T0129378

# UNDERSTANDING CHINA: DANGEROUS RESENTMENTS

*George Du Bois, Ph.D.*

Order this book online at www.trafford.com
or email orders@trafford.com

Most Trafford titles are also available at major online book retailers.



Printed in the United States of America.

ISBN: 978-1-4907-4505-3 (sc)
ISBN: 978-1-4907-4507-7 (hc)
ISBN: 978-1-4907-4506-0 (e)

Library of Congress Control Number: 2014915059



*Trafford rev. 10/14/2014*

www.trafford.com
**North America & international**
toll-free: 1 888 232 4444 (USA & Canada)
fax: 812 355 4082

*For*

*My three Graces,*

*Daniele, Christine, and Valerie*

*and for*

*Dorothy Bonett, Dick Long & Allan Joseph*

Courtesy of the University of Texas Libraries,
The University of Texas at Austin.

*Contents*

# *Note on Pronunciation of Chinese names*

Pronouncing Chinese names looks more formidable than it is. This brief guide to vowels and to those consonants pronounced differently from English should help.

| Vowels | Consonants |
|---|---|
| a as in f*a*ther | c as in i*ts* |
| e as in *uh* | x as in *sh*ow |
| ei as in s*ay* | zh as in *J*ane |
| i as in s*ee* | |
| o as in l*aw* | |
| u as in t*oo* | |

Of all the names in the book, Cixi is the one that looks most different from the way it is pronounced. Try it now. The rest with very little practice should be easy.

# *Acknowledgments*

I am grateful to many people who helped this book reach its final form. Barbara Center and, especially Dorothy Bonett, both life-long China scholars, made helpful suggestions concerning the chapters dealing with China before the 20th century. Dr. George H. Callcott, Professor of History and former Vice-Chancellor of the University of Maryland for Academic Affairs, read the entire manuscript, suggested the title, and made helpful suggestions concerning the organization of the book. Dr. Richard Long, a retired State Department official, was most helpful in our many lunches to discuss such matters as power transition theory and current events in the South China and East China Seas. Dr. Jack Fritz, a retired World Bank official, read the entire manuscript and made helpful suggestions. Allan Joseph, a businessman who has traveled to and resided in China and who teaches a course on modern China, made many helpful suggestions on the politics of the two republics of China–Nationalist and Communist. Allen Dean, who was concerned with China at the Central Intelligence Agency, provided his insight. Dr. John Hewetson and Dr. Fred Spahr read the manuscript to point out statements that needed further clarification and offered suggestions on writing style. My wife Daniele Sureau Du Bois edited the entire manuscript, suggested the subtitle of the book, and made suggestions for the book cover. My anthropologist daughter Dr. Christine M. Du Bois was particularly helpful in clarifying my thoughts and in offering excellent advice whenever I had a question concerning content or style. Robby Hamilton supplied on-site photos. I wish to thank the Agnes and Sophie Dallas Irwin Memorial Fund for their generous grant many years ago to sustain me in my long period of research. I am also indebted to the many scholars whose books I have studied over the years.

# 1. China Awakens

In the early 19th century when China was still admired by intellectuals in the West, Napoleon remarked, "China is a sleeping giant. Let it sleep, for when it awakens, it will astonish the world." That moment has finally arrived, and the nations of the West are not sure whether China is ultimately a friend or a foe.

Answering that question must take into account both China's past unhappy relations with the West (*resentments*) and some aspects of its brilliant 2,000-year-old Confucian culture (*lingering heritage.*) Without such considerations, any analysis of future relations looks essentially at the future as mere questions of economic tensions, military power and hegemonic ambitions.

Understanding China's *resentments* requires an examination of two factors that together (the "Western Impact") make that nation's relations with the West unique: 1) the distinctive mistreatment of China by Western nations beginning in the 19th century and 2) the consequent quasi-destruction of a remarkable civilization developed over 4,000 years. Both contribute to China's psychological sense of grievance.

The most egregious example of Western mistreatment is Britain's attack on China in 1842 to force it to permit unlimited importation of opium, reaching the astounding cumulative total of 800,000,000 pounds by 1899. In that period, China experienced a full share of the negative aspects of colonialism but none of the positive ones. The contrast with India is instructive. In India, the British took control of the country and exploited it. In China, no one took control, but the Western nations individually extorted concessions from the Chinese by treaty, and thanks to most favored nation clauses, whatever one nation extorted from the hapless Chinese redounded to the benefit of all.

Both India and China suffered exploitation, but only India *gained* some benefits. When the British departed from India, they left behind, for instance, a well-trained modern civil service and an extensive railway system. No Western nation trained Chinese civil servants, and none built a large railroad system. On balance it was probably more advantageous to be an outright colony than to retain a powerless national independence. The abuse that China experienced in the 19$^{th}$ century still rankles the proud Chinese.

Although many historians capably describe the Western mistreatment of China, they hardly mention the *resentment* some Chinese feel from the quasi-destruction of a culture that had stood at the forefront of world civilization for millennia. (The term "quasi" is used deliberately. Those aspects of the culture not destroyed by the Western Impact are the *lingering heritage* that statesmen today should also take into account in analyzing China–to which we turn three paragraphs below.)

Chinese civilization had usually been in the vanguard of world civilization for over 2,000 years–the richest, most populous of civilizations. Statesmen today need an understanding of the nature of that civilization, significantly dismantled by Western arms and the introduction of culture more appropriate to a modern society than to a traditional agricultural society like China. Western political creeds, education, science, mathematics and industrialism rendered China's own way of life obsolete. Here the contrast with Islamic civilization is instructive. The Islamic Golden Age of advances in philosophy, science, art, and architecture ended with the Mongol conquest of Baghdad hundreds of years before Islamic lands suffered Western exploitation. The West did not cause the decline of Islamic civilization. The West was, by contrast, *a major cause of the rapid decline* of Chinese civilization from power and splendor to impotence and derision.

Both Western exploitation and cultural destruction reverberate, consciously and unconsciously, in the Chinese psyche today and are likely to influence future decisions of Chinese leaders. China suffered a compound fracture. In this respect, it is unique in the present world. The West should be very careful not to aggravate those feelings of resentment. Welcoming China into a significant role in peace-keeping in the modern world is likely to prove more rewarding than viewing China as a potential threat. China's reaching great power status is now inevitable.

In addition, some aspects of China's brilliant civilization–the *lingering heritage*–may also play a role in the decisions of China's leaders. An evaluation of China's political stance, for example, should take into account China's long tradition of authoritarian government. Democracy has essentially *never* existed in China; yet China was long perhaps the most sophisticated of civilized nations. China's great contribution to political theory, the doctrine of the Mandate of Heaven, the first theory of justifiable revolution against tyranny, serves today as a warning to China's leaders that present rampant corruption threatens the regime. Thus, the lingering heritage serves as a backdrop to contemporary anti-corruption campaigns.

Lingering heritage affects the economy as well. An evaluation of the future nature of China's economy should recognize that after thousands of years of experience with government monopolies, particularly in the salt and iron industries, there is little likelihood that China will develop a totally market economy. An evaluation of China's future financial strength should also take into account the traditional reliance on family for one's security in old age. China has already taken modest steps to liberalize its one-child policy, allowing the creation of families of larger size. Such an event could lift a significant financial burden from the government in the future if the next generation of elderly can count on larger families, nuclear and extended, to support them.

An evaluation of China's traditional attitudes toward other countries should also help inform policy makers as to prospects of war between China and the United States. China has not aggressively annexed territory for the last 1,500 years without ostensibly legitimate reasons.

The themes of China's resentments and lingering heritage appear throughout this account, though to differing degrees in different parts of the book.

The **first part** of the book surveys the first 4,000 years of Chinese history (2070 B.C.E. to 1911 C.E.), elucidating China's extraordinary heritage. Knowledge of China's civilization, especially the last 2,000 years, is important today to statesmen and businessmen, for many features of and attitudes derived from that civilization endure and potentially influence the actions and attitudes of China's leaders and people today. Many aspects of culture are slow to change.

The **second part** of the book examines China's sad history during the 19$^{th}$ century C.E., when the leaders of China adamantly refused to jettison their culture and adopt a majority of Western ways. This section thus explores the historical reasons for Chinese resentments. Why, after all, should the Chinese change their civilization in order to imitate ruthless men whom they considered "sea devils?" The splendor and cultural brilliance of Chinese culture had radiated like a bonfire throughout East Asia and deeply influenced Korea and Japan. Here the contrast with Japan is instructive. China, the *propagator* of culture in East Asia, resisted all but minimal changes to its culture in the 19th century. Japan had been a frequent borrower of culture (from China) including the written script, the tea ceremony, Chinese architecture, and Zen Buddhism. Well aware of the advantages of cultural borrowings, the Japanese set out to adopt Western ways with a speed and enthusiasm unmatched in history while China stood still. As a result, China experienced stagnation and then chaos, whereas Japan developed a powerful economy.

China's civilization was such that most of its previous conquerors astonishingly had adopted Chinese culture in preference to their own. History was not to repeat itself. In its encounters with the West, China was confronted for the first time in the 19th century C.E. with a culture more dynamic than its own. Finally, even the conservatives realized–but too late–that substantial change was necessary.

The **third part** of the book ties the themes of lingering heritage and resentment together. It starts with an examination of the years from 1911 to 1976 when China experienced revolution, political chaos, civil war among warlords, civil war between Nationalists and Communists, invasion by Japan, and ill-advised policies under Mao Zedong. It then examines the three decades of extraordinary economic growth under Deng Xiaoping and his successors in a tacit alliance with the United States. It closes with an examination of the most recent few years when China and the United States have each taken actions creating a degree of mutual distrust and making war between these powerful nations a possibility. American policy makers need to understand that a muscular approach to China will not work. It can only initiate a spiral of confrontations and military spending that increases the prospects of an unnecessary war.

# 2. Ancient China

## (ca. 2070 to 206 B.C.E.)

The most striking facts about Chinese civilization are its long duration and its cultural brilliance. Though historians long doubted Chinese accounts about events prior to the 11th century B.C.E., archaeologists in the 20th century C.E. proved that much in these accounts must be considered historical. The dawn of Chinese civilization has receded some 1000 years to the 21st century B.C.E.

### A. The Legendary Emperors

Many of the emperors of China's high antiquity may be recognized, not as actual rulers but as stages of development of the Chinese people. Such is the case with Fu Xi, reputed to have taught the "black-haired people" to live in houses, fish with nets, keep domestic animals, and live in family groups. His illustrious successor Shennong is supposed to have taught the Chinese the art of farming. Still a third legendary emperor, Huangdi, also known as the "Yellow Emperor," is alleged to have established a single government, invented bricks, and built roads; his wife's great achievement was teaching the Chinese how to raise silkworms.

In these legends a progressive increase in the level of civilization is discernible. Some of the succeeding legendary emperors, though, acted much more like actual rulers and may have been historical persons. Foremost among them were Yao, Shun and Yu, who gave the Chinese people eras of peace, prosperity and good government. Yao rejected his own son as his successor in favor of Shun, whom he chose because of his moral qualities–the first instance in Chinese history of virtue as a necessary characteristic of a legitimate ruler. Yao's choice was wise, for Shun's was a model of benevolent government. Yu, in particular, is beloved of the Chinese. He labored ceaselessly for 13 years to prevent the floods that periodically ravaged China and founded the Xia dynasty, the first of China's great ruling families, when the people urged that his son succeed him.

The importance of Yao, Shun and Yu depends not upon whether they were actual historical personalities but rather on the fact that their examples partially shaped the ideal of a ruler's conduct for some 2,500 years. In the 5th century B.C.E., Confucius, greatest of all Chinese philosophers, held up these three sovereigns as models for the Chinese to emulate. Living in a troubled era of constant warfare, he urged his countrymen to return to the peaceful ways of these rulers. Thus, characteristically, the Chinese looked to the past for a golden age, not to the future, as is the case with modern peoples.

## B. Pre-History

Archaeology has shown that after ca. 2070 B.C.E. peoples of a reasonably advanced culture inhabited China. Hundreds of sites in the Yellow River ("Huang He") valley disclose the existence of people who produced exquisite black, red or gray pottery. They lived in villages, kept dogs, pigs, sheep and cattle, buried their dead face down, used knives and sickles, and grew millet and eventually rice.

The pottery people practiced *intensive* agriculture farming small plots by hand rather than *extensive* agriculture by animal-drawn plough. They were gardeners rather than farmers. In intensive agriculture a high degree of cooperation is required within the family. Unless all members attempt to maximize the yield of each square foot of ground, there might not be enough food for the family's own needs, let alone a surplus to exchange for salt, cooking oil, tools, cloth, etc. A family that worked together survived; a family that quarreled or pursued individualistic goals risked impoverishment or starvation.

The traditional Chinese family system with all power concentrated in the oldest male was a consequence of the intensive agriculture practiced by the pottery people. It only awaited Confucius and his followers to give it a moral and political rationalization to serve as the most important factor in the longevity of China's brilliant civilization. The history of China would have been quite different had extensive farming of large areas by plow been adopted. In farming by hand, the Chinese committed themselves to many of the features of their civilization for the next 4,000 years. The plow, the *sine qua non* of extensive farming was invented in the early Middle East but did not reach China until the late-middle part of the Zhou dynasty, about 1,500 years after the dawn of Chinese civilization. By then, it was too late for plow cultivation to supplant the firmly established pattern of farming by hand. Fields were already miniscule Rare was the peasant whose acres were all of a single piece, and their size made extensive farming impractical.

The prehistoric "pottery peoples" of China were not as sophisticated as the Chinese people of later ages, but they were far from primitive. Their only severe handicaps were ignorance of the use of metal and lack of a system of writing. Archaeologists hypothesize the derivation of China's first dynasty, the Xia dynasty (roughly 2070 to 1550 B.C.E.), from the black pottery people.

No Xia texts exist, but archaeologists have excavated settlements with post-and-beam type palaces on platforms of stamped earth surrounded by the modest dwellings of the common people. The Xia made a great advance in the arts of civilization by learning the techniques of bronze casting. Bronze originated in the ancient Middle East and gradually radiated in all directions, arriving late in China by virtue of the long distance involved and the impenetrability of the mountain ranges to the south and deserts to the west of China. Bronze entered China from Siberia in the north, and it is for this reason above all that Chinese civilization originated in the central plain of China in the great Yellow River ("Huang He") valley.

The Xia used bronze for weapons and artifacts used in religious ceremonies, particularly ancestor worship, a practice initially limited to the royal family but which over the centuries all Chinese families adopted. The Confucianists would, a thousand and more years later, use this practice as one foundation upon which to build one of the most remarkably stable civilizations the world has ever seen. Ancestor worship also required the Chinese to look to the past for guidance.

## C. The Shang Dynasty (ca. 1550 to ca. 1045 B.C.E.)

With the Shang dynasty begins a more certain history of the Chinese people, for the Shang unlike the Xia had a fully developed written script, another great advance in the arts of civilization. In the last years of the 19th century C.E., peasants in the modern province of Henan began uncovering "oracle bones" as they tilled their fields. By the turn of the century scholars realized that these ancient bones were inscribed with the earliest known form of the Chinese script. Later excavations uncovered the great metropolis of Anyang, ancient capital of the Shang in the extreme north of present-day Henan province, and yielded over 100,000 of these bones, the shoulder blades of oxen and the plastrons (i.e. the underside of the shell) of a species of long-extinct turtle. A prodigious effort by scholars has succeeded in deciphering a large number of the inscribed characters.

Used to foretell the future, the bones were inscribed with questions relating to the weather, sickness, crops, the prospect of military success, etc. The officials in charge, who formed a semi-priesthood, heated the "oracle" bones with a redhot poker until they cracked. They then interpreted the cracks to obtain answers to the questions and often inscribed the answers on the bones. The characters used indicate that the Chinese script is indigenous to China and not an offshoot of some other hieroglyphic script like that of Egypt.

The Shang people were well acquainted with urban living. Their great capital of Anyang contained elaborate palaces, temples, mausoleums and houses, as well as the circular dwellings with a subterranean floor of the common folk. Building materials were mud bricks and wood (the most characteristic Chinese building material throughout history); true bricks and tile do not appear until later ages. The Shang mastered the techniques of weaving textiles and raised silkworms. Their jewels were of jade, and they carved marble. They used place-value in writing numbers, though the round symbol for zero was not invented until later in India. They invented the decimal system in use throughout the world today. They observed eclipses of the sun and moon and understood the difference between the solar and lunar years. Militarily, they used the crossbow and fought in armies composed of common soldiers on foot and nobles in bronze chariots. Armies of up to 5,000 men were not uncommon. Agriculturally, they cultivated wheat and barley in addition to the rice and millet of the pottery peoples. To the domestic animals previously known they added oxen and elephants. Commercially, they traded animals, furs, slaves, tin and copper (the components of bronze), and ivory over a wide area. They used the cowry shell as money. Craftsmen specialized in pottery, basket making, silk weaving, and the carving of bone, wood or stone. Artistically, they excelled in the production of bronzes. Their work in this medium was so strong that no succeeding age ever equaled it. To the connoisseur of Chinese bronzes, the work of the Shang is beyond comparison.

At Anyang the Shang king (the "Wang") was responsible for city government. Subordinate officials maintained public buildings, constructed irrigation systems in the surrounding countryside, and collected the tribute paid by rulers of lesser courts. The Wang presided over a federation of his own people and peoples on the periphery of his domain. The Wang owed protection to the peripheral peoples who paid him tribute; he was responsible for leading military campaigns against the ever-encroaching northern nomads. The peripheral peoples, in turn, owed duties to the Wang, particularly rallying to him in time of war and providing him with labor. The Wang was also responsible for determination of the calendar, a grave responsibility for rulers in almost all early agricultural societies since planting at the correct moment meant the difference between adequate food supplies and widespread famine.

The organization of Shang family life left its imprint on later ages of China until, like ancestor worship, it was eventually incorporated into Confucianism, one of the bonds that indissolubly welded the Chinese into a single people with a strong and enduring civilization. Patriarchal family organization, probably a continuation of Xia practice, existed in Shang times with all power concentrated in the father. It only awaited Confucius to give this organization an ethical rationalization to make it an enduring feature of society as well as government for thousands of years.

In religion, the people of the Shang era recognized Shangdi ("the Ruler Above"), a personalized deity with whom the Wang interceded on behalf of the people. Of lesser importance were a whole host of animistic deities, such as the gods of the earth, the rivers, and the sky. In later ages Shangdi became depersonalized and replaced by Tian, an impersonal "Heaven." The lesser gods, however, continued in the full affection of the people and eventually became important in Daoism.

After the Shang had ruled almost 500 years, nomadic incursions in the west caused the Zhou people, a semi-civilized people of the western borderlands, and others on the periphery to conclude that the Wang was failing to protect them. Several groups gradually coalesced into an alliance and overthrew the Shang. The conduct of Shang Zhou, last of the Shang kings, was held up in future ages for the edification of rulers on how to lose the throne. According to the Chinese accounts, he was one of the most cruel and debauched emperors in Chinese history. On one occasion he banqueted beside a wine-filled pool while naked youths and girls pursued each other among the trees. He cut out the heart of his uncle in anger and compelled his enemies to walk a greased pole over a fiery pit. Shang Zhou's greatest mistake was to imprison the ruler of the Zhou tribe, the Duke of the West. Ransomed by his people, the Duke prepared for war. His death transferred the burden of revenge to his son, Wu Wang, who defeated the tyrant's armies. Shang Zhou fled to his palace where he committed suicide, and Wu Wang founded the next great Chinese dynasty, the Zhou.

The conquest of the Shang by the Zhou witnesses an early enunciation of the doctrine of the Mandate of Heaven. According to the *Book of History*, a compilation in later times of ancient documents, Wu Wang, in addressing his troops prior to final victory, asserted that Shang Zhou by his misdeeds had lost the favor of Heaven and that he, Wu Wang, had been selected as the new ruler of the black-haired people.

The Mandate of Heaven, stressed by the Confucian philosopher Mencius, stamped Chinese political theory with a moral character. An immoral ruler had no legitimate power. It is the first doctrine of justifiable revolution in world history; not until many, many centuries later can one find such a theory in any other civilization. Heaven expressed its withdrawal of the Mandate in the event of misrule by such natural phenomena as droughts and floods. The people then had the right to rebel and depose the unjust ruler. He who succeeded militarily in establishing a new dynasty was viewed as the new recipient of Heaven's favor and was subject to the same obligation to exercise his power benevolently in the interests of the people.[1] Rebellions were usually far-flung and saw struggles among various leaders of the revolt until one emerged triumphant and established a new dynasty that *from its inception was considered legitimate.* Might made right, and China then experienced a long period of peace.

No dynasty that seized power under the Mandate ever attempted to repudiate it. Aside from the fact that the emperors were as much influenced by the doctrines of Confucianism as any of their subjects, the new ruling house could not renounce it without admitting that its own rule had no foundation other than naked military force. Each dynasty continued to admit the possibility that another champion of the people might some day legitimately overthrow it. One task undertaken by new dynasties was to write the history of their predecessors, one of the motives being to show that the former dynasty had indeed abused its power. The doctrine of the Mandate of Heaven contributed to the huge wealth of documents that permits far more knowledge of the Chinese past than that of other ancient civilizations, the histories of which often depend upon the informed guesses of archeologists.

A brief comparison of the doctrine of the Mandate of Heaven with the superficially similar Western doctrine of the Divine Right of Kings, advocated by such rulers as the early Stuart monarchs of England, highlights the "modernity" of this ancient Chinese political theory. Under the Western doctrine, as under the Chinese, the ruler supposedly received his authority from Heaven. Unlike the more liberal Chinese doctrine, however, the theory of the Divine Right of Kings envisaged no possibility that the right to rule might legitimately pass from one dynasty to another in the event of

---

[1] As Mencius said, "The people are the most important element in a nation...the sovereign is the lightest."James Legge The Mencius, Book 7, Part 2, Chapter 14, No.1.

misrule. The Western doctrine placed the ruler above the people in importance; the Chinese doctrine subordinated him.

The loss of the Mandate by the Shang is also an early instance of the so-called dynastic cycle–periodic changes of ruling houses. The founders of dynasties, the successful competitor among several engaged in a general rebellion, were usually men with the force of personality and wisdom necessary to establish their own rule firmly. They corrected the abuses of the preceding dynasty, often redistributed land, and usually ushered in periods of vigorous, good government. As the rulership descended hereditarily, though, sooner or later emperors preferred the delights of their harems to the exercise of government, or they were young children and allowed power to fall into the hands of palace eunuchs, the military, great families, or their own relatives, many of whom sought maximum self-enrichment in the shortest possible time. One explanation of the dynastic cycle is the progressive withdrawal from taxation of land owned by the families of those who had obtained influence. Toward the end of a dynasty the burden of taxation fell more and more heavily upon the peasantry until, triggered by famine, widespread rebellion occurred.

Other aspects of the doctrine of the Mandate of Heaven bear mention. First, since the doctrine justified successful revolution, to it belongs a fair share of the blood shed in numerous revolts, particularly those of China's secret societies–the colorfully named but deadly serious secret societies–the Yellow Turbans, Eight Trigrams, White Lilies, White Clouds, Little Daggers, Heaven and Earth Society, Complete Truth Society, Elder Brothers and numerous others active at the close of dynastic cycles. Second, the successful competitor in the struggle for succession could consolidate his control with relative ease since success brought acceptance of his rule by the people. Third, since retention of the Mandate depended upon benevolent rule and moral example, it behooved the emperor to surround himself with scholars who had devoted their lives to studying Confucianism. Fourth, the doctrine helped maintain the social preeminence of Confucian scholars from dynasty to dynasty. Fifth, the doctrine was instrumental in establishing and preserving the unity of China. Since Heaven ruled over all lands, it followed as a corollary that there was but a single Mandate and that the ruler of China was in theory the ruler of the entire civilized world. Finally, the leaders of today's Chinese Communist Party still face the cultural memory of the doctrine of the Mandate of Heaven, especially in dealing with present widespread corruption by Party officials.

After 500 years of Shang rule in the central plain of China, and with the Zhou, semi-barbarians who presided, actually or nominally, over one of the most confusing, chaotic and productive eras in Chinese history, China moved on to its longest and perhaps its most important age.

## D. The Zhou Dynasty (1045 to 221 B.C.E.)

Having defeated the Shang, Wu Wang sought to reward family members and military leaders who had contributed to his success. He divided the central plain of China into fiefs and distributed them to his followers. Magnanimously, he included the defeated Shang among the recipients of his favor and assigned them an important fief where they ruled as subordinate members of Chinese feudal society.

## 1. Chinese Feudalism

The Chinese feudal system resembled the feudalism that existed almost 2,000 years later in the West and based society on personal rights and duties between officials of greater and lesser importance. Below the Wang were five grades of nobility roughly equivalent to the Western ranks of duke, marquis, count, viscount and baron. Each noble in the feudal hierarchy had duties to his superior. Among them were duties to pay tribute, usually in kind (gifts of wheat, cloth, etc. passed upward from rank to rank), to provide military service, to reside periodically at the superior's court, and through elaborate rituals to pay homage to the latter. In return each member of the hierarchy had duties to his inferiors. The Wang, for instance, owed his nobles military protection by leading them in battle, justice in the event of disputes among them, and enjoyment of their lands by solemn ceremonies of investiture. The principal difference between Western and Chinese feudalism was that in China family relationships often competed with feudal relationships.

Below the nobles were the peasants. According to ancient Chinese documents, land tenure was based on the "well-field" system which divided land into nine equal parts according to the following diagram: #. Eight peasant families participated in each "well-field" cultivating the interior plot for the lord and the exterior plots for themselves. Additionally, they supplied the lord with corvée labor on roads, walls, etc. To the peasants, the nobility in return gave military protection and provided justice through their courts. Historical information about peasants comes from the ancient *Classic of Poetry*, a collection of 305 poems and songs.

## 2. The Rise of Independent States

Some of the early Zhou emperors are credited with outstanding achievements, as, for instance, the Emperor Mu (1001 to 946 B.C.E.), the first Chinese ruler to invade the Yangzi (formerly "Yangtze") region and, to introduce civilization into that great river valley. From Mu's initiative, eventually by the Tang era, some 1,700 years later, the Yangzi valley would wrest primary importance away from the Yellow River ("Huang He") valley.

The expansion of their territory by the early Zhou emperors to about four times the size of that of the Shang contributed to the dynasty's downfall. Given greater distances and the difficulty of communication, the Zhou were unable to maintain control over their vassals. Gradually the holders of fiefs began to pass them on as an inheritance to their sons. They reduced the tribute paid as taxes to the Zhou. They also began to use the title of Wang within their territories and to adopt royal rituals.

Last of the effective Zhou rulers was You Wang. Enamored of a court beauty, You murdered his queen and disinherited his son. On one occasion, to amuse his demanding mistress, he foolishly lit the beacon fires used to summon the nobility to battle. Like the little boy who cried "wolf," You later found to his chagrin that this act was a grievous error. A discontented noble formed an alliance with the Qin people, occupied Chang'an, the Zhou capital located near the present-day city of Xi'an, and put You to death. No one came when the beacon fires were lit.

The Zhou in 771 B.C.E. moved their capital far to the east to the city of Luoyang, an area safer from barbarian incursion. The Zhou lost what little remaining control they had over the nobility, and for three centuries China slowly fragmented into about 250 independent states whose rulers used the title of Wang within their domains. Some of these Wangs gradually became subordinate to various Ba Wangs or hegemons, an intermediate layer of authority in the complicated political structures of the era. No Ba Wangs ever claimed the title of Emperor, though, and the Zhou in their new capital continued to occupy a figurehead position for about 500 years. They served principally a religious function in making sacrifices on behalf of the people as a whole; rarely were they active in the political arena, though upon occasion they were asked to determine the legitimate heir to one or another of the now-independent fiefs. The continuance of the fiction that the Zhou ruled China for the ensuing five centuries is worthy of note. The ideal of the unity of the Chinese people was already firmly established in the Zhou era.

## 3. The Decline of Feudalism

Two factors appear to have played an important role in he gradual decline of feudalism in China during the middle and late Zhou periods: 1) changes in land tenure due to the development of a money economy and additional land reclamation and 2) the introduction of iron.

The system of feudal land tenure with its incidental rights and duties up and down the social scale constitutes a distinctive politico-economic system. Relationships in a feudal society are quite restricted. One's political and economic relationships are only with those who have an interest, superior or inferior, in the same particular piece of land.

During this era coins came into general use and, by reason of the greater flexibility of money in permitting broader economic relationships, nobles began to demand a rental payment in coin for the use of their land instead of the feudal payments of labor and crops. As money payments replaced feudal payments, all the other rights and duties of the feudal system slowly disappeared. The noble class, which controlled the destinies of Ancient China over many centuries, transformed itself into the landlord class that played a major role in Chinese society into the 20th century C.E.

The Chinese also brought new land into production by extensive irrigation and the drainage of marsh areas. Much of this reclaimed land was never subject to feudal obligations. The total percentage of land held under feudal tenures continuously declined and, with it, the economic and political importance of the feudal system itself.

A second reason for the decline of feudalism was the transformation of Ancient China from a bronze-age society into an iron-age society. The introduction of ironworking techniques is believed to have occurred in the 6th century B.C.E. The use of iron gave greater military power to those states that possessed the technical secrets of extraction, casting, etc.

Superimposed upon an already moribund feudalism, the Iron Age led to the final destruction of social stability. War became the order of the day among all states, and the rulers of the separate kingdoms embarked on a course leading to their annihilation.

The most enduring innovation of the Zhou period was the creation of a new social/political class. The proliferation of independent states required a great increase in the number of literate advisers to local rulers. They were in great demand and could shift easily from service to one ruler to that of another. These scholars achieved a degree of independence that they would retain for over two millennia and at least an inchoate identification as a separate social class.

## 4. Political and Military Events of the Late Zhou Period

By the 5th century B.C.E., the process of fragmentation of the Zhou territory began to reverse itself. Vacant lands between the 250 or so independent states had filled up, border disputes were common, and ambitions for expansion led to the absorption of weaker states by stronger. By the late 4th century B.C.E. more powerful neighbors had absorbed all but a dozen states. Of these Qin in the west, under an ambitious dynasty, was the strongest, and in 333 B.C.E. six states under the leadership of their hegemon, the Ba Wang of Chu, challenged Qin. Despite the weight of numbers, Qin emerged triumphant. A western border state, Qin had achieved a degree of political and military efficiency previously unknown in China. The rulers of this aggressive state were the first to establish a substantial central bureaucracy, primarily for the purpose of constructing and administering the extensive irrigation systems critically needed in their parched western lands. Always militant, the Qin rulers were the first in China to organize armies, in which foot soldiers and cavalry predominated, a development that rendered obsolete the chariot armies of their opponents. Reluctant to permit a diffusion of power, the Qin moved to abolish feudalism by permitting the alienation of fiefs. In accordance with Legalist philosophy discussed below, they established an identity card system, maintained a police force, and punished even slight transgressions of law in a draconian manner.

A decisive moment, unrecognized at the time, came in 247 B.C.E. when Zheng established the Qin dynasty. Known as Qin

Shi Huangdi ("First Emperor"), the title he adopted when he had extended his realm to all China, this vigorous, energetic Legalist ruler is one of the most remarkable men in history. Reaching his maturity in the 230's B.C.E., he embarked on a swift and stunning career of conquest. His victories stamp him as one of the world's great conquerors. Han fell to his arms in 230 B.C.E.; Zhao in 228 B.C.E.; Qi in 226 B.C.E.; Wei in 225 B.C.E.; Chu, his most formidable opponent, in 223 B.C.E.; and Yan in 222 B.C.E. After six centuries of *de facto* division, despite the continuing nominal authority of the Zhou dynasty, China was reunited by his genius.

## 5. Cultural Advances

By the moment of the final triumph of the Qin, China had progressed far in civilization from the era of the Shang. Except in bronzes where the forms and designs of the Shang were superior to the endeavors of the Zhou, the Chinese advanced in all areas of civilization. Tools of the late Zhou included the iron plow (introduced from lands to the west), scythes, axes, and saws. Major agricultural inventions included rotary-fan winnowing machines and multi-tube seed drills, each used in China about 2,000 years before its use in the West. Invention of a breast-strap harness that allowed a horse to breathe while pulling led to greater agricultural production than could be achieved with oxen. The technique of cultivating crops in rows with intensive weeding in between also increased production many centuries before the technique was adopted in the West. Large-scale irrigation was initiated. New domestic animals included mules, donkeys, camels, and water buffalo. Chickens were raised, and advances were made in the production of fertilizer. Treatises on agriculture appeared.

Petroleum and natural gas were used as fuels some 2,300 years before their use in the West. The year was calculated to have 365 1/4 days. Blast furnaces produced cast iron over 1,000 years before its production in the West. Use of the piston was understood 1,900 years before it appeared in the West. Medically, circulation of the blood was discovered some 1,800 years before its discovery by the English physician William Harvey. The number of market places increased. Dwellings were often spacious with pleasant gardens. Walls and moats surrounded towns and there was a general increase in urbanization. Coins came into use. Additional characters were devised for the written script. A type of liquor was made from fermented millet. Chopsticks replaced use of the fingers in dining, and rhyme was used in poetry over ten centuries before its first use in Latin or Arabic. Periodic censuses were taken, and the dead were buried in coffins. Long sections of wall were built to keep nomadic raiders out of China, and the crossbow was perfected. A general from the state of Wu, Sun Wu, wrote *The Art of War*, the world's first treatise on warfare, a book that profoundly influenced Mao Zedong some 2,400 years later. Artistically, the era saw the invention of lacquer, an art for which the Japanese offshoot of Chinese civilization is now most noted.

The Zhou period is best remembered for the development by the inchoate scholar-official class of a wide variety of philosophic schools. All of them were intellectual attempts to chart a way out of the chaos of the "Period of the Warring States," the late Zhou period from the 6th to the 3rd centuries B.C.E. The story of Confucius's trip over the mountains is illustrative of the effects upon people of the military opportunism of the era. Leaving his native state of Lu because of strife there, Confucius met an old woman weeping by a grave in the mountains. To his inquiry about the cause of her grief, she replied that a tiger had killed her father, her husband and, now, her son. When Confucius asked why she didn't leave that dangerous place, she replied that there was no oppressive government there.

Drawing upon a common stock of ideas developing since the dawn of Chinese civilization. The so-called "Hundred Schools" of thought proposed solutions to the lack of harmony around them. The most significant were the Yin-Yang philosophers, the Moists, the Legalists, the Daoists and the Confucianists.

The period witnessed similar developments on a worldwide basis–Socrates, Plato and Aristotle in Athens, the Buddha in India, many Prophets in Israel, and Zoroaster in Persia.

Of all the Chinese philosophical concepts, one especially is symbolic of the problems of the time: Yin and Yang, the two forces of the universe. This subtle concept has been depicted graphically in one of the most expressive symbols in history:

The Chinese believed that the entire universe, not merely the physical universe perceptible to the senses but also the spiritual universe, consisted of Yin and Yang, each of which contained a small amount of the other. Yin was the principle of darkness, cold, wetness, softness, passivity, femininity, and the earth. Yang was the principle of brightness, heat, dryness, hardness, activity, masculinity, and the sun. Everything from the trees and rocks to the qualities of courage and obedience has one or another of various combinations of these two principles.

The two outstanding characteristics of Yin and Yang were mutual inequality and mutual reciprocity. Just as female was inferior to male in Chinese society, Yin was considered inherently unequal to Yang; yet, just as men and women cooperated with each other in the Chinese family system, Yin and Yang complemented each other in the universe. Yin combining with Yang, male with female, reciprocity with inequality; all occurred in such a way that the ultimate result was a pervading harmony in nature and in humans' social relations with each other. The Yin-Yang concept, although of earlier date than the Period of the Warring States, profoundly influenced Confucianism and Daoism, especially in its emphasis on harmony. The Period of the Warring States, however, when life was insecure and peace nonexistent represented a moment when the Yin and Yang of society were out of joint. The symbol is most often seen today on the flag of South Korea, a land strongly influenced by Chinese civilization.

Mozi, founder of the Mohist school in the 5$^{th}$ century B.C.E., like Confucius, was a native of the state of Lu, located to the east of present-day Beijing. He was the first of the world's philosophers or religious thinkers to give central prominence to the ethical doctrine of universal love. He believed in the existence of a Supreme Being with personal attributes, whose will it was that men should love each other just as Heaven loved men. While Mozi never carried his doctrine to the point of returning good for evil, of turning the other cheek, the similarity of his ethical message to that of Jesus, who preached 500 years later, is evident. Through universal love, Mozi sought to reestablish a harmony in which the large states would not attack small ones and the strong would not plunder the weak. That the principal criticism Mozi had to meet over and over again was the charge of impracticality indicates that the ancient Chinese, no less than their modern counterparts, were an intensely practical people. His followers formed an ascetic sect under strict military discipline; they defended small states invaded by more powerful neighbors. The sect disappeared soon after the Qin reunification of China.

In contrast to Mozi's faith in human good will, the Legalist school argued that to depend upon human good will for the harmony of society was an absurdity since history showed that little good will existed among humans. Legalism, associated with a thinker named Han Fei, advocated a stern system of laws and punishments. In a way reminiscent of the modern scientific concept of conditioned reflexes, the Legalists believed that men, if punished often and severely enough, would ultimately become peaceful and law-abiding and harsh penalties would no longer be necessary to maintain social harmony. Society was to be based on law and punishments, not on morality.

The theories of Legalism were put into practice in 221 B.C.E. by the state of Qin, most powerful of the states that vied for supremacy in the late Zhou period. Though Legalism influenced the administrative structure of future dynasties by creating an extensive bureaucracy, it came to an early end as a school of thought. The Chinese persisted afterwards in preferring a society based on ethics and human relationships rather than on the impersonal mechanism of law. Its demise is attributable to its excessive aggressiveness.

Of the thinkers associated with Daoism the best known is Laozi ("Old Master"), who lived from 604 to 517 B.C.E. Chinese sources tell us that his real name was Li ("plum"), that he was curator of the Royal Library of Zhou, and that he once gave rather patronizing advice to the young Confucius. Some modern scholars doubt that he ever existed. Be that as it may, writings attributed to him exist and have contributed to Chinese life over the centuries.

Daoism was the only one of the more important ancient schools that sought harmony outside a social context. It was the only school that co-existed with Confucianism down through the centuries. Confucianism was, above all, concerned with the relation of man to man; Daoism with the relation of man to nature. Fundamentally, the two surviving schools directed their attentions in opposite directions. Confucianism was the cornerstone of Chinese culture; Daoism was a doctrine to which one turned when not involved in the major events of life and which offered greater peace of mind and tranquility than the often severe, practical doctrines of the dominant Confucian creed.

Central to Daoism is the concept of the Dao, literally the "Way." The Dao was the way of nature and, by extension, the way of the wise man seeking to order his life in conformity to nature. Civilization was artifice, out of harmony with nature. Similarly, knowledge was worthless since it led to the complexity and quarrels of civilization. Daoism viewed the other schools of thought in China as useless in that they sought to reform society–an impossibility–and harmful in that they prevented men from returning to a life of primitive simplicity. The Daoist must spend his life in contemplation of the Dao. He must seek to influence others by his example and reject thought, which can lead only to arguments. Thought, knowledge, civilization: all useless. The Dao was not to be found in the things of man, only by bringing man into harmony with nature, of which man was but a part.

Paradoxically, Daoism was a doctrine of inaction in order to arrive at a goal–people living in "primitive simplicity." As Laozi said:

> . . . a sage has said, 'I will do nothing...and the people will be transformed of themselves; I will be fond of keeping still, and the people will of themselves become correct . . . .I will manifest no ambition, and the people will of themselves attain to the primitive simplicity.' [2]

The student of Western history will find some familiarity in the Daoist exaltation of nature. More than 2,000 years after Laozi, Jean-Jacques Rousseau advocated a return to living in rustic simplicity. Rousseau, however, never influenced Western thought or life to the same extent as Laozi and his famous disciple, Zhuangzi. Their view of the world permeated Chinese consciousness over centuries of time.

Confucianism ultimately became the most important of the ancient schools of philosophy. Of its founder, Kong Fuzi (Latinized to Confucius), Chinese history has much to say. He was born in Lu, one of the Warring States, in 551 B.C.E. After the death of his father, he worked after school to support his mother. He became skilled in archery and music in his youth. He married at the age of nineteen, had one son, who later became one of his disciples, and divorced at the age of twenty-three shortly after he began his career

[2] The Tao Teh King, James Legge (translator), Part 1, p.101

as a teacher. Despite his extreme physical ugliness, he attracted many students who became devoted to him. He spent a good part of his life travelling from one feudal court to another, unsuccessfully seeking a ruler who would put his ideas into practice (it is recorded, however, that he did serve briefly as Minister of Crime in his native state of Lu). He died at the age of seventy-three. Much of his thought descends to us through his disciples who collected his sayings into the *Lunyu* ("*Analects of Confucius*").

Confucius's most important follower was Meng Zi (Latinized to Mencius), who lived from approximately 372 to 289 B.C.E. Like Confucius, he lost his father at a young age. His mother has been proclaimed a model of motherhood for countless generations of Chinese. In her dedication to the proper development of her son's character, she changed residence three times. Initially, they lived near a cemetery. When his mother found that Mencius was imitating an undertaker, she moved. Unfortunately, there was a slaughterhouse near their new home, and the young Mencius began to mimic the cries of the animals as they were being slain. His mother moved again, this time to the vicinity of a marketplace, only to find that the boy was beginning to act like a merchant. Finally she chose a home near a school, and thereafter, Mencius devoted himself to scholarship. In his manhood, Mencius, faithful to the model of Confucius, traveled throughout China seeking a ruler who would give him high office and put his ideas into effect. In this quest he was even less successful than his master.

One of the most profoundly conservative thinkers in history, Confucius found his model for an orderly society in the past. *Confucius stamped Chinese intellectuals with what was to be perhaps their outstanding characteristics for the ensuing 2,500 years: judging the propriety of future action by reference to the precedents of the past.* That characteristic eventually became a restraint on any extension of the emperors' activities much beyond defense, the punishment of crime, and water control. Confucius's hierarchical philosophy with emphasis on the family, including the ancestors, also fit the needs of a land where the average farm was 10 acres or so. Confucius was a genius in matching a political and social structure to the underlying economy and buttressing it with a strong moral content. He gave China's civilization almost 2,000 years of relative stability at a high level of prosperity for an agricultural civilization.

Because Confucianism only became the framework of Chinese civilization in the Han dynasty a century and a half after Mencius's death, a more detailed analysis of Confucianism will be deferred to the next chapter. A deeper knowledge of the advanced civilization built upon Confucianism helps to understand the attitudes and rhetoric of China today.

Oracle Bones

Some of the 5,000 Terracotta Statues of Soldiers in Qin Shi Huangdi's Tomb near the city of Xian (Note the individualized facial features.)

Confucius

## E. The Qin Dynasty (221 to 206 B.C.E.)

Having established control over all the black-haired people, Qin Shi Huangdi attempted to remold Chinese society under Legalist concepts. Like that of other schools of philosophy, the Legalist aim was to bring order out of the chaos of the Period of the Warring States. The theory that obedience to laws should be rigorously exacted from the people until further compliance would be forthcoming without resort to force, however, carried its own death wound. The excesses of Qin rule soon brought rebellion and a general revulsion from Legalist theories, although some aspects of Legalism continued under future dynasties.

Upon seizing power, Shi Huangdi and his chief minister Li Si, who had been instrumental in the Qin triumph, undertook a series of enormous public works to protect the frontiers from nomads, particularly the Xiongnu, a Turkic tribe (?) later known in Roman history as the Huns (?), and to broaden the agricultural base of the empire. Chinese sources attribute to Shi Huangdi the construction of the irrigation system that renders a large part of the western province of Sichuan fertile to this day. He also improved the canal system throughout China. To keep the nomads at bay, he joined together smaller pre-existing walls on the northern frontier, creating the original Great Wall of China. Additionally, he built an extensive system of roads–lined with trees–of a width of "fifty paces." His standardization of axle widths, moreover, standardized the ruts in the roads of all regions and facilitated cross-border trade. Shi Huangdi accomplished all his public works in the mere 12 years that he occupied the imperial throne before his death in 209.

The Chinese consider Shi Huangdi a tyrant. His public works required onerous taxation. It is recorded that he received a tax amounting to "the greater half." Moreover, Shi Huangdi was no greater respecter of persons than pocket books. Estimates of peasant deaths from forced labor in building the original Great Wall of China have reached 1,000,000. Shi Huangdi also required mass exchanges of population from region to region to break down regional loyalties developed during the Zhou period, a policy that, like forced labor, did not endear him to his long-suffering subjects.

Nor did he satisfy himself with provoking the enmity of the defeated feudal nobility and the common people; his order, at the urging of Li Si, to burn the books of all the schools of thought that opposed Legalism earned Shi Huangdi the opposition of most of China's intellectuals and the opprobrium of history as the first of the great book burners. Since writing at that time was done vertically on thin bamboo strips tied together to form a "book," the literature was bulky and difficult to hide. Attempts to preserve the writings of other schools entailed considerable risk. Much of the literature, including the *Classic of Music*, was lost, and many of those who tried to hide writings were buried alive.

Finally, Shi Huangdi kindled popular resentment by the brutality and severity of punishments meted out to those who opposed his policies of heavy taxation, forced labor, forced migration and suppression of freedom. Common punishments included branding, having one's nose or feet cut off, being buried alive, and being torn apart by chariots. As a result, Legalism came into strong disfavor as a school of thought. The excesses of Shi Huangdi discredited that philosophy, and it perished with his dynasty. Upon Shi Huangdi's death in 210 B.C.E., his incompetent son lost his father's iron grip on the country. Within three years rebellion broke out and the Qin dynasty ended in 206 B.C.E., succeeded by one of China's most important and long-lived dynasties, the Han.

Shi Huangdi had many accomplishments balancing his excesses. He moved to abolish the remnants of a moribund feudalism by permitting the alienation of land holdings–a development opening the way for the Confucian society that succeeded the Qin. His construction of canals, roads, and the first version of the Great Wall improved China's defenses and infrastructure. His further conquests extended Chinese control to the far southeast coast for the first time. He established the central bureaucracy that was the nucleus of government thereafter, an aspect of Legalism that lingered for millennia.

Most importantly, Shi Huangdi succeeded in unifying China after the troubles of the Period of the Warring States. Thanks to his foresight, China remained a unitary state for more than two millennia afterwards. There are several mutually unintelligible Chinese *spoken* languages that today include Mandarin (over 800 million speakers), Yue (about 60 million around Guangzhou–formerly "Canton"), and Wu (about 77 million around Shanghai). Smaller separate language groups total over 200 million speakers. That the problems posed by China's mutually unintelligible spoken languages did not have the same consequences as linguistic differences in Europe–continual warfare between nations speaking different languages–is primarily attributable to Shi Huangdi's standardization of the Chinese written script, which proved a stronger force in unifying the country than the spoken languages in dividing it. A Mandarin speaker and a Yue speaker cannot converse but can read the same book, newspaper, or document, an important mutual intelligibility that has been a major factor in the stability of Chinese civilization for over 2,000 years.

Compared to the other strong men of history–Julius Caesar, Alexander the Great, Genghis Khan and Napoleon–Shi Huangdi in retrospect was the most important of them all. In terms of accomplishments enduring for millennia and affecting billions of people, Shi Huangdi was probably the most influential secular individual who ever lived.

# 3. *Imperial China*

# (206 B.C.E. to 960 C.E.)

The history of China after the fall of the Qin dynasty in some respects resembles that of previous centuries. Intensive agriculture, ancestor worship, the family system, and many ethical values of the feudal period provided continuity. Yet differences are significant, especially in the realm of central government.

## A. The Han Dynasty (202 B.C.E to 220 C.E.)

Of all the dynasties of Imperial China, the Han is perhaps the most important. Tentative beginnings were made in creating many of the institutions that still characterized China as late as the early 20th century.

### 1. The Early Han Emperors

The founder of the Han dynasty, Liu Bang, was a man of humble birth, fond of drink and pretty women. From a minor post under the Qin, Liu Bang turned bandit in the confusion following the collapse of that dynasty. Before long he made a bid to succeed Shi Huangdi as ruler of a unified empire. His principal opponent, the General Xiang Yu, was an aristocrat who sought to reinstitute feudalism. In five years of strife between the two, Xiang's troops won most of the pitched battles, but Liu, a master of politics, won the war. Xiang, cruel, arrogant, and quick-tempered, alienated the people; Liu, affable and good-natured, gained a reputation for clemency to his enemies. Desertions from Xiang's armies swelled Liu Bang's ranks and eventual victory was his. In establishing the Han dynasty, he took the title Emperor Gaozu.

The new emperor wisely realized that after the excesses of the Qin, the Chinese were weary. Eliminating the cruelties that had distinguished the reign of Shi Huangdi, he generally maintained the centralized authority forged by the Qin; but, to appease those who argued for a reestablishment of feudalism, he granted a limited number of fiefs to imperial relatives. Under his relaxed rule and that of his immediate successors, China gradually recovered its prosperity.

In the decades following the founding of the dynasty the only substantial problem faced by the Han emperors was occasional revolts of the imperial princes. Finally, to prevent a reemergence of a totally feudal society, the Emperor Jingdi, in the year 144 B.C.E., abolished primogeniture. With fiefs divided among the several sons of deceased imperial princes rather than inherited by the eldest, the number of fiefs increased rapidly but constantly shrank in size and importance. Historians of the latter part of the Han era rarely considered the fiefs worthy of mention.

## 2. Han Wudi

Jingdi's successor was the outstanding emperor of the Han, if not of the entire imperial era. Coming to the throne as an adolescent, Han Wudi reigned for 53 of the most significant years in Chinese history (140 to 87 B.C.E.)

The title "Wudi" means "military emperor" or "warlike emperor," and this dynamic individual fully justified his title. In the decades of peace under the early Han emperors China had recovered its strength, and Han Wudi reconquered south China, which had split off into independent kingdoms after the fall of the Qin. Under his rule China also invaded Korea for the first time. The Chinese protectorate established as far south as the present Korean capital of Seoul came to have over 300,000 Chinese colonists who eventually spread their culture to the mysterious islands of uncivilized Japan.

Han Wudi also sought to make China's borders secure by campaigns into the homelands of the nomads who periodically threatened China's northern and western flanks, particularly the Xiongnu. The Great Wall of China, unfortunately, offered only a partial protection from nomads to the north because of difficulty in maintaining armed garrisons at spaced intervals throughout its 1500-mile length. Without such garrisons the nomads would have had little trouble climbing the Wall. Seeking to further bolster China's defenses, Han Wudi also resorted to the age-old tactic of fending off an enemy by creating pressure on his flanks. One nomadic enemy of the Xiongnu, the Yuezhi tribe, had retreated westward after an unsuccessful struggle with the Xiongnu. Consequently, he dispatched Zhang Qian to locate the Yuezhi in the unknown lands to the west of China and to forge an alliance with them against the common enemy.

The discovery of the west by Han Wudi's envoy, Zhang Qian, is one of the most important chapters in the history of exploration. The mission promised little early success since the Xiongnu quickly captured Zhang Qian. Only after ten years did he manage to escape and pursue his mission. Finally, in the transCaspian region to the north and east of Persia far beyond the limits to which any Chinese had ever ventured before, Zhang Qian located the Yuezhi. From a military point of view the mission was a failure; settled beyond the reach of the Xiongnu, the Yuezhi firmly declined the alliance offered by the Chinese emperor. From the point of view of the historian, though, the mission was of great significance, for in his travels Zhang Qian reached outposts of Persia and ascertained that China was not alone in possession of a high degree of civilization.[3] Zhang Qian is considered a national hero in China today.

Yet, while Zhang Qian opened China to contacts with other civilizations, intercultural exchange remained limited. The only major foreign influence on China prior to the 19th century C.E. was Buddhism, which arrived in China from India some 200 years after Zhang Qian's journey.

The most important part of the story of China's contacts with other cultures, though, is not the intercourse that developed after the discoveries of that remarkable explorer but the centuries of isolation. Chinese history was almost half over before Zhang Qian's discovery. By the time foreign influences began to trickle into China, the pattern of its intensive agriculture was already of

---

[3] The most immediate influence on China of Zhang Qian's travels, according to Chinese sources, was the introduction of alfalfa and the cultivated grape, the first of a long series of new crops, including oranges, lemons, lychees, onions, broad beans, peas, lettuce, almonds, sugar beets and cane, figs, spinach, onions, and fast-maturing varieties of rice, that was to play a role in maintaining China as a stable, agricultural civilization

ancient date. The importance of family including deceased and unborn generations and the pervasive obligations of filial piety were already established. Confucianism with its strong moral content had already become the epicenter of Chinese political thought and structure. The Chinese were already far advanced in the technology of water control, irrigation, and agriculture. They knew how to produce steel and understood the circulation of the blood. China had little need of the ideas or technology of other lands.

The protection offered by China's frontiers against the unsettling effects of foreign influence–the Himalayas, the Gobi desert, and the immense stretches of grassland and forests to the north–was a key factor in the stability of Chinese civilization. Other ancient civilizations–Hindu, Persian, Roman, Greek, and Egyptian–stretched contiguously in a broad belt from northern India to the shores of the Mediterranean. China, sheltered by formidable physical barriers, had remained isolated for over 2,000 years from any unsettling foreign ideas and had developed a unique and brilliant civilization. The significance of China's isolation can hardly be overemphasized.

Great as were Han Wudi's victories, they were a severe economic strain on the country. Even defense expenditures in the peaceful interludes proved burdensome, for the garrisons maintained at short interval along the Wall's vast length were expensive. The resulting chronic shortage of funds gave the imperial bureaucracy its first real lessons in economics.

The history of coinage under Han Wudi serves as an illustration of what the imperial officials went through until they finally began to realize the most basic principles of a monetary system. Faced with a coin shortage, Han Wudi authorized minting of new coins to which he assigned an arbitrarily high value. Almost simultaneously, however, new deposits of copper ore were discovered, and private minters flooded the country with so many new coins that money became almost valueless. The government thereupon sought to check the evil by re-establishing a central monopoly over minting and issuing coins smelted according to secret formulas, such as a copper coin with a special red border. Expectations were frustrated when the formula for the red border was broken and the home counterfeiting industry again inundated China with an excess of coins. Illegal minting was not finally halted until some years later when a wiser government realized that the basic reason for the coin chaos was the arbitrary value assigned to the money. The dynasty then began issuing coins of a value only slightly higher than the value of the copper itself. Its profit margin gone, the counterfeiting industry disappeared. The Grand Historian, Sima Qian, recorded that under an amnesty granted to counterfeiters a million people were set free.

Other economic steps taken by Han Wudi's government proved more successful in providing sufficient revenues to support his military activities than upping the value of coins. One was the establishment of monopolies over iron, salt and fermented drink, which met opposition from Confucian scholars as not validated by precedents from former ages. While the monopoly of fermented drink proved unenforceable and disappeared after 17 years, the other two persisted. The combination of a free market and state ownership of industry found in China today has more than a score of centuries of precedent.

Another innovation was the establishment of an "ever-normal-granary" system whereby the state sought to stabilize the price of grain by buying grain when crops were abundant and releasing it into the market when harvests were poor. The system provided some relief to struggling peasants and provided the government with another source of revenue. Since no precedents existed for the system, it too met with opposition from Confucian scholars.

### 3. Establishment of a Confucian Society and Government

During Han Wudi's reign Confucianism became the basic ideology of China. His policy in this regard was not totally innovative, for every emperor, starting with Han Gaozu had included at least some Confucian advisors within his entourage. Through their persuasion Han emperors became increasingly conscious that Confucianism served as a rational justification for centralized, autocratic rule.

Quoted below are a few representative excerpts from the writings of Confucius and Mencius, as well as from another principal document of the Confucian school, the *Zhong Yong* ("*The Doctrine of the Mean*"). These excerpts not only contain the seeds from which Confucian civilization was to germinate but also illustrate the Chinese style of writing philosophy. Broad theoretical outlines are not stated directly and then developed in a logical fashion–stories are told, pithy sayings are quoted, etc.

> Confucius said, "The mind of the superior man is conversant with righteousness; the mind of the mean man is conversant with gain."[4]

> Mencius said, "The great man is he who does not lose his child's heart."[5]

---

4 *The Analects of Confucius*, James Legge (translator), Part 4.

5 *The Mencius*, James Legge (translator), Book 4, Part 2, Chapter 12, No. 1.

Confucianism exalts those virtues that the great religions of the world have valued. The "superior man" despises the pursuit of gain and prizes sincerity, humility, kindness, courage, generosity and justice. Such a moral content is unusual for a political philosophy. Confucianism is not a religion but a political philosophy.

> Mencius said, "If a ruler give honor to men of talents and virtue and employ the able, so that offices shall all be filled by individuals of distinction and mark, then all the scholars of the kingdom will be pleased, and wish to stand in his court.[6]

Like Socrates, but unlike the majority of religious thinkers, Mencius considered knowledge a principal virtue. For him the "scholars of the kingdom" are the true superior men. The Confucian view that knowledge was an ethical value was of far-reaching effect in the later conduct of the Chinese central government. The highest knowledge was that of the Confucian classics,[7] and admission to the governing class depended upon mastering them with all their moral content. No parallel exists in the modern world for ethical training as a qualification for governing.

The Chinese, in fact, concluded that the most critical activity of the bureaucracy, the *sine qua non* of the peace and prosperity of the empire, was the selection of its own personnel. Of the Six Boards initiated under the Han emperors, the Chinese considered the Board of Civil Office the most important.

---

6 *The Mencius*, James Legge (translator), Book 2, Part 2, Chapter 5, No. 1.

7 The Classics included the Classics of Poetry (or Songs), Rites, History, and Filial Piety, the Analects of Confucius, The Mencius, the Spring and Autumn Annals, the Great Learning, and the Doctrine of the Mean.

> The Master said, "A transmitter and not a maker, believing in and loving the ancients, I venture to compare myself to old P'ang."[8]

> The Master said, "I am not one who was born in the possession of knowledge; I am one who is fond of antiquity, and earnest in seeking it there."[9]

The Confucianists looked far into the past to the age of the early emperors, Yao, Shun and Yu for guidance in governing. They believed it was a time when the people were prosperous and virtuous, and rule was benevolent. Confucius himself devoted much of his life to collecting and editing ancient literature. He was incorrect, however, in claiming to be merely a transmitter of ancient knowledge. The hereditary aspect of Chinese feudal society is conspicuously absent from his thought. Confucius looked to the "superior man" for leadership, not to the man of high birth.

Constant reference to the past made Confucianism one of the most conservative political philosophies in history. Utopia was in the past. Men did not turn their thoughts to innovation in order to realize some perfect society in the future; men studied the ancient ways to conserve the best of the past. Unless there was a precedent in the past, any proposed new type of governmental activity met strong opposition from China's scholars. With this doctrinal tendency to minimize government and let the people make most decisions, China was during much of its history a decentralized society, especially from the Song dynasty onward (960 to 1911 C.E.).

---

8 *The Analects of Confucius*, James Legge (translator), Part 7.

9 Ibid. Part 7.

Wherever the innovating emperor might turn in governing the most populous empire on earth, he was sure to be greeted with advice based on the Confucian classics. The scholars in his court would often remind him that his proposals had no precedent in antiquity or that the proposed activity was contrary to the methods of his own imperial ancestors and thus contrary to filial piety.

The Confucianists did not limit their admonition to follow ancient ways to the emperors of China. They urged even the peasant farmer to follow the old ways–in this case the ways of his own direct ancestors rather than those of the early emperors Yao, Shun and Yu. The incorporation of ancestor worship, a practice described on the oracle bones of the Shang dynasty, reinforced the conservative Confucian love of the past since it too required men to look backwards, to take into account the wishes of the deceased. Like the carryover of ethical values, from feudal times, ancestor worship was an important thread of continuity between feudal times and the imperial era.

Few were the emperors strong enough to resist the advice of their counselors against innovation. A glance at the emperor as a man rather than as an institution will elucidate some practical limitations placed on abuse of his power. Future emperors were no more immune in their childhood than anyone else from constant inculcation of filial piety and other Confucian virtues. Like all who aspired to future position, heirs apparent developed a fitting veneration for those doctrines.

Upon succeeding to the throne, the emperor had limited contacts. Aside from the corps of imperial concubines who served his pleasure and the eunuchs who served his household, the people with whom the emperor was most in contact were his civil servants, all of whom had devoted their energies for 10 to 40 years to mastery of the Confucian classics and owed their positions of power and prestige to knowledge of Confucian doctrines, not, as in the modern West, to expertise in finance, labor relations, urban planning, public health, agriculture, etc.

While the emperors generally eschewed innovation, they were active in punishing crimes, defending the empire militarily, and building or maintaining public works, especially those for water control and irrigation–all vital fields of governmental activity legitimated by long-standing precedents. All were tasks that the people could not accomplish on their own.

Of immense importance were the activities of the central regime in managing the river systems. Chinese civilization was economically based on agriculture, and upon the ability of the peasant to produce a good crop depended the ultimate prosperity of all.

The Yellow River ("Huang He")–aptly called "China's sorrow"–was particularly prone to overflow its banks. During the Ice Age winds from Siberia had deposited a fine yellow dust, loess, up to a depth of 150 feet along the upper reaches of the Yellow River. This soil appears never to have supported forests and is subject to a high rate of erosion. Consequently, the Yellow River is continuously depositing huge quantities of sediment and in prehistoric times created the flat fertile central China plain to the east of the original loess country. Humans enclosed the river with dikes to prevent flooding and to create an agricultural civilization. Contained, the Yellow River then began depositing its cargo of loess in its own bed. The bed of the river rose higher and higher above the surrounding countryside (some 20 feet today in its lower reaches), and the bursting of a dike spelled disaster. From the early days of the empire, the central authorities (often in vain) devoted much of their energy and revenues to the construction and maintenance of the dike system along the river. Despite their efforts, on occasion the Yellow River even switched its course to reach the sea, now north, now south of the Shandong peninsula, a situation roughly equivalent to a change of course by the Hudson River to discharge into the ocean at Boston rather than at New York City. Even without dramatic changes in course destroying thousands of villages, the Yellow River's frequent inundations during periods of high rainfall brought famine to millions. The only three natural disasters in human history that have cost more than 1,000,000 lives were Yellow River floods. The most costly was the flood of 1332-33, which killed 7 million people As late as 1931, a flood killed an estimated 1 to 4 million people.

Such has been the importance of taming China's waterways that it is arguable that inability to perform this task on a purely local basis was the reason for the existence of a single central authority in the first place. Europe with its more dependable rainfall and complacent rivers has been able to sustain political division and a greater diversity of culture. Geography often expresses itself politically.

The central China plain also saw frequent drought-caused famines. The winds of the South China Sea discharged most of their moisture over the hills of south China. The tropical southeast coast and the great Yangzi valley received abundant life-sustaining moisture. The remoter Yellow River valley to the north was considerably dryer, receiving barely enough average annual rainfall to support agriculture. In years when precipitation was below average, famine was a constant danger. A partial solution to that problem was the construction of irrigation systems throughout the

Yellow River valley, an activity in which central support was of prime importance.

The central government also had military responsibilities. The primary role of China's military establishment was to defend the frontiers against the nomadic peoples with whom the Chinese shared the great geographic compartment of East Asia. The wealth of China served as a constant temptation to the nomads to attempt conquest. The military also suppressed banditry and peasant rebellions.

The Chinese had a severe handicap in defending against the nomads. They were often more skillful than their Chinese adversaries in horsemanship, one of the supreme military skills of pre-modern ages. Accustomed to the saddle from childhood and inhabiting lands more suitable for the breeding of animals than agriculture, they maintained cavalry superiority and constantly threatened north China with their incursions. The emperors were obliged to maintain standing, professional armies quartered in garrisons shortly spaced all along the Great Wall of China–a significant drain on imperial revenues. The magnitude of their task is shown by their failures. Of the 2,133 years that the empire lasted from Qin Shi Huangdi to Sun Yatsen (formerly "Sun Yat-sen"), north China was under nomadic control approximately 40 percent of the time and south China, whose terrain is less suitable for cavalry maneuver, was under nomadic control 20 percent of the time. Despite periodic domination by nomads, however, Chinese civilization remained intact. Only political control passed to the nomads who soon adopted Chinese culture even including methods of governing. Stable China culturally absorbed its conquerors.

Another tenet of Confucianism is the obligation of filial piety.

> Mencius [said], "There are five things which are pronounced in the common usage of the age to be unfilial. The first is laziness in the use of one's four limbs, without attending to the nourishment of his parents. The second is gambling and chess playing, and being fond of wine, without attending to the nourishment of his parents. The third is being fond of goods and money, and selfishly attached to one's wife and children, without attending to the nourishment of one's parents . . .[10]

> Mencius said, "There are three things which are unfilial, and to have no posterity is the greatest of them."[11]

Intensive agriculture required concentration of authority in the father and obedience by younger generations; but filial piety included far more than simple obedience. It included, among many other duties, producing children who would someday perpetuate the rites of ancestor worship and support the elderly.

The great importance of the family was a principal source of Confucian strength in its contest with rival schools. The Confucianists built upon a real and limited base, readily understandable by all. While the universal love of Mozi may have seemed theoretical and impractical under the circumstances of the Period of the Warring States, the family did not suffer from the same accusations; it was a daily reality permeating the life of the Chinese at all times. Confucianism won acceptance by

---

10 *The Mencius*, James Legge (translator), Book 3, Part 2, Chapter 30, No. 2.

11 Ibid. Book 4, Part 1, Chapter 26, No. 1.

incorporating the familiar. Is it not more practical to show the proper respect for one's parents and to support them in their old age than to love all mankind as the Moists advised?

The Chinese family–including collateral relatives, deceased ancestors, and unborn generations–was an institution even more important than the imperial government. An old Chinese proverb says that the sky is big and the emperor is far away. Of all the institutions of the Utopian past, the Confucianists attributed highest value to the family and made it the framework of Confucian morality and society. It was a principal context within which the Chinese exercised the ancient virtues. The Confucianists believed that the root of all harmony within society was found in familial relationships, especially in the practice of filial piety by younger generations.

Since as-yet-unborn generations were a part of the family, the father, as the manager of family property in Imperial China, had an additional incentive toward conservatism. It was his duty, imposed by custom, to preserve family property prudently for the benefit of future generations; in no sense of the word was the property his to dispose of for his own benefit. His position was not unlike that of a modern trustee.

> The philosopher Zeng Zi said, "Let there be a careful attention to perform the funeral rites to parents, and let them be followed when long gone with the ceremonies of sacrifice; then the virtue of the people will resume its proper excellence."[12]

[12] *The Analects of Confucius*, James Legge (translator), Part 1.

> Mencius said, 'The nourishment of parents when living is not sufficient . . . . It is only in the performing their obsequies when dead that we have what can be considered the great thing.'[13]

Within the family one of the emphasized ways of demonstrating filial piety was through ceremonial rites, particularly sacrifices to the ancestral spirits. As Chinese society gradually developed, rites in all phases of life from the emperors on down took on an increasing importance. To some extent, knowledge of correct ceremonial procedures became a substitute for thought–another restraint on change..

The importance accorded to deceased members also inclined the Chinese to conservatism. Since the tending of ancestral graves was an important responsibility, the Chinese tended to lose geographical mobility and its concomitant exposure to new ideas. "The Brothers' Search for Their Father," a tale included in Lin Yutang's *The Wisdom of China and India*, illustrates the importance of ancestral graves. It tells of two brothers whose father had mysteriously disappeared a thousand miles from his native village. For two years the brothers searched for his remains in order to return him to the family plot.

> Someone addressed Confucius, saying, "Sir, why are you not engaged in the government" Confucius said, "What does the *Shujing* ["*Book of History*"] say of filial piety? 'You are filial, you discharge your brotherly duties. These qualities are displayed in government.' This then also constitutes the exercise of government."[14]

---

13 *The Mencius*, James Legge (translator), Book 4, Part 2, Chapter 13, No. 1.

14 *The Analects of Confucius*, James Legge (translator), Part 2.

One of the distinguishing features of Confucianism is its constant stress on duties. Various duties flowed from son to father and father to son, from subject to emperor and emperor to subject. While it may be true that for every duty there is a corresponding right, the Confucianists failed to accord rights an equal significance. A society conceived of largely in terms of duties rather than rights tends to be conservative.

The saying also reflects the Confucian concept of society as a whole, as a single extended family. The obligation of subject to ruler was no different from that of son to father. The emperor was neither merely the representative of his people nor merely the ruler of the state. He was, in a sense that George Washington could never have hoped to be, the father of his people, and they, his children. The discharge of obligations within the family was *of the same nature* as the discharge of obligations to the central government on the larger scene of society.

> Confucius said, "He who exercises government by means of his virtue may be compared to the north polar star, which keeps its place and all the stars turn toward it."[15]

> The Master said, "When a prince's personal conduct is correct, his government is effective without the issuing of orders. If his personal conduct is not correct, he may issue orders, but they will not be followed."[16]

The Emperor theoretically did little more than present a role model of virtue to the people in his personal life, and in his

[15] *The Analects of Confucius*, James Legge (translator), Part 2.
[16] *Ibid.*, Part 2.

public life punish crimes, defend the empire militarily, and build or maintain public works, especially those for water control and irrigation–all fields of governmental endeavor legitimated by long-standing precedents. An Emperor or official who tried to do more than these limited, albeit important tasks, was rare in Confucian China. Fortunately for the Chinese, a few emperors broke with ancient precedent and maintained granaries for famine relief.

> "The duties of universal obligation . . . are those between sovereign and the people, between father and son, between husband and wife, between elder brother and younger, and those belonging to the intercourse of friends. Those five are the duties of universal obligation."[17]

Nowhere is the interrelation between the family and government more clearly seen than in the "Five Relationships:" emperor-people, father-son, husband-wife, elder brother-younger brother, and friend-friend. Throughout the centuries these five stimulated an extensive literature analyzing and defining the duties contained within each. A glance at their major characteristics in many ways serves to summarize traditional Chinese society. First, four of the five were relationships that the West conceives of as private relationships. Second, three of the five were actual family relationships and the remaining two by analogy to father-son and elder brother-younger brother can be conceived of in terms of the family. Finally, four of the five were relationships of superior to inferior. Such was Chinese society: familial and hierarchical. Such a society was ill equipped institutionally to stave off the

---

[17] Doctrine of the Mean, James Legge (translator), 1893

threat posed in the 19th Century C.E. by Western military power, industrialization and science. So long as the Chinese did not face the problem of accommodating themselves to a more dynamic culture, so long as China remained isolated and agricultural, the Confucian organization of society worked admirably for more than a score of centuries. China stood for millennia at the forefront of civilization.

A dynasty bent on maintaining itself in power could not but find Confucianism a highly attractive instrument for the perpetuation of its rule. The excesses of the Qin had discredited Legalism, and Mohism and Daoism were too impractical to serve as a basis for governing a sophisticated and highly complex civilization. Confucianism was a practical doctrine. It urged the regulation of society through the family, an advocacy in accord with the economic realities of an agricultural society. It advocated staffing the central government with the most talented men available. It glorified the emperor as the holder of the Mandate of Heaven and made the relationship of emperor-subject–involving the subordination of the latter to the former–one of the key relationships of society. On the other hand, in finding in Confucianism a rational and ethical basis for the perpetuation of their own rule and in establishing a civil service based on expertise in its doctrines, the Han emperors perhaps unwittingly imprisoned themselves and their successors for the next 2,000 years. In traditional China the emperor might violate Confucian precepts but could not change them.

Han Wudi and his successors not only established the general Confucian tone of succeeding ages; they also established specific governmental institutions through which Confucianism expressed itself. One innovation was the organization of the government into six ministries, the Boards of War, Punishments, Works, Revenue,

Rites, and Civil Office, a structure maintained intact in China until the revolution in 1911 C.E. The Japanese revived it in their puppet state in Manchuria, and it did not finally disappear until the Japanese were driven from that region in 1945 C.E.–a venerable history testifying both to Chinese conservatism and to Han organizational ability.

Two other key practices of the Imperial era also found their beginnings under Han Wudi. Dispatching officials periodically from the capital to check upon the activities of provincial authorities eventually became institutionalized in the Censorate, an independent body of officials who exposed corruption and criticized government at all levels. Han Wudi also started choosing some of his officials by written examinations on the Confucian classics–a rational way to choose those of highest merit. He established an imperial academy in 124, B.C.E. with some 50 students studying for the civil service examinations. This technique of staffing the bureaucracy was the most important innovation in Chinese history other than the adoption of Confucianism itself as the guiding principles of society. These examinations had no counterparts elsewhere for 2,000 years.

## 4. Wang Mang

Of the seven emperors who succeeded Han Wudi, several were quite able. Realizing that the empire was again approaching exhaustion from Han Wudi's expensive campaigns, they reverted to the precedent of Han Gaozu and provided China with almost one hundred years of a relatively uneventful cooling-off period. The major problem of the era was one internal to the government, repeated attempts by the families of the empresses to seize effective power in the state. In perhaps typical fashion Han Wudi had supplied his successors with a solution to this problem. Having chosen his heir apparent, he executed his consort so that, should his son come to the throne as a minor, her family would be unable to manipulate her regency to their own benefit. Wisely or foolishly, Han Wudi's successors did not follow his brutal but effective precedent and, in 8 C.E., the family of an empress succeeded in seizing power and placed on the throne one of the most interesting but atypical emperors in China's long history: Wang Mang, first and last emperor of the so-called Xin (or "New") dynasty.

A man of temperate living and distinguished scholarship, Wang was one of China's great social idealists but one whose extreme disregard of Confucian restraints on innovations contributed to his downfall. Provoking the enmity of the wealthy, he limited ownership of land for families with fewer than eight members to approximately 200 acres, distributed their excess lands to others, and banned the selling and buying of land. He abolished the slave trade (usually limited to household servants), extended Han Wudi's state trading system in grain to textiles, and instituted low-interest loans to peasants. Further affecting the livelihoods of countless Chinese, he added imperial monopolies of liquor, coinage, forestry, and fishing to the salt and iron monopolies established by Han Wudi.

Wang attempted to change China too radically and too fast. He was opposed by the Confucianists, who found no precedents in former ages for these reforms, despised by large landholders, sabotaged by corruption in his expanded bureaucracy, plagued by disastrous floods in the Yellow River ("Huang He") valley, and troubled by a revolt of the Red Eyebrows, one of the first of China's secret societies. Wang was cut down by an ordinary soldier in his palace only fifteen years after his seizure of the throne.

## 5. The Decline of the Han Dynasty

Succeeding Wang Mang in 23 C.E. was a prince of the Liu family, Han Guang Wudi, who reestablished the Han dynasty, put down the Red Eyebrows, and reasserted China's strength against the nomads. Han Guang Wudi certainly ranks with the most spirited of China's innumerable emperors, but, insofar as the Han dynasty is concerned, he was the last of the Liu family to have great ability. The depressing political events of the last 200 years of the Han period are of little interest. None of his many successors were men worthy of particular note. With weak emperors on the throne, often children, an "aristocracy" of land-owning families exercised much political influence in the provinces. Intermarriage among these families lent an aura of heredity to their social and political position. Having used the Liu weakness to gain provincial leadership, they would compete with future dynasties for power–a pattern often repeated in Chinese history.

Gradually the palace eunuchs came to be the real power behind the throne and when, toward the close of the 2nd century, the military moved to assert power over them, it was but a matter of time before an adventurer would oust the Han. After many rebellions, the dynasty collapsed in 220, and China split into three kingdoms.

## 6. Cultural Advances

Under the Han dynasty, China laid the foundations for a remarkable civilization that led the world over most of the next 2,000 years. Its ultimate destruction after contact with Western culture would leave a sense of loss and resentment that help to explain China's present attitudes and suggest changes in United States policies concerning China.

Technologically, the era was a fruitful one. One of the most important inventions in world history, paper, was perfected by Cai Lun in 105 C.E. Together with printing, also a Chinese invention of later date, it eventually made possible the modern world. A few years later Zhang Heng invented the world's first seismograph. Seeking to produce salt, the Chinese developed deep drilling techniques to reach underground brine. They also learned to make steel from cast iron by the 1st century C.E. Other technological developments during the Han period included invention of the crank handle, pumps, the belt drive, and watertight compartments and sternpost rudders for ships. Mathematical advances included negative numbers and the extraction of square and cubic roots.

Buddhism made its first appearance in China, via the Silk Road of Xinjiang, and by the end of the Han period several small centers of Buddhist activity were active in China.

Daoism at this time underwent important changes and, allying itself with folk superstition, transformed itself from an esoteric philosophy into a hierarchically organized church. The founder of the Daoist church, one Zhang Daoling, the first Celestial Master, is said to have lived during the later Han. His alleged descendants maintained a hereditary Daoist hierarchy officially recognized in 748 and not abolished until 1927. The Celestial Masters of Daoism are still active today on Taiwan.

Artistically, the era saw the invention of glazes and proto-porcelain, a significant step in the development of true porcelain in later centuries. In literature, the Han is most noteworthy for its high level of achievement in the writing of history. China produced the greatest historians of any ancient civilization. Foremost among them was Sima Qian during the reign of Han Wudi. His great work, *Records of the Grand Historian*, established a model for future historians. Encyclopedic in scope, it sets forth innumerable important documents in their entirety and has specialized sections on such aspects of Chinese life as music, economic policy, famous men, rivers and canals, etc. Covering Chinese history from the very beginning to Sima's own day, it established a high standard of literary quality. It is owing to Sima that the writing of history was thereafter considered the highest form of literature in China. Only in dealing with his own times is Sima occasionally biased. His dislike of Han Wudi is discrete but apparent. He may be forgiven for these lapses from historical objectivity, for he had suffered at the hands of his Emperor. Enraged at Sima's eloquent defense of a general who had surrendered his army to the nomads, Han Wudi subjected the historian to the penalty of castration. Throughout the rest of his life, Sima was an embittered man. As Mencius had said, the most unfilial act was "to have no posterity." Sima's sole reason for wanting to live was to finish his great historical treatise. Somewhat later Sima's high standards were maintained by Ban Gu and his sister, Ban Zhao, who turned their talents to history rather than to adventure like their equally famous brother Ban Chao, whose conquest of nomadic Xinjiang is the one bright spot in the political history of Han Guang Wudi's feeble successors. Ban Zhao, China's most celebrated woman scholar was equally talented in poetry as in history. Many other achievements too numerous to mention in a short survey also contributed to the reverence with which future ages have always contemplated the Han; to this day the people of North China still refer themselves as the "Han people."

# B. The Three Kingdoms (220 to 280) and the Minor Dynasties (280 to 589)

## 1. The Three Kingdoms

After the collapse of the Han dynasty China was split into three Kingdoms for some 60 years, Wei in the north, Wu in the south and southeast, and Shu in Sichuan. The period is of interest because it was the only time in Chinese history when one or the other of these three key economic areas was not sufficiently powerful to dominate the other two. Prior to the era of the Three Kingdoms the north was the principal economic region in China; afterwards primacy passed to the south and southeast. Yet for at least one brief moment China divided itself naturally into three regions of equal importance. Reunification of China by the Jin dynasty in 280 was a key event in Chinese history. It prevented China from becoming a series of quarreling independent kingdoms like Europe after the fall of the Western Roman Empire.

The era is one of the periods best known to the Chinese people. It is the subject of *Romance of the Three Kingdoms*, written during the much later Mongol (or Yuan) dynasty, one of the "Four Great Classical Novels." This extremely important milestone in the development of the Chinese novel so thoroughly idealizes the period that the Chinese to this day have a great affection for the "heroes" of the era. The truth is quite the contrary, an era of intrigue, warfare, and cruelty.

## 2. Cultural Advances

Advances in the arts of civilization were many. Pei Xiu, one of history's great cartographers, invented the grid system of rectilinear subdivisions in the 3rd century. Agriculturally, biological pest control began some 1,600 years before its use in the West when the Chinese began to use yellow citrus killer ants to protect mandarin orange trees from ravaging by black ants, caterpillars, and other insects. Medically, the Chinese understood vitamin deficiency diseases. By trial and error, they were able to determine needed diets to overcome scurvy, beriberi, and rickets.

## 3. The Minor Dynasties

Reunification occurred in 280 when Sima Yan of Wei conquered the kingdom of Wu and founded the Jin dynasty. In keeping with the troubled nature of the times, only twenty-four years after the reunification, a dispute broke out among the Jin princes, one of whom made the fatal mistake of summoning the Xiongnu south of the Great Wall to his assistance. For the first time but hardly the last, various nomadic groups swiftly established control over a vast area of China and by 316 controlled the entire north. The Jin retreated to the south and maintained a tenuous existence at Nanjing (formerly "Nanking") until an ambitious general ended the dynasty by usurping the throne in 420. In the meantime the Xiongnu dynasty in the north had suffered the same fate, succumbing to the ambitious founder of a new ruling line. There is little point in tracing further the history of individual dynasties either in the Chinese south or the nomad north. The following table of ruling houses should suffice to indicate the chaotic nature of the period:

North

| Dynasty | Dates of Rule |
|---|---|
| *Han Zhao* | *304 to 329* |
| Later Zhao | 319 to 352 |
| Cheng Han | 265 to 420 |
| Early Liang | 313 to 376 |
| Later Liang | 386 to 403 |
| Southern Liang | 397 to 404 |
| | 408 to 414 |
| Northern Liang | 397 to 439 |
| Western Liang | 401 to 421 |
| Early Yan | 349 to 370 |
| Later Yan | 384 to 408 |
| Southern Yan | 398 to 410 |
| Northern Yan | 409 to 436 |
| Early Qin | 351 to 494 |
| Later Qin | 384 to 417 |
| Western Qin | 385 to 390 |
| | 409 to 431 |
| Xia | 407 to 431 |
| Northern Wei | 386 to 535 |
| Western Wei | 535 to 554 |
| Eastern Wei | 534 to 550 |
| Northern Ch'I | 550 to 577 |
| Northern Zhou | 557 to 581 |
| South | |
| Jin | 280 to 420 |
| Liu Song | 420 to 477 |
| Ch'I | 479 to 501 |
| Liang | 502 to 556 |
| Ch'en | 557 to 587 |

The northern dynasties were Mongol, Xiongnu, Turkic, and Xianbei with a sprinkling of Chinese. The southern dynasties were all Chinese. Usurpers usurped from usurpers and foreign invaders conquered foreign invaders.

## 4. Effects of the North-South Partition

The principal phenomenon of the period was a vast migration of Chinese refugees, not merely the wealthy but also millions of simple folk, to the south to escape nomadic incursions. Estimates indicate that the population of the south increased more than fivefold during this period. Afterwards, Chinese history was largely determined by the people of the Yangzi (formerly "Yangtze") Valley and the southeast coast. The primacy of the Yellow River (now called "Huang He") lands, the ancestral home of Chinese civilization, ended. Certain characteristics of central and south China began to impose themselves on Chinese civilization. For the first time rice became an important part of the Chinese diet. Tea was mentioned for the first time in Chinese history, and a tea industry arose in Jiangxi and Zhejiang provinces. Suitable cups and pots for tea were needed, and it is probably more than coincidental that the early porcelain industry in the later Tang period centered in the two southern provinces where tea was most popular. Not until several hundred years later did tea become a standard drink in the north. Similarly the luxuriant landscape of the south gave rise to a considerable literature on botany.

A second major effect of the partition was the spread of Buddhism. The northern invaders came from Central Asia, where Buddhism was the principal creed. By 405 approximately 90 per cent of the population of the north had embraced the new faith. Buddhism also spread gradually to the Chinese-ruled south where, as in the earlier Period of the Warring States, the instability of life caused a quickened interest in a new creed.

Among the doctrines of Buddhism are the following: 1) the world is one of pain and suffering, for "birth is painful, old age is painful, death is painful, sorrow, lamentation, dejection and despair are painful;" 2) men are trapped on the wheel of existence and are continually reincarnated into this world of pain and suffering; 3) a man's state in the world is dependent upon his deeds in previous existences; 4) the pain and suffering of the world are attributable to selfish craving; 5) it is possible to overcome selfish desire and reach *nirvana*, an extinguishment of personality, in which pain and suffering cease and the cycle of rebirth is broken; and 6) one may attain *nirvana* by following the Eightfold Path:

Right Views
Right Intention
Right Speech
Right Action
Right Livelihood
Right Effort
Right Mindfulness
Right Concentration

The Confucianism of the Han, which depended largely on the leisure and bookish scholarship of settled times, lost some of its importance. The Chinese welcomed a faith that offered escape from pain and suffering. By 554, China had 2,000,000 Buddhist monks and nuns and many thousands of monasteries. Buddhism took its place as one of the three great creeds of China.

The nomad dynasties, particularly the Northern Wei, actively encouraged Indian missionaries and pilgrimages of Chinese to the holy places of India. Altogether some 186 Chinese are recorded as having traveled to India between 259 and 790.

One of the most famous of these Chinese pilgrims, Faxian, left China in 399. In India he divided his time between three sedentary years in the Buddhist center of Pataliputra and three itinerant years throughout most of the sub-continent. In addition to copying a great number of sacred texts, Faxian left to posterity an invaluable journal describing his travels. From the historian's point of view this journal is of greater interest than Faxian's labors to advance the cause of Buddhism in China, for it is in large measure thanks to him that historians are aware that India at that time was ruled by one of the most vigorous dynasties in its history, the Guptas. In addition to Faxian's journal, only a few Tibetan, Sinhalese, and Arabic chronicles cast light on the Gupta Empire. Indian sources themselves are mostly limited to coins and carved inscriptions. Unlike the Chinese for whom history was the greatest form of literature, the Indians were little interested in recording their own past. Buddhism contributed to this Indian attitude, for that faith teaches that life, the subject matter of history, is not worth living. Fortunately, the Chinese in adopting Buddhism rejected Buddhism's attitude toward the recording of history. Buddhist or Confucianist, the Chinese remained the greatest writers of history among all pre-modern peoples.

Faxian's impression of India under the Guptas was favorable. He wrote with admiration of the mildness of the imperial administration, the wealth and prosperity of the country, and the liberties of the common people. Faxian's descriptions of buildings and murals that no longer exist go far toward filling in gaps in our knowledge of the aesthetic side of the Gupta era.

After a twelve-year absence from his native land, Faxian finally returned to his native city of Ch'angan with his collection of texts. Thereafter, he devoted the rest of his life to writing his famous journal and to translating the sacred texts.

Of even greater fame than Faxian is another pious monk, Xuanzang, who left China in 629 to collect additional Buddhist texts in India despite an imperial prohibition on foreign travel. Xuanzang left an impressive picture of the monastic university at Nalanda with its 10,000 students, 100 lecture halls, great libraries, and immense dormitories. Like Faxian, his predecessor, Xuanzang arrived in India at one of the peaks of Indian civilization under the rule of the great Harsha. Xuanzang's journals contain a wealth of information in detail, country by country and mile by mile, on the commerce, agriculture, languages, customs, institutions, superstitions, philosophies, religions, political relations, and prominent personalities of the lands of India and central Asia. So accurate were his observations that they have been of invaluable aid to modern archaeologists. His journal is even more impressive than Faxian's.

The partition of China eventually came to an end as a new dynasty, the Sui, reunified the country. Gradually the north and south had become more culturally homogeneous. The northern warrior dynasties, heavily outnumbered by the more civilized Chinese, realized that they could not govern the north without adopting most aspects of Chinese culture. Eventually, they even adopted the Chinese language. The process of their sinefication was aided by intermarriage with their Chinese subjects. The nomads thereby gained allies to help shore up their rule, while wealthy

Chinese found intermarriage an important factor in protecting their own economic interests. The northern Chinese incorporated a few nomadic words in their language and adopted a few minor aspects of nomadic culture concerning food and food preparation. The resulting blend was, nonetheless, overwhelmingly Chinese. China absorbed these conquerors just as it had absorbed various semi-civilized tribes throughout its history. The stage was set for reunification, the ideal of a unified empire having persisted for almost 400 years.

## 5. Cultural Advances

Despite China's political woes and the kaleidoscopic conditions of the era, many artistic developments occurred. In good times or bad, some men advance the cause of civilization.

One of the heroes of world poetry is Shen Yue, who lived in the period of the Minor Dynasties. Not until Shen did any poet deliberately base his work on the various tones of the spoken Chinese language. The "flats and sharps" of this new type of poetry gave a musical quality and a rhythm that Western poetry can only hint at. Thanks to Shen, the Chinese composed a great body of poetry, especially during the later Tang dynasty, which must be heard, not merely read, to be fully appreciated. Yet at the same time this poetry must also be read to be fully appreciated. The colorful, picturesque characters of the Chinese script add visual pleasure to the enjoyment of the poem. Prose writing became flowery and ornate as writers turned away from the straightforward, simple and direct style of earlier periods.

Painting advanced as Xie He enunciated the famous Six Canons of Painting:

1. Rhythmic vitality
2. Anatomical structure
3. Conformity with nature
4. Suitability of coloring
5. Artistic composition
6. Finish

Previously the trade of craftsmen for decoration, painting became a fine art during the Minor Dynasties. The painters of later dynasties, especially the Song, were to create a great body of masterpieces.

Another advance came in calligraphy. The Chinese wrote with a special brush having a handle of bone, wood or more precious materials, and a tip of bristles. Supposedly, the Qin general, Meng Tian improved the brush, and later generations further refined it, using tips of rabbit hair for slender, delicate writing and of sheep hair for the formation of bolder characters. The invention of the writing brush permitted a transition from the relatively sharp, angular style of the "ancient" form of characters to the more graceful "modern" style. Wang Xi Zhi, the greatest early master of calligraphy, elevated the art to a new level during the Minor Dynasties period. Wang created abstract masterpieces using the "grass script," a swirling, sweeping form of handwriting.

Other advances are traceable to the period of the Minor Dynasties. The Chinese invented stirrups for horses and learned techniques of manufacturing glass. The first of China's local gazettes appeared, covering events, customs, and personalities of southern Shaanxi and northern Sichuan. On a more mundane level, the era saw the invention of dice and umbrellas.

Even during troubled political times during the Three Kingdoms and Minor Dynasties period, Chinese civilization advanced. As long as a conqueror was willing to adopt Chinese ways, it made no different that they were foreigners, a remarkable feature found in few other civilizations.

## C. The Sui Dynasty (589 to 618)

For almost 400 years after the collapse of the Han dynasty, the idea of political unity was never lost and the title of Emperor was constantly used. Reunification required only an individual shrewd enough to defeat his rivals and skillful enough to expel the nomads. Such a man was the Emperor Wen, founder of the Sui dynasty. His reunification of China prevented China from remaining a series of quarreling independent kingdoms like Europe after the fall of the Western Roman Empire.

The Sui era resembles the earlier Qin dynasty. Both periods saw a unification of China; both brought vigorous but cruel men to the Dragon Throne; both were preludes to a succeeding dynasty of greater mildness and remarkable cultural achievement; both mercifully were brief.

The Emperor Wen of Sui began his rise to power by deposing a boy ruler of the Northern Zhou dynasty in 581 and soon afterwards allegedly put to death 59 princes of the royal blood. Within eight years by military success or skilled negotiation, he was master of all China.

His accomplishments were many. By redistributing much land to the peasants, he shored up his regime. On the one hand, landless peasants had always presented the threat of rebellion to China's dynasties, and, on the other, too much land in the hands of the great aristocratic families had always presented the threat of usurpation of the throne. Redistribution of land at the start of new dynasties was always useful to fend off threats from both directions simultaneously. To maintain social stability, like Han Wudi and Wang Mang before him, he also established state granaries, to buy grain when plentiful and sell grain when scare, stabilizing the price at levels peasants and simple townsfolk could afford.

To protect the revenues of the throne, the Emperor Wen established military agricultural colonies along the northern frontier. By providing their own food, those units spared the central treasury considerable expense. He further economized by reorganizing his bureaucracy for greater efficiency.

With the expenses of government reduced, he undertook a major improvement to China's transportation network. All dynasties kept their capitals in the north because of the never-ending threat from the nomads. Over time, however, climate change had made the region warmer and dryer, no longer as productive agriculturally. The Emperor Wen began to improve China's canals to facilitate easy transportation of grain to the north from the Yangzi (formerly "Yangtze") valley, before his death in 604, possibly at the hands of his son the Emperor Yang.

The Emperor Yang of Sui accomplished even more than his father. He laid out a new capital, Chang'an near the site of a former capital of the same name. The new city, said to be the first planned city in the world, was approximately 30 square miles in area. It became a model for the later Japanese cities of Nara and Kyoto. He also made changes to the civil service examinations that endured for fourteen hundred years.

Most importantly, the Emperor Yang completed the canal projects of his father, thereby earning a reputation comparable in cruelty to that of Qin Shi Huangdi, whose Legalist philosophy he followed, The Emperor Yang's reign was an exception to the normal practice of Confucian rule. Just as Qin Shi Huangdi is said to have expended 1,000,000 lives in building the first Great Wall, the Emperor Yang spent as many in building China's famous Grand Canal, the world's longest canal at 1,114 miles linking six different river valleys. He conscripted more than 5,000,000 peasants to dredge and link up already existing local canals. Decapitation was the penalty for evaders and flogging the penalty for laggards. The deaths of 1,000,000 peasants and the enormous disruption of peasant life led to the very social instability that the Emperor Wen had sought to obviate by his land and grain policies. Repulsive though the Emperor Yang's cruelty was, he left to the succeeding Tang dynasty a superb system of internal communication between the great river valleys. As a later Chinese historian aptly remarked, the Emperor Yang "shortened the life of his dynasty by a number of years but benefited posterity to 10,000 generations. He ruled without benevolence, but his rule is to be credited with enduring accomplishments."[18] When his military campaigns in Manchuria and Korea drained his treasury and proved unsuccessful, revolts broke out, and the Sui Dynasty lost the Mandate of Heaven.

---

[18] Joseph Needham, Science and Civilisation in China, Cambridge University Press, Volume 1: Introductory Orientations, p. 123 (1954)

## D. The Tang Dynasty (618 to 907)

### 1. Political Events

The Chinese people must have rejoiced when members of the Li family, a family of mixed Chinese and sinefied nomads, revolted against the Emperor Yang. The first emperor of the Tang dynasty was Tang Gaozu but the guiding spirit behind the revolt was his son, Li Shimin, a mere lad of 16 who badgered his hesitant father into rebellion. Nine years later Tang Gaozu abdicated and his dynamic son ascended the throne under the title Tang Taizong, said by some to have had no equal on the throne of China. His reign is noteworthy for energetic campaigns deep into Central Asia against the nomads and for significant redistribution of land, a common practice at the start of a new dynasty. His crowning achievement was his greatly increased use of written examinations for recruiting officials. While Han Wudi and others had made sporadic use of written examinations, Tang Taizong made them a principal means of staffing his bureaucracy, though many officials were still appointed directly. Significantly, he extended eligibility to farmers and eliminated the necessity of any preliminary "recommendation" by provincial officials. Wealthy aristocratic families continued, nonetheless, to supply most of the candidates, for their sons were most likely to have the leisure to pursue a course of demanding studies. Learning the literary allusions in the Confucian classics alone could take many years. Tang Taizong also strengthened the examination system by enlarging the Imperial Academy at Chang'an. Some 3,260 students were resident at the Academy, and total enrollment was 8,000, a large increase from the Han dynasty.

Buddhism reached its heyday under the Tang, and Confucian influence on the emperors weakened. The Tang rulers paid less attention to historic precedents than the rulers of other dynasties. One very "unConfucian" innovation was a system of price controls. Every month the Tang established prices for three qualities of many items, including food and textiles.

After Tang Taizong's death, the Empress Wu exercised imperial power, the only woman ever to have officially occupied the throne. She ruled competently for 15 years. Her grandson Xuanzong was a diligent emperor in the early part of his long reign but lost his vigor as old age approached. In 751, one of the decisive battles of world history occurred when Islamic troops crushed Xuanzong 's troops along the Talas River in Central Asia. Islam thereafter rapidly expanded to the borders of Gansu, westernmost province of China proper, and Central Asia was lost for a thousand years to Chinese control.

A few years later a major internal rebellion broke out. Xuanzong was captivated by Yang Guifei, his favorite concubine. She, a capricious beauty, had jokingly "adopted" her own favorite, An Lushan, as her son. At her urging, Xuanzong ultimately promoted him to command of the finest troops of the Empire. An Lushan, though, treasonously marched on the capital in 775, and the emperor fled to the west. En route, in a little town in Shanxi province, occurred an incident greatly romanticized in the literature and poetry of later ages. Xuanzong's mutinous troops demanded the execution of Yang Guifei to which the reluctant emperor finally agreed.

The An Lushan rebellion was put down only with the aid of armies raised by the provincial governors, who during the remaining century and a half of the Tang period retained more and more of the tax revenues from their regions and exercised greater and greater independence from central control. The trend was gradual and might have been reversed by a single dynamic emperor, but even though some of Xuanzong's successors were able, they died after brief reigns. Another result of the rebellion and weakening of central control was the demise of the system of price controls. For the next thousand years, Chinese dynasties would generally adhere to precedent, and markets in land and goods would be open markets. Ultimately the Tang dynasty was powerless and in 907, a military adventurer pushed it aside.

The most significant event of the latter half of the Tang dynasty was the great religious persecution of 845. Nestorian Christianity, Zoroastrianism, and Manichaeism were virtually eliminated and Buddhism began a thousand years of gradual decline. The persecution, so atypical of Chinese religious attitudes, appears to have been directed primarily at Buddhism, which, argued Han Yu, a major intellectual of the period, was a foreign creed. Blaming Buddhism in particular for China's political and cultural problems, he called for a return to Confucian values as well as an end to the flowery style of literature characteristic of the Minor Dynasties that obscured correct Confucian thought. The principal factor in the persecution, though, was the drain on the imperial treasury from tax exemptions for the Buddhist monasteries, a drain compounded by the schemes of great aristocratic families to disguise their own lands as belonging to the monasteries. With much revenue already being retained by provincial strongmen, the dynasty sought to recoup its fortunes by the persecution.

Some 4,600 temples were destroyed and 260,500 monks and nuns were compelled to return to civil life. Buddhism, which had threatened to replace Confucianism as the principal creed of

China, never recovered from the blow; in no dynasty after the Tang did Buddhism demonstrate any of its earlier intellectual vigor or exuberant growth. The next major dynasty, the Song, followed Han Yu's advice and returned to a straightforward, simple and direct prose style.

## 2. Cultural Advances

Under early Tang rule China experienced a "golden age." The arts flourished, medicine and technology advanced, and cultural exchange with other civilizations reached a peak.

Two of the greatest Chinese poets, Li Bo and Du Fu, members of a group called the "Eight Immortals of the Wine-Cup" wrote some of the world's greatest verse They followed the example of Shen Yue in basing their verses on the tone values of spoken Chinese. Li Bo's famous poem "Drinking Alone By Moonlight" is set forth below. The Eight Immortals were sociable drinkers, so Li Bo invented two drinking companions for himself:

A cup of wine, under the flowering trees;
I drink alone, for no friend is near.
Raising my cup I beckon the bright moon,
The moon, alas, is no drinker of wine;
Listless, my shadow creeps about at my side.
Yet with the moon as friend and the shadow as slave
I must make merry before the Spring is spent.
To the songs I sing the moon flickers her beams;
In the dance I weave my shadow tangles and breaks.
While we were sober, three shared the fun;
Now we are drunk, each goes his way.

May we long share our odd, inanimate feast,
And meet at last on the Cloudy River of the sky. [Milky Way].[19]

Wang Wei and others among China's greatest painters flourished and originated China's greatest contribution to world painting; artists began to paint landscapes for the first time. Much of their inspiration came from Daoism, which called for men to eschew the artificialities of town life and to live in harmony with nature. Illustrative of the talent and great achievements of Tang painters is the apocryphal story told of Wu Daozi, a great muralist of the Tang period, none of whose works have survived. According to the story, Wu asked one night for lodging at a monastery. Rebuffed by the monks, he lingered only long enough to paint a vivid representation of a donkey on one of the monastery walls. When the monks awoke the next morning, they found, much to their chagrin, that Wu's donkey had descended from the wall and had kicked their furniture to bits.

The techniques of producing translucent porcelain–known fittingly in the West as "china"–were developed. Tang polychrome earthenware figures of mounted horsemen, animals, and men and women, often burial items, are also highly esteemed by collectors today. Among the most interesting figures are those of foreigners whose "unChinese" characteristics–large noses and heavy beards–are exaggerated.

Foreign contacts were extensive. The early Tang period was the most open of all Chinese eras to cultural exchange with people of other civilizations, an attractive era. Under the protection of the

[19] Juyi Bai and Arthur Waley, More Translations from the Chinese, Alfred A. Knopf (1919), p. 27

court, many foreign religions established themselves in China, notably Nestorian Christianity, Zoroastrianism, Manichaeism, Judaism, and Islam. Foreign trade in silk, spices, ivory, incense, rhinoceros horn, and other items of small bulk and great value flourished along the Silk Road linking China to the Mediterranean. The capital, Chang'an, teemed with Persians, Arabs, Koreans, Vietnamese, and Japanese. China would not be as open to foreigners and foreign culture again for more than a thousand years.

Chinese culture radiated like a bonfire through neighboring lands including Korea and Vietnam. The splendor of the Tang dynasty had a strong effect on backward Japan in particular. The Japanese had already borrowed the Chinese script in the 5th century; now, dazzled by the cultural brilliance of the Tang, they began to borrow wholesale. Prince Shotoku sent students to China to study Chinese culture, an exodus to more advanced lands that the Japanese would copy in the 19th century.

The Japanese drank deeply of Chinese Buddhism, then in its heyday in Tang China. Buddhism eclipsed Shinto and became virtually a state religion for over a thousand years. Architecturally, the Japanese built the city of Nara in the Yamato plain as a miniature version of the great Chinese capital, Chang'an, built by the Emperor Yang of Sui. The best surviving examples of Chinese architecture of the era are found at Nara, not in China. Many of the arts that make Japan visually and literarily so reminiscent of China also came to the islands during this first, almost frantic wave of cultural borrowing including the tea ceremony, music, and poetry. The islanders, however, rejected some aspects of Confucian society without which any attempt to create a true copy of China was impossible. The revolutionary doctrine of the Mandate of Heaven, for instance, was incompatible with the divine nature of their emperor, a direct descendant of the Sun Goddess. Similarly, the warrior class remained at the top of Japan's social structure.

Printing on paper became common around this time in Tang China, leading to a great increase in literacy. A greater availability of books facilitated a full flowering of the civil service examination system in the succeeding Song dynasty. Another Chinese invention of the Tang era that helped to shape the modern world was gunpowder. The mechanical clock also dates from the Tang. Medically, the Chinese treated goiter with thyroid hormones, and diagnosed diabetes from urine samples. They also understood the angle of variation between true north and magnetic north. All in all, early Tang China stands as one of the most attractive ages in the long history of mankind. Those Chinese most familiar with their country's history, consciously or unconsciously, are offended by the loss of a civilization that could produce such an age at the hands of the West in the 19$^{th}$ century.

Buddhist Statues in Luoyang Grotto

金無鬱蒸之氣
微風徐動有淒
清之涼信安體
之佳所誠養神

Chinese Calligraphy

Tang Tomb Pottery

## E. The Five Dynasties and the Ten Kingdoms 907 to 960)

The 53 years following the collapse of Tang were ones of constant warfare, misgovernment, and abuse of the people, a period strongly resembling the earlier troubled ages of Chinese history, the Period of the Warring States (5$^{th}$ to 3$^{rd}$ centuries, B.C.E.) and the era of the Minor Dynasties (280 to 589 C.E.) Five dynasties rapidly succeeded each other in control of a large part of the north. The great aristocratic families that seized power or attempted to seize power from each other were largely decimated by the continual warfare. The south, divided into independent kingdoms, remained out of the imperial grasp, and refugees from the northern wars swelled the southern population. One felicitous result was an increase in general prosperity in the succeeding Song dynasty, for the south was agriculturally more productive than the Yellow River ("Huang He") plain.

Politically, the principal event of long-range significance was the establishment of control over a broad area of the north, by the Khitan, a Mongolic tribe.

Lamentably, the practice of foot binding, one of the most abusive customs in the long history of humankind, a custom which eventually inflicted suffering on hundreds of millions of young girls, began among the elite in one of the kingdoms in the south, a badge of exemption from manual labor. By the 17$^{th}$ century foot binding was universal among the elite and widespread among ordinary Chinese though less prevalent among women who had to work in the fields. One estimate suggests that as many as two billion Chinese women were subjected to foot binding between the 10$^{th}$ and 20$^{th}$ centuries. The Communists effectively outlawed the practice in 1949.

# *4. Imperial China*

# (960 to 1796)

## A. The Song Dynasty (960 to 1279)

### 1. Political Events

Zhao Kuangyin, founder of the Song dynasty, was chief general of the Later Zhou, last of the Five Dynasties. Sent north to repel the Khitan, Zhao was awakened at dawn by his mutinous chief officers and forcibly clothed in the imperial yellow. Reluctantly he consented to become emperor but stipulated that no harm should befall the members of the ruling Later Zhou house. Marching on the capital, he seized power and established the Song dynasty.

Concerned lest his dynasty should suffer the fate of the preceding Five Dynasties, Zhao summoned his generals and offered them lands, riches and titles in return for their resignations. Obediently they complied, and the game of political musical chairs that had endured since the fall of the Tang dynasty came to an end. Thereafter the war-weary independent kingdoms of the south peacefully submitted, and unity was reestablished. To Zhao's credit is the fact that of all the great dynasties in Chinese history, his was the only one peacefully instituted.

### a. Relations with the Nomads (960 to 1126)

Zhao was unique in Chinese imperial history, as he was the only founder of a great dynasty unwilling to turn arms against foreign invaders established in the north. Quickly he made peace with the Khitan, leaving them in control of a considerable area inside the Great Wall. This initial period when the Song controlled most of northern China and all of southern China is known as the Northern Song.

Zhao's immediate successor unsuccessfully tried to expel the Khitan, but thereafter five Song emperors maintained a pacific policy toward the Khitan for over a hundred years. Historians make radically different evaluations of their rule. Some praise them for their pacifist tendencies as the most enlightened sovereigns who ever ruled in China; others condemn them as a "sorry spectacle" for their failure to secure the empire against the nomads. There is some truth in each view. Enlightened they were, for the peace they gave China led to a period of great prosperity and cultural achievement; short-sighted they also were, for, once the friendly Khitan succumbed to other nomads in the north, the time was approaching when the greatest nomad onslaught in history would engulf Song China itself.

The relative peace established with the Khitan came to an end when the Jurchen tribe, vassals of the Khitan in the Amur River valley of northern Manchuria, revolted and drove the Khitan far west into Central Asia. Emperor Huizong unwisely accepted the advice of a conservative faction at his court to take advantage of the

Khitans' defeat and seize territory in the north. The Jurchen moved swiftly, captured the Song capital of Kaifeng (in eastern Henan Province) in 1126, and drove the Song permanently to the south. A surviving Song prince established a new capital at Hangzhou. The period after 1126 is known as the Southern Song. Warfare between the Southern Song and the Jurchen continued sporadically until both were swept away by the Mongol hordes of Kublai Khan a little over a hundred years later.

### b. The Innovations of Wang Anshi (1067-1085)

Only occasionally did the imperial government depart from its position of limited government and rule by moral example. Han Wudi (140-87 B.C.E.) established salt and iron monopolies and created a state trading system in grain. The usurper Wang Mang (9-23 C.E.) went much further, extending Han Wudi's trading system to textiles, creating imperial monopolies in liquor, coinage, forestry and fishing, banning the selling and buying of land, abolishing the slave trade, and introducing novel taxes. Tang Taizong (627-49 C.E.) established price controls over a wide variety of commodities. The last statesman of this stripe was Wang Anshi, Prime Minister to the Song Emperor Shenzong (1067-85). His innovations contrast markedly with the traditionally limited activities of central government.

Although some commentators have described Wang Anshi's reforms as a Chinese experiment in socialism, Wang Anshi was not dreaming of a classless society. His motive for the reforms was to increase tax revenues in preparation for defense of China against nomads again menacing the frontier. Reforms favoring the peasantry would result in more prosperity throughout the empire and yield the higher tax revenues.

The Young Shoots law was a decree designed to free peasants from their dependence since time immemorial on the village moneylender. Under it the government performed the role of an agricultural credit bank lending seed money to peasants in the springtime. Interest rates on these loans, repayable after harvest, were only two percent a month. Private moneylenders demanded sharply higher rates often amounting to 50 per cent total interest over the growing season. Wang Anshi and his group of "Innovators" believed that easy credit would induce peasants to bring additional land under cultivation. The Song government would receive increased tax revenues from harvests on more land being tilled–in addition to its interest profit.

The Remission of Services law attempted to reform the system of annual days of labor on public works owed by the peasantry to the government. In addition to occasional individual hardships caused by calling up peasants at harvest or planting time, the system of taxes paid in labor prevented the government from concentrating its public works in districts where they were most urgently needed. It was impractical to transport large numbers of peasants from district to district. While people could not easily be shifted, though, money could, and Wang Anshi substituted a tax paid in money for the traditional tax paid in services.

The Equalization of Loss law revived the system of ever-normal granaries created originally by Han Wudi. Under it the Song government purchased grain on the open market in provinces with a temporary glut to keep prices from falling so low that the peasants incurred losses. The grain was stored in state granaries throughout China and sold at times when crops were poor and famine threatened. The law provided food for the peasants and kept prices from skyrocketing to the advantage of wealthy hoarders and speculators.

Among other economic reforms of Wang Anshi were 1) the establishment of a budget commission to plan the annual expenditures of the central government with an eye to savings; and 2) reorganization of local land registers to bring back into taxation lands that through local corruption and false returns had gradually filtered out of the tax system.

A reform related to the defense of the empire was the Horse Breeding law, an attempt to overcome China's military disadvantage in numbers of cavalry compared to the nomads. Wang Anshi decreed that families in the northern and northwestern provinces where some terrain was suitable for horses be supplied with a horse and sufficient fodder for the winter months. He established a system of inspection to verify that the "foster parents" of each horse were giving it proper care. By the time dissident Literati overturned Wang Anshi's reforms the system had produced 30,000 cavalry mounts. Had it continued a few years longer, it might have permitted the Song to resist the successful nomadic invasions that occurred soon afterwards.

These reforms were out of keeping with the traditional inactivity of the central government. Although perhaps of great desirability from an idealistic point of view, they appear to have failed because of the human element involved. At the time of the reforms there were simply not enough trained officials capable of administering such a vast expansion of central activity efficiently. Wang Anshi's attempts to overcome that handicap by training additional officials merely compounded the problem, for many of the "new men" came from families lacking in traditions of governmental service and devoted themselves with fervor to self-enrichment through corruption.

The most important reason for the failure of Wang Anshi's innovations was the general opposition of the entrenched Literati class. led by Sima Guang. Compared to Wang Anshi, who was conceited, obstinate and personally unkempt, one of the most appealing characters of the whole episode was the Emperor Shenzong, an unostentatious ruler genuinely interested in the welfare of his people, who was obliged to listen patiently to the flood of "memorials" addressed to the throne by conservatives attacking Wang Anshi's programs.

Their criticism of the "Innovators" shows how deeply conservative traditional Chinese society was. Over and over they stressed that various reforms were not in accord with the ways of the imperial ancestors, that they were not in keeping with the traditional functions of Chinese government, that they departed from the Confucian precept of rule by moral example alone, and that they closely resembled the principles of the long-discredited Legalist School–central control of all aspects of Chinese society through positive law–the school that had committed the unforgivable sin of burning the Confucian literature.

Although the conservatives occasionally argued that Wang Anshi's reforms failed to accomplish their purpose, the bulk of their complaints were a defense of traditional ways. Since it is mostly through their eyes, their leader Sima Guang being one of the great historians of China, that one sees this unusual episode in Chinese history, it is difficult to determine the degree of inefficiency involved.

Despite the opposition of the Literati, Wang Anshi's reforms lasted for eighteen years until the death of Shenzong in 1036.

Repealed by the succeeding regime, the Emperors Zhezong and Huizong revived them from 1193 until 1226, an additional thirty-three years. The dispute between the Innovators and the Conservatives became a moot point in the latter year when the nomadic Jurchen conquered all of north China. Instituted to strengthen the empire militarily, the reforms had had the opposite effect. A China wracked by internal dissension was an easy prey for the Jurchen. Thereafter for almost 800 years the Chinese steadfastly declined to alter the scope of activity of their central autocracy; extensive intervention in the lives of the people by the imperial authorities, for better or worse, was simply out of keeping with the all-embracing Confucianism of late Imperial China.

## 2. The Examination Culture and Social Change

Western historians have adopted the term "Literati" for both the Confucian officials of the government and the local elite. All ultimately traced their beginnings as a distinct social class to the scholar-officials of the Han dynasty. All shared in the Song "examination culture." For the next thousand years, the examinations served as China's political and social and intellectual framework.

During the earliest years of the Han dynasty, selection for the bureaucracy was solely on the basis of recommendation of scholars by provincial authorities. The first modest use of civil service examinations to identify the most talented recommended scholars for official posts began under Han Wudi.

It fell to Tang Taizong, second emperor of the Tang dynasty, to make the results of the examinations the principal means of entering the imperial bureaucracy. He also eliminated the need for a preliminary recommendation and extended eligibility to farmers. Taizong's motive in making the examinations of chief importance in admission to the governing class was to curtail the self-perpetuation of the bureaucratic families who controlled the power of recommendation. New blood constantly infused into the bureaucracy would prevent the establishment of a hereditary counterweight to the omnipotence of the emperor himself.

The decision of Zhao Kuangyin, founder of the Song dynasty, to select the personnel of his government exclusively by examination on the Confucian classics was the momentous step by which Confucianism reestablished itself permanently as China's dominant philosophy. Zhao's motives were self-interested. By staffing his government almost exclusively with scholars chosen by merit and beholden to him, he sought to protect his dynasty from future military men and from those remaining great aristocratic families that had survived the carnage of the Minor Dynasties period. Facilitating his goal was a great increase in the woodblock printing of books that, in turn, facilitated a great increase in literacy. To create a large pool of candidates for the civil service examinations, he initiated a vast enlargement of the Imperial Academy. The goal was a school in every prefecture.

The number of students preparing for the civil service examinations illustrates the institution's evolution. Under the Han, the imperial academy accommodated 50 students; under the Tang, 8,000; at the end of the Song, 400,000. Historians call the culture of China from the Song dynasty forward "the examination culture." One's social position depended on one's participation in the examination system, not on birth into an aristocratic family.

Examinations were given at three different levels, prefectural, provincial and imperial. Candidates for the imperial degree (*jinshi*) were limited to those who held provincial degrees (*juren*), who in turn were chosen from the ranks of the holders of prefectural degrees (*shengyuan*).

Those who had only a *shengyuan* degree, those who failed the exam, and those who had seriously studied for the exams became the new local elite of China. They served as secretaries to prefectural officials, as teachers, as leaders of village associations, and as managers of local projects, such as irrigation works, schools, charitable foundations, and other grassroots tasks. Most were also landlords. With the cooperation of such a large number of educated men spread throughout the empire, the Emperors withdrew from many previous imperial activities, further decentralizing China.

Successful competitors for the *juren* degree at the provincial level were eligible for minor provincial posts with their attendant possibilities of "squeeze," a practice whereby officials charged with collecting a required amount of taxes would collect a greater amount and pocket some of the difference before remitting the balance to their superiors. Officials at every level on the way up kept some of the excess monies; finally the emperor received the taxes he required. Squeeze in limited amounts was considered compensation for often-underpaid officials. Only when it became excessive was it considered corruption.

The odds were quite slim of competing successfully at the imperial level for the *jinshi* degree leading to appointment to the imperial bureaucracy; by the end of the Song period less than one per cent passed annually. To those who earned the degree, high office and riches were commonly, though not automatically, available. A special honor was conferred upon the 25 *jinshi* with the highest scores each year. They entered the prestigious Imperial Academy, a reservoir of the finest minds in China. There, while awaiting call to high office, members spent their lives in study of the Confucian classics. Frequently they were selected to grade the examination papers of later candidates who aspired to emulate them.

Ranking behind the Literati in the Chinese social scale were, in order of prestige, farmers, artisans, merchants, and the "mean people" (barbers, actors, servants, prostitutes, and the like). According to Confucian theory the merchant was a social parasite producing nothing tangible like the farmer and the artisan. The merchant lived off the labor of others. At times during Chinese history the merchant's low prestige was evidenced by discriminatory dress regulations. A decree during the Minor dynasties period, for instance, required merchants to wear a white turban and one white and one black shoe. Curiously, even the business of mining suffered a moral stigma. It was felt that since no one had planted the minerals, no one was morally entitled to harvest them.

## 3. Interpretations of Confucianism

Thanks to the examination culture, the Song period in China witnessed the greatest intellectual ferment since the era of Confucius, Laozi, and their followers over a millennium earlier. The intense concentration on the Confucian classics stimulated many and varied commentaries.

Some scholars scoured the existing literature for moral role models for the emperor, his officials, and the people. Theirs was a traditional approach like that of Han Yu of the Tang period, who had called for simple, straight-forward writing, an end to China's flirtation with Buddhism as its dominant doctrine, and a return to a pure Confucianism.

Other scholars searched Chinese history for precedents that could lead to the solution of contemporary political, social, and economic problems. As Confucius had said, the proper courses of action were to be found in the past. Their findings varied since the stronger emperors of the past, Han Wudi for instance, had occasionally overruled their Confucian advisors and pragmatically taken novel steps. Some Song scholars considered those past actions precedents for an expanded role of government. Others adhered to the traditional view that the emperors should interfere minimally in the life of the people. These opposing approaches led to the rancorous political struggle between Wang Anshi, Sima Guang, and their followers described above.

Still other scholars sought to buttress Confucianism by giving it a metaphysical content. What had previously been a creed largely based on simple sayings of the early Confucian masters became a creed incorporating various aspects of Taoism and Buddhism–a triumph wrapped in an irony. The justification for this Neo-Confucianism was to be found in the patterns of nature, especially moral patterns. Some said that human intuition could discern these patterns. The dominant view, though, was that only observation of the actual world would reveal the patterns ("the investigation of things"). By such observation, educated gentlemen would be able to cultivate their own moral qualities, regulate their families, and bring social harmony and peace to the State. The great master of this view was Zhu Xi, a 12th century philosopher whose stance eventually became the official version of Confucianism on which the examination system was based. Important sources for Zhu were the sayings of Confucius and Mencius, and the ancient *Classic of Rites.*

## 4. Economic and Demographic Changes

With many decades of peace, the population of Song China expanded to an estimated 100 million by the end of the dynasty. Several cities had over 1,000,000 inhabitants. Noteworthy was the growth of cities beyond the centers of political power. Some had a population of hundreds of thousands, and at least one counted a million. With the demographic surge, the economy expanded, and the number of smaller market towns also increased substantially. Some regions began to specialize (e.g. in textile production, the growing of tea, and porcelain manufacture).

Food production greatly increased. Fast-ripening, drought resistant strains of rice were introduced from Champa (southern Vietnam). The growing season declined from 150 days to 100. With crossbreeding experiments, it declined to 60 days by the end of the Song era. Growing two rice crops and one winter wheat crop became common in the south. A greater supply of organic fertilizers (human waste), resulting from the growth of population, also increased food production.

Song China was also an advanced and sophisticated land in technology and industry. It was at a level of economic development not seen in Europe until the 18$^{th}$ century. Steel production reached 125,000 tons a year, a five-fold increase from that of the Tang dynasty, a remarkable level for the time. Coal was used as an industrial fuel. Production of tin and lead each increased about 50 times that of the Tang. The imperial kilns in the town of Jingdezhen in northeastern Jiangxi Province produced large quantities of porcelain. Silk cloth of various sorts was another important manufacture. Both were major items of an expanded international trade encouraged by the emperors. Paper money began to circulate generally for the first time. Even the production of coins was 20 times greater than during the Tang dynasty. Instruments created for facilitating transactions on credit complemented the increased money supply in expanding China's economy.[20]

Important improvements in naval architecture occurred as China developed a significant fleet. Some ships were so large that they could transport several hundred passengers and crew. The magnetic compass, a Chinese invention of uncertain date, was used for the first time for navigation, and excellent navigational charts were developed. Chinese merchants sailed as far as India. Since merchants had a low social standing, Literati families did not participate directly in this trade. They did participate indirectly, though, by various arrangements with merchants. All in all, the Song period was one of the most prosperous in Chinese history.

## 5. Cultural Advances

Song China, though less cosmopolitan than Tang China, is one of China's most attractive ages,. The printing of inexpensive books spurred a great increase in literacy and a lively intellectual life. Significant advances occurred in mathematics, literature, the fine arts, and social mores.

Technological advances were numerous. Significant inventions included the two-gated canal lock, which greatly improved

[20] Before the Chinese invented paper money in Song times, the accumulation of substantial capital for any purpose whatsoever was risky. China lacks natural gold deposits, and most of its coinage has always been in copper. Thus, the accumulation of large sums involved hundreds of thousands, if not millions of coins. Hiding such bulky quantities of coins from bandits was of extreme difficulty, and the Chinese preferred to keep their wealth in land rather than money. It is probable that the sheer bulk of copper coins contributed to the invention of paper money by the bankers of Sichuan under the Song. Paper money was of greater convenience in large transactions than wagon loads of coins.

transportation on the Grand Canal, the chain drive, the spinning wheel, and movable type. The latter dates from about 400 years before Johann Gutenberg. Because of the thousands of characters of written Chinese, however, and because composed of fired clay, movable type failed to supplant woodblock printing. A great school of algebraists flourished. Inoculation against smallpox was known during the Song period but not widely practiced until the late 16th century, more than 200 years before Edward Jenner developed his method of vaccination in England in 1796. The era also saw important treatises on botany, including the earliest account in any language of citrus varieties. Gunpowder, considered one of China's "Four Great Inventions," along with the magnetic compass, paper, and printing, was used for the first time militarily in the form of grenades.

The Chinese always considered historical works the highest form of literature, and Sima Guang was one of the greatest practitioners. He wrote an outstanding history covering the 1,500 years preceding the Song era. The era also saw the beginning of some 200 local histories, the writing of which swelled to 1,000 in the Ming era (1368 to 1644) and to 5,000 in the Qing era (1644 to 1912), treasure troves of information for historians.

In the fine arts, porcelain came into its own. Song potters strove for simplicity and elegance. Their wares, usually of a single color, sometimes incised, sometimes with designs in relief, sometimes translucent, and sometimes with carefully controlled crackling of the surface are delicate and beautiful.

Painting also flourished. Though excellent work was done in genre and scenes of court life, the glory of the Song was small pictures of birds, animals, or flowers and, especially, monumental landscapes. Somewhere in a painting of mist-shrouded mountains and lakes, hills and valleys is a tiny figure of Man, a sage contemplating Nature, a fisherman bringing in his boat, or a woodchopper. Without Man there would be no true portrayal of Nature, for Man is a part of Nature but far smaller, a Daoist view.

Mostly monochromatic, the landscapes are visual illustrations of Neo-Confucianism. They seek to capture the essence of what it is to be a tree, a mountain, a lake, a rabbit, or a bird. They show the patterns of Nature, generic Nature, not the characteristics of a particular tree, mountain, lake, rabbit, or bird. The aim of the Neo-Confucianist artist was not to paint realistically but, through observation of the world, to paint philosophically. The paintings are an expression of the ideal rather than the real. The thought behind these paintings is similar to Plato's theory of forms.

Since Chinese painters used the same writing brush as Chinese calligraphers, the Literati with their years of practice in forming the complex characters of the Chinese script always had an advantage in the techniques of painting, Art remained a scholar's art. It was unique in that these scholars were also the leaders and governors of the country. Aesthetic refinement and political savvy went hand in hand. The pine tree standing isolated on the edge of a ravine appears in many Chinese paintings as a symbol of the steadfastness of the scholar in the face of adversity.

Northern Song landscapes achieved a sense of depth. Southern Song landscapes tended to be minimalist. A further development occurred when Su Shi popularized writing landscape poems on landscape paintings, a felicitous combination of poetry, calligraphy, and painting.

In addition to the initiation of the "examination culture," the great flourishing of philosophy, and the significant economic and technological advances, Song China had great accomplishments in historical literature and the fine arts. The Chinese have every reason to be proud of the civilization they were to lose in the 19th century.

## B. The Yuan (or Mongol) Dynasty (1279 to 1368)

### 1. The Mongol Conquest

A cataclysm swept over China in one direction and drove to the plains of Hungary in another: the Mongol empire, the largest empire the world has ever known. Its founder, Genghis Khan, was the dispossessed son of a tribal chief. Enduring great hardship, by the age of thirty he had a handful of followers. By his late 40's he had welded all the Mongol tribes into one vast military organization under his command and had established his capital at Karakorum in Mongolia.

The Mongols appear in most respects to have been unattractive. Among other repugnant habits, they were forbidden to wash from cradle to grave, they were inclined to excessive drunkenness, they tenderized their meat under their saddles as they rode, and their men were forbidden to engage in any occupation other than hunting and war. Their viciousness in war was often extreme. Any town or city which offered the slightest resistance to the Mongols suffered a cruel fate: every man, woman and child was put to the sword. It was this policy that led to a characterization of the Mongols as "the most savage and pitiless race known to history."

First, the Mongols destroyed the Jurchen; then, they detached Sichuan from Song China; finally, reacting to a bellicose policy of the Song court, they invaded south China. Hostilities endured 45 years, for the mountainous terrain was largely unsuitable for the Mongol cavalry, and the Chinese were their most tenacious opponents. Fighting was not continuous, though, for Genghis's successors Ogedei and Kublai were frequently occupied in other parts of the now-vast Mongol empire. In the end not even the Chinese could withstand the Mongol onslaught. In 1279 they defeated the last of the Song pretenders, and for the first time all China was in the grip of a foreign invader. They ruled from Beijing, chosen as capital for the first time by a ruling dynasty.

## 2. Mongol Rule

Although Marco Polo, who served as a minor official under Kublai Khan, has left an indelibly favorable impression of Mongol rule, the historical facts are considerably more ambiguous.

On the positive side, the Mongols established an excellent postal system with relays of 200,000 fast horses. They extended the Grand Canal to Beijing. They constructed a network of imperial highways connecting all parts of their vast Empire, and by maintaining order over most of the great Eurasian land mass, they made possible foreign trade and an exchange of peoples on a scale never before dreamed of. Moscow had a Chinese quarter; Chinese engineers brought their irrigation techniques to the Tigris and Euphrates valleys; scores of Europeans, among them the merchant Marco Polo and the missionary John of Montecorvino, sojourned in China and took back to Europe new geographical and technical knowledge.

Artistically, the Mongols introduced carpet weaving and indirectly stimulated the development of two major Chinese art forms, the novel and the drama (or "Chinese opera"). Reluctant to rely on the scholar class in governing China, they generally preferred to employ foreigners, such as Polo. Many of the "unemployed" Literati, liberated from governmental duties, wrote dramas and novels, including the famous plays "*Romance of the West Chamber*" and "*The Orphan of Zhao*," the first Chinese drama known in Europe. Many of the great traditional Chinese dramas still performed today date from the Mongol period. They also turned their energies to painting in the Song Dynasty style and created many masterpieces.

On the negative side, after Kublai's death, the Mongols spawned a succession of seven weak emperors, and China bogged down in a sea of corruption (18,000 officials were dismissed). They issued a national paper currency and came close to drowning China in a sea of inflation. They considered executing all Chinese of the family names Zhang, Wang, Liu, Li and Zhao (a large percentage of the population). They imposed vexatious restrictions upon the Chinese. They weakened the examination system by first discontinuing it and later reinstituting it only on a very limited basis. Most unwise perhaps of all, the Mongols adopted Chinese ways only to a limited extent and attempted generally to retain their own customs and identity. Such a practice was contrary to that pursued by the nomadic rulers of the Minor Dynasties, by the Khitan, and by the Jurchen, all of whom became sinified.

For once China was unable to absorb its conquerors; and, after twenty years of rebellion, the Chinese expelled them in 1368. Their empire of which China was only a part was too vast to administer properly. After a few decades of luxury had dulled their fighting spirit, the empire simply dissolved. Today the Mongols are limited geographically to Mongolia and of limited importance on the world scene.

## C. The Ming Dynasty (1368 to 1644)

### 1. The Early Ming Emperors

When the Mongols retreated from China, the foreigners, including Europeans, who had been so visible during their rule, disappeared with them; yet paradoxically, Ming times are the true beginning of the age of the "Western Impact." The Europeans had left possessed of new geographical and technical knowledge; they would soon be back. Confucian civilization had received a shock at the hands of the Mongols; ultimately it would crumble at the hands of their European servants.

The founder of the Ming dynasty, Zhu Yuanzhang, a man with a snoutlike face, nicknamed the "pig emperor," was on a par with Confucius as one of China's ugliest great men. Born of peasant parents, who died in a famine, Zhu in turn became a shepherd, a Buddhist monk, and the leader of one branch of the Red Turbans, another of China's secret societies whose rebellions were an expression of popular opposition to misrule. Leaders of the Red Turbans fought with each other from 1356 to 1367 for the opportunity to establish a new dynasty while the Mongols remained immobilized in their strongholds. After ten years, having eliminated his Chinese competitors, Zhu sent an army of a quarter of a million against the Mongol capital, Beijing. The last of the Mongol emperors fled northward, and Zhu established the Ming dynasty with its capital at Nanjing (formerly "Nanking"). One of his first acts was to confiscate much land from wealthy families and redistribute it to China's peasants, a goal of all the Red Turbans' leaders. Like Han Wudi and Tang Taizong, Zhu was also active in the early years of his reign in campaigning against various nomadic tribes to the west and, especially, to the north.

His reign is noteworthy for internal developments in the machinery of government. Two of his innovations with regard to the examination system are of great importance. To his credit he extended eligibility for the first time to grandsons of merchants and ushered in a modest increase in social mobility; previously eligibility was limited to those who had not had a merchant ancestor in the previous three generations.

From Ming times forward the principal possibility for some members of merchant families to escape from their humiliating status as parasites was the civil service examinations. Obtaining degrees would raise the prestige and prospects of the entire family. Capital which might have been accumulated for trade or industry was diverted to provide the younger generations with leisure for study. Even disposable funds not needed for education were unlikely to be accumulated for industry, for such was the desire of the merchants to share in the prestige of the Literati that they emulated the latter in their choice of investments. Land was the favorite investment of the Literati, and prosperous merchants were quick to become landlords, not industrialists, and to intermarry into less wealthy Literati families. China remained agricultural.

Nor did the Literati exercise a social control over the merchant class solely by siphoning off some of the best talent in that class into their own ranks; individual Literati also exercised a very personal control over individual merchants. Except during the short-lived Qin dynasty, China was a land governed primarily on the basis of ethical principles rather than by law. *China had no commercial code of law to protect contracts and property.* The Chinese merchant depended for his protection on members of the Literati. The aggrieved

Western merchant sought redress in the king's courts; the aggrieved Chinese merchant sought redress through his carefully cultivated "connections" with the Literati.

Unfortunately, although Zhu liberalized eligibility for the examinations, he sterilized their content by prescribing a rigid literary form, the "Eightlegged Essay." Gone were any questions on practical matters of defense, taxation, and the like.

Candidates wrote a poem and an eight-legged essay of eight sections containing eight paragraphs of prescribed structure and content. The most difficult to compose must have been the fifth and sixth which were rhythmically arranged in four and six word phrases. The resulting essay was often trite or pedantic and by omitting questions on mathematics helped minimize Ming technological advances. On the other hand, the poetry requirement indicates that Chinese civilization, unlike others, considered aesthetic sensitivity a part of the mental equipment necessary for governing.

A typical subject for the essay was Confucius's statement, "The superior man bends his attention to what is radical. That being established, all practical courses naturally grow up. Filial piety and fraternal submission, are they not the root of all benevolent actions?"[21] A typical subject of the poem was "the green of the hills and the sound of the oars."

The student emerged from the many rigorous years of preparation for the examinations with much mental maturity and analytic ability but factually ignorant concerning practical matters. One of the hallmarks of the traditional Chinese official was that, unlike his counterparts in other civilizations, he was an amateur

---

21 The Analects of Confucius, James Legge (translator), Part 1.

rather than a professional. He tended to look askance at such studies as mathematics, which in his view was a narrow specialty not relevant to the art of governing. Although professional training in accounting might seem more useful to the tasks of the Board of Revenue than knowledge of the myriad literary allusions of the Confucian classics, most Literati were firm in the belief that the narrow specialist would never be able to provide that government by moral example, which the *jinshi* could provide. They spent much of their leisure and some of their official time in such refining activities as painting, calligraphy, and the composition of verse.

The examination system was a key factor in the stability of traditional Chinese civilization as well as in its dissolution in the face of the Western Impact. In view of the complexities of the Chinese script, the achievement of mere literacy was no mean feat, and beyond literacy itself lay the complexities of memorizing and understanding the Confucian classics. After these fatiguing labors the Literati were for the most part indifferent to other forms of learning, an indifference that prevented them from profiting by new knowledge in multiple disciplines. Learning tended to exhaust itself in the classics. Had not the rewards been so high, perhaps the Chinese might have reserved some of their energies for nonConfucian studies. A perceptive comment in this regard came from the pen of the Jesuit priest Matteo Ricci, who lived in China in Ming times:

> It is evident to everyone here that no one will labor to attain proficiency in mathematics or in medicine who has any hope of becoming proficient in the field of philosophy. The result is that scarcely anyone devotes himself to these studies unless he is deterred from the

> pursuit of what are considered to be the higher studies by reason of family affairs or by reason of mediocrity of talent. The study of mathematics and that of medicine are held in low esteem, because they are not fostered by honors as is the study of philosophy, to which students are attracted by the hope of glory and the rewards attached to it. This may be readily seen in the interest taken in the study of moral philosophy. The man who is promoted to the higher degrees in this field prides himself on the fact that he has attained to the pinnacle of Chinese happiness.[22]

More harmful to China perhaps than the low esteem in which mathematicians and physicians were held was the indifference of the Literati to ideas and knowledge developed by other civilizations, an indifference which became a tragic resistance in the 19th Century as Western influences rendered China's agricultural civilization obsolete. China most of the time remained an intellectually closed world; only in the introduction of Buddhism had there been an intense Chinese interest in foreign learning before the 20th century. Throughout much of late imperial history the examination system reinforced the barriers of geography to keep China isolated.

So complete was the self-immersion of the Literati in the study of the classics to the exclusion of other subjects that the examination system was the key to a successful system of voluntary thought control. Despite the benefits of moral philosophy as an ideological control in softening the conduct of an absolutist central government, the ablest men in China voluntarily subjected

22 Matteo Ricci and Nicola Trigault, China in the Sixteenth Century. The Journals of Matthew Ricci: 1583-1610 (trans. Louis J. Gallagher), Random House, 1953

themselves to an exhausting course of studies leading to the conclusion that the status quo was the best of all possible worlds. The vast amount of time spent not long ago in Communist China studying the thoughts of Chairman Mao Zedong, the all-encompassing ideology of recent Chinese society, had ample precedent.

Under Zhu Yuanzhang the Censorate whose origins are traceable to Han times reached full development. The early Han emperors dispatched officials periodically from the capital to check on provincial authorities. To assure their unbiased reporting of the misconduct of provincial officials who might rank higher in the hierarchy, the central government carefully removed its inspectors from the normal chain of bureaucratic command. The practice of independent inspection became institutionalized on a permanent basis under the Ming dynasty. Headed by two Censors-General, its key operating personnel were 56 provincial censors organized into 15 circuits throughout the provinces of China. Other censors watchdogged the imperial capital and the central bureaucracy stationed there.

Although it had no power itself to punish misdeeds, the Censorate, through memorials to the throne, was a powerful force for clean, competent government. It exposed corruption and criticized the government at all levels. Lesser functions were auditing accounts of the taxing authorities, surveillance of state property, supervision of the construction of public buildings and dams, and management of public charities.

The Censorate was a means of preventing oppression of the people by provincial officials–and possible transfer of the Mandate of Heaven–through the two great evils of the Chinese bureaucracy: nepotism and squeeze. Since Confucianism valued loyalty to the family above all else, nepotism reached its height in traditional China. Rare was the official who always put the public interest ahead of the obligations of filial piety and resisted family pressures for sinecures, preferences in government contracts, and the withdrawal of land from tax registers.

The problem of squeeze was more ambiguous. It was always difficult to draw the line between reasonable and excessive squeeze. The official who squeezed excessively was not committing an act of a different kind from normally sanctioned conduct but merely of a different degree. Even those officials most dedicated to the public welfare were compelled to resort to the practice to avoid humiliating poverty. A provincial official had wide latitude in interpreting his duties and setting the amount of taxes due; it was expected that his administration would be a highly personal one. The Censorate functioned as the eyes and ears of the throne to determine the balance between just compensation and oppression of the people. A wealthy Chinese landowner or merchant did not have recourse to law to protect him against official extortion. Confucianism stressed regulation of society through individual moral qualities as opposed to the impersonal law advocated by the discredited Legalist School.

## 2. The Voyages of Zheng He

Zhu's successor was an emperor of no outstanding ability. His tenure was brief, however, for his uncle Zhu Di, better known to history as the Yongle Emperor, usurped the throne. Like Zhu Yuanzhang, he was vigorous in campaigns against the nomads and successfully asserted Chinese military superiority, giving China some 200 years of peace.[23]

His reign is significant for the extraordinary voyages of the eunuch admiral Zheng He. Given advances in naval architecture, it was inevitable that sooner or later the Chinese would cross the massive barrier to the east, the Indian Ocean. After some 1,500 years in which China's main contacts with Mediterranean lands were overland via the Silk Road of central Asia, suddenly the Chinese for thirty years became the greatest naval power in the world. Here one encounters the most intriguing mystery in Chinese history.

In the annals of naval exploration, Zheng He merits a place alongside Christopher Columbus, Vasco da Gama, Ferdinand Magellan, and Captain Cook. Exactly why the Yongle emperor provided him with the opportunity to earn a reputation as one of the great sailors of history is unclear. Several explanations, none genuinely satisfactory, have been offered: 1) a desire to win suzerainty over other civilized nations; 2) a desire to win new allies in the event of an attempted reconquest of China by the Mongols; 3) the need to import horses, sulfur, copper ore, spices, etc., upon which the coastal areas of China had grown to depend; 4) the decline in importance of the land routes with the collapse of the Mongol Empire; 5) a search for a nephew of the Yongle emperor, whose claim to the throne threatened the latter's position; 6) court intrigue between the Literati and palace eunuchs; and 7) the ambition of the Yongle emperor to leave his imprint on the pages of

[23] With his gaze fixed on the northern frontiers, the Yongle Emperor committed his greatest mistake by transferring his capital from Nanjing ("Southern Capital") to Beijing ("Northern Capital"). Chinese civilization was now clearly most vibrant in the center and south of the country; and the Ming emperors, far to the north in Beijing, increasingly lost touch with the mainstream of Chinese life.

history. All of the aforementioned reasons appear to contain some element of truth.

The first of Zheng He's great expeditions set sail in 1403 from Suzhou in southern Jiangsu Province, a vast armada of 63 ships and 27,870 men. In all seven of Zheng He's expeditions some 250 vessels and 70,000 men took part. Ibn Batutta, a seasoned Arab traveler, described the larger ships as having four decks with public rooms and spacious cabins with closets. He noted that some crew members brought their wives and children; others brought a concubine.

The range of these voyages was remarkable for the times. In addition to reaching Java, Malacca, Bengal, and Sri Lanka, the Chinese fleets visited the Somali coast of East Africa and, sailing up the Red Sea, reached the port of Jeddah, from where seven Chinese traveled overland to the holy city of Mecca. The cargoes brought back by these expeditions were as varied as their ports of call. Among items delivered by Zheng He to the Yongle emperor were the king of Sri Lanka, who had refused to recognize Chinese suzerainty, and a live giraffe from East Africa. Unfortunately, no record is available of Zheng He's solution to the interesting problem of how to feed and care for a giraffe on board ship. Most important were such intangible items as the recognition of Chinese suzerainty by some 16 states extending from Malacca to the Persian Gulf and a wealth of information on sea lanes, navigation problems, available harbors and foreign customs.

Then, suddenly, the voyages ceased. Again, several reasons have been advanced for China's failure to capitalize on the exploits of the great eunuch admiral: 1) the deaths of Zheng He and the Yongle emperor, the prime movers behind the voyages; 2) the threat of a new Mongol invasion, a concern that concentrated the court's attention once more on the land frontiers to the north; 3) realization that the financial resources of the government were too slender to support an aggressive foreign policy on a virtually global scale; and 4) rivalry between the palace eunuchs and the Literati, who seized every opportunity to downgrade the achievements of the eunuch admiral. Again, all of the aforementioned reasons appear to contain some element of truth.

Not only were no further expeditions undertaken but even the construction of seagoing vessels was prohibited. So complete was the about-face in policy that the imperial court attempted to suppress even the memory of Zheng He's seven expeditions. The ancient policy that forbade Chinese vessels to leave coastal waters was revived. A spirit of isolationism prevailed in Beijing.

Zheng He's expeditions dwarfed the Portuguese feat that changed the course of history when Vasco da Gama became the first European to sail the Indian Ocean 64 years after Zheng He's final voyage. Had the Ming dynasty maintained China's newfound naval supremacy, the Europeans would have immediately confronted the most powerful and wealthiest nation on Earth. China withdrew behind its borders, however, and the Portuguese, British, Spanish and Dutch encountered little difficulty in dominating one by one the kingdoms and principalities of southern Asia. The personnel of the early voyages were not the finest representatives of the West. The chances of returning from the long voyage to Asia were 50-50 at best, and only the most reckless soldiers of fortune were attracted to them. The Chinese long used the term "Ocean Devils" to describe Westerners.

There might have been no history of Western colonialism in Asia, had China not turned inward. China was to pay dearly for its missed opportunity when Western arms, victorious everywhere, finally turned to China in the 19th century. Given the enormous advantage in resources that China enjoyed in the 15th century, one is compelled to conclude that the ultimate reason for the Western triumph lay in the domain of psychology; the Chinese simply lacked the tremendous urge for expansion that the kingdoms of the European peninsula possessed.

The Yongle Emperor, the imperial sponsor of Zheng He's remarkable voyages, was the last forceful emperor of the Ming; and, in the ensuing 200-odd years, history was destined to repeat itself wearily as a succession of talentless or unresponsive emperors, often dominated by palace eunuchs if they had inherited the throne as children, gradually spelled the end of Ming relevance.

## 3. The Zheng Family, Pirates and Patriots

The Ming dynasty's decision after the Yongle Emperor's death to prohibit the construction of seagoing vessels created a naval vacuum rapidly filled by pirates who ravaged the Chinese coast from the 15th century onward. The fate of the Ming dynasty eventually became bound up with one group of these pirates, the Zheng family, pirates and patriots, who supported the last of China's native dynasties militarily while filling their own coffers with loot from Dutch, Spanish and Portuguese merchantmen.

The first of this remarkable family, Zheng Zhilong, emigrated to Taiwan to serve as an interpreter to the Dutch, who had begun to colonize that sparsely settled island in 1623. Turning pirate, Zheng Zhilong assembled a fleet of a thousand ships by 1626 and moved his fleet to Xiamen (in Fujian province).

The Ming then sought an alliance with Zheng Zhilong to alleviate the Dutch threat to China's southern coasts. Fearful of the growing power of the Manchus in the north, the Ming were reluctant to fight on two fronts. Zheng Zhilong entered into the proposed alliance and, with greater foresight than the Ming, began to prepare for the possibility that the Manchus might succeed in conquering the Empire. A man of vision, he conceived of Taiwan, protected by his fleet, as a last refuge of Ming civilization–a precedent for the refuge sought on Taiwan by the Nationalist government of Chiang Kaishek in 1949. Zheng Zhilong began to encourage Chinese emigration to the island. As he foresaw, the Manchus invaded in 1644, and all of north China fell rapidly to their arms. Zheng Zhilong was taken prisoner by the Manchus and executed in that year.

The task of realizing his vision fell to his better-known son, Zheng Chenggong (known as "Koxinga"), whose refusal to surrender the fleet to the Manchus was a contributing cause of his father's execution. Though he surrendered his father's life, Koxinga remained faithful to the concept of Taiwan as a last bastion of the Ming. After a number of years of military operations on the mainland with a force of 50,000 cavalry, 70,000 infantry and a formidable fleet of 3,000 ships, he found himself endangered by a Manchu pincers movement from west and north. Viewing the Ming's military situation on the mainland as hopeless, Koxinga decided to challenge the Dutch for complete control of Taiwan.

Delayed by monsoons, Koxinga appeared off the coast of Taiwan near the Dutch fortress of Casteel Zeelandia in the spring of 1661. Taking advantage of a river too shallow for the larger Dutch ships, he landed troops to the rear of Casteel Zeelandia and blockaded the Dutch by land and by sea. When the Dutch surrendered after a six-month siege, only 500 survivors remained. Koxinga was in complete control of the island.

To make his control unchallengeable, Koxinga, like his father, encouraged Chinese immigration to the island. He decreed that immigrants be given land exempt from taxation for three years and supplied the necessary transportation of settlers with his vast fleet. The Chinese population of the island grew from some 25,000 to 400,000 in approximately 50 years.

Unfortunately, death struck again and Koxinga died, probably from tuberculosis, at the age of thirty-nine in the spring of 1663. At the time of his death he was preparing to extend his rule by taking the Philippines from the Spanish, a substantial extension of his father's original vision of creating a haven of Ming culture off China's shores. Like his father before him, Koxinga died before realizing his plans, and the mantle of the Zheng family fell to his son Zheng Jing, who continued to encourage Chinese immigration, undertook occasional military expeditions against the Manchus, and governed the island ably. Upon his death in 1681, the fortunes of the Zheng family declined, and in 1683 after a naval victory, the Manchus annexed the island and ended the saga of the Zheng family.

Even though unable to keep Taiwan free as a bastion of Ming civilization, the Zheng family influenced future history, for they initiated the great migration of Chinese into other lands. Future generations of Chinese emulated the acts of the pioneers on Taiwan and gradually created the substantial and influential Chinese communities found today from the United States to Southeast Asia.

## 4. Economic Advances and Social Tension

The economic expansion begun under the Song continued during the long period of peace under the Ming. Regional specialization accelerated; the number of market towns increased; and production rose. Facilitating these advances were a significant increase in population, the rise of banking houses, the establishment of an efficient empire-wide postal system, and in the late Ming period an influx of Mexican silver via trade with the Spanish in the Philippines.

As more merchant families grew wealthy, social tensions with the Literati increased. Wealth competed with education for social prestige, but without a strong system of legal protection for contracts and private property, merchants continued to depend on personal connections, including intermarriage with Literati families, for protection.

Moreover, agriculture progressed *pari passu* with commerce and industry. The Song dynasty saw the introduction of lentils and rice that matured in 100 days–eventually in 60 days–and required less moisture, permitting two crops a year and the utilization of additional land. The Ming dynasty saw the introduction of corn, peanuts, potatoes, and sweet potatoes–all from the New World. The sweet potato was of particular importance because it tolerated sandy soil and allowed use of much marginal land. Complementing the introduction of new crops were two new farming practices: 1) stocking rice paddies with fish, and 2) crop rotation instead of allowing one half of the land to lie fallow each year, resulting in a vast increase in agricultural production.

Many of the new crops increased the efficiency of agricultural labor. After his wheat or rice had been sown, the Chinese peasant did not have to wait in partial idleness till harvest time but could plant other crops with different growing seasons.

## 5. The Jesuits Arrive

Some Westerners reached Ming China. The most famous of these was the perceptive Jesuit Matteo Ricci, who arrived in 1582. Before his death in Beijing in 1610, Ricci had well earned his reputation as one of history's greatest missionaries. Recognizing the profound cultural conservatism of the Chinese, Ricci was quick to adopt Chinese dress, eat Chinese food, learn the Chinese language, study the Confucian classics, and point out similarities between the teachings of Confucius and the Gospel of Jesus. In bringing Western knowledge of cartography to Beijing, Ricci tactfully showed the Middle Kingdom at the center of his map of the world. He admired such aspects of Chinese culture as the value placed on peaceful relations with other nations: "Policies of war are formulated and military questions are decided by the Philosophers only, and their advice and counsel has more weight with the King than that of the military leaders. In fact very few of these and only on rare occasions, are admitted to war consultations. Hence it follows that those who aspire to be cultured frown upon war and would prefer the lowest rank in the philosophical order to the highest in the military."[24]

Ricci and his Jesuit colleagues and successors, practically alone among the thousands of Christian missionaries eventually sent to China, realized that their faith would have to be sinified if it

[24] Louis J. Gallagher (translator), *China in the Sixteenth Century: The Journals of Matthew Ricci*, Random House (1942), an English translation of Matteo Ricci and Nicolas Trigault's *De Christiana expeditione apud Sinas suscepta ab Societate Jesu*.

were to succeed in China. The Dominican and Franciscan orders viewed the Jesuit strategy as a threat to the purity of the faith; and a long simmering quarrel broke out, only resolved officially in 1742 when the Pope forbade Chinese Christians to participate in rites honoring Confucius and their ancestors. Christianity's first attempt to convert China ended.

## 6. Cultural Advances

An evaluation of Chinese culture under the Ming is difficult. While the age is lacking in the exuberant creativity of the Han, Tang and Song periods, some significant advances were registered, and it is not justified to describe the Ming as stagnant and fossilized. It has been aptly remarked that the Ming has had a bad press.

Two of the "Four Great Classical Novels" date from the Ming era. *Water Margin* tells of a group of 108 outlaws granted amnesty by the government and sent on campaigns to defeat rebel forces and repulse foreign invaders. *Journey to the West* is a fictionalized account of the pilgrimage to India by the Buddhist monk Xuanzang during the Minor Dynasties. Both have influenced movies, television series, and plays in later times throughout East Asia.

In other fields the Ming had noteworthy achievements. Talented Ming painters produced many masterpieces. They used more colors than their Song predecessors and developed new techniques. They also combined calligraphy with painting more frequently. Architecture and porcelain reached peaks of excellence under the Ming. The greatest of China's architectural treasures, the Forbidden City of Beijing, was the creation of the Yongle Emperor. Ming potters went beyond the monochromes of the Song by developing the lovely polychrome porcelain of later Chinese history. Ming achievements in the so-called minor arts, such as cloisonné, carpets, ivories, jade, and rosewood furniture, were also significant. All in all, Ming China saw progress in many aspects of civilization, though the era saw little technological progress, a deficiency that boded ill as China came in contact with the European nations.

"Mountain Landscape, in style of Guo Xi, Southern Song dynasty"
Freer Gallery of Art, Smithsonian Institution, Washington, D.C.: Gift of Charles Lang Freer, F1909.190

"A Myriad Bamboo, Section 1, in style of Song Ke, Yuan Dynasty"
Freer Gallery of Art, Smithsonian Institution,
Washington, D.C.: Purchase, F1938.18

## D. The Early Qing Dynasty (1644 to 1796)

The Manchus, the last foreign conquerors of China, were an amalgamation of various tribes living in the northeastern area beyond the Great Wall. A hapless Ming emperor invited them south of the great wall to help crush a rebellion. They decided instead to take all of China.

### 1. Avoiding the Mongols' Mistake

Aware of the animosity the Mongols had provoked by excluding the "Literati" from government, the Manchus employed Chinese scholars in all offices, always paired with a Manchu as co-officeholder. The Manchu's main function was to check up on his Chinese counterpart. That the Manchu was usually less qualified for his duties and obtained promotions more easily led gradually to some decline in Literati prestige and morale. China's scholars could not quite overcome the stigma of serving an alien dynasty. Still, the system of dual offices, by including rather than excluding the Literati, made them more tolerant of foreign rule than was the case under the Mongols. Moreover, the Manchus, well aware that many of the Literati considered them uncivilized, subscribed to most conventional aspects of Chinese culture. Seeking to reduce the cultural gap between themselves and the more advanced Chinese, they exhibited an unyielding devotion to the most orthodox version of Confucianism, a stance that would contribute to their downfall in the years after 1839 when they faced aggressive Western nations.

While the Manchus generally adopted Chinese culture in matters of language, food, dress, ancestor worship, and Confucianism, the latter as useful politically to foreign as to native emperors, there were exceptions. To preserve their own identity, they prohibited intermarriage with their new subjects who outnumbered them by some 35 to 1. To their credit, they forbade the foot binding of Manchu women. To protect themselves against rebellions by the more numerous Chinese, the emperors forbade Manchu men to work and required them to live in military garrisons in eight provincial cities. These garrisons or "banners," were organized along pre-existing clan lines. The Manchus also visually asserted their political dominance by requiring all Chinese males to shave their foreheads and wear the queue, a long pigtail characteristic of the Manchus.

## 2. Early Qing Emperors

The first century and a half of Manchu rule was one of China's golden ages. Two of the ablest emperors in the China's long history had exceptionally long reigns: the Kangxi emperor (1662 to 1722) and his grandson, the Qianlong emperor (1736 to 1796). For over 100 years China enjoyed a greater prosperity under their rule than that in any contemporary European country.

Like the most vigorous of the Han and Tang emperors, Kangxi and, especially, Qianlong sought to eliminate threats from the nomads. During Qianlong's reign, China reached its greatest territorial extent. He penetrated deep into central Asia and in 1759 incorporated much of Turkestan into the Empire as Xinjiang province. He completed the process of bringing the Mongols into the empire. Lamentably, he practiced a degree of genocide on one rebellious group of Mongols, the Zunghar Oirat Mongols. A Qing scholar estimated that 30 per cent of the Zunghar Oirats were massacred, and 40 per cent died of smallpox spread by Qianlong's troops. His treatment of leaders of other conquered enemies was milder. By bestowing official titles and honors and wealth upon them, he gained their loyalty. He incorporated them into the empire rather than humiliate or eliminate them.

Not content to govern from his palace in Beijing, Kangxi undertook six trips during his reign to inform himself personally of the conditions and needs of his empire. He reduced inefficiency and corruption in his bureaucracy. He encouraged industry, granting tax exemptions to the textile and dye industries. He rebuilt China's most important industrial complex, the imperial porcelain works at Jingdezhen, a vast complex of 3,000 kilns using assembly line methods many centuries before Henry Ford. Rebels had destroyed the complex early in Kangxi's reign. He attempted unsuccessfully to eliminate the custom of foot binding among the Chinese. He undertook water control projects that fostered agriculture and helped to prevent the floods of the Yellow River–"China's Sorrow"–that had ravaged the central plain throughout history. Very early in his reign, Kangxi issued 16 maxims for use in the *lijia* system (or Community Compact), a system inherited from previous dynasties. As an expression of orthodox Confucianism, the maxims were a means of strengthening the dynasty. A local magistrate required villagers to attend the lectures twice a month. Accompanied by ritual, incense, musicians, drums, and other embellishments to convey the seriousness of the occasion, the maxims sought to guide the conduct of the populace.

Unfortunately, one of Kangxi's reforms, the Tax Edict of 1712, had unintended consequences that a hundred or so years later would help weaken the Manchu dynasty financially just as the era of the Western Impact began in earnest. Kangxi undertook a survey of land ownership and taxation throughout China to match tax burdens to land productivity. The reform was particularly beneficial to peasant farmers, often abused in Chinese history by successful efforts of the great provincial landowners to shift tax burdens downwards. It also initially stabilized the fiscal basis of the dynasty. With little understanding of the need for economic flexibility when circumstances change, however, Kangxi decreed that the new tax rates, payable in silver, would remain in effect in perpetuity. Chinese scholars concentrated on the Confucian classics rather than on economic theory, and the Literati who advised him were unable to foresee the long-range consequences of what seemed to be a reform so beneficial to both the peasants and the government.

Kangxi's son, the Yongzheng emperor (1722 to 1736), was a man of some ability and a hard worker. He continued his father's efforts to eliminate corruption, simplified the making of policy decisions, and streamlined some other aspects of his bureaucracy. Yongzheng's short reign was also notable for his elimination of legal discrimination against the "mean people." those at the very bottom of Chinese society. Discrimination in practice, though, continued unabated.

Many Western and Chinese historians consider the reign of Yongzheng's son, Qianlong, the apogee of the Qing golden age, a valid evaluation for the period up to about 1775. A hands-on administrator for much of his sixty-year reign, Qianlong maintained and often completed the projects of his predecessors, especially those involving water control and irrigation. He sought competent officials for his bureaucracy and managed affairs in a pragmatic way. He also maintained stores of grain for famine relief.

From about 1775 as old age approached, Qianlong devoted less time to his government and more to pleasure including collecting art and supposedly writing 40,000 poems. He left government in the hands of a favorite, Heshen, probably the most corrupt official in China's long history. Over 24 years, Heshen embezzled or extorted the equivalent of 12 years of imperial revenue and helped deplete the imperial treasury just as the era of belligerent Western encroachment on China was about to begin.

The financial situation of the empire was also affected, first favorably, then negatively, by growth of the population. At first, increased population led to more trade and strengthened the merchant class. Provincial Literati began to move into the cities and engage in commerce, both internal and foreign, and in manufacturing. Constituting about 25 per cent of global trade, Chinese porcelain, tea, silk, lacquer ware, and other manufactures flowed to the far corners of the known world. With little need or desire for foreign goods, China had a favorable balance of trade.

Unfortunately for the Manchus, though, population outstripped agricultural resources, perhaps by 1775 at about the same time that

Heshen began to loot the imperial treasury. The average acreage of a peasant family started a decline from about 10 acres to about 6. Grain surpluses disappeared, and peasants were increasingly unable to pay their land taxes. A landless rural underclass began to form, and social instability began to increase. The inflow of silver from foreign trade, however, temporarily masked the dynasty's looming fiscal problems from the decline in land-tax revenues and from corruption.

Toward the end of Qianlong's reign the balance of trade began to shift. As it deteriorated, China was no longer awash in silver to compensate for reduced land taxes. Ironically, the shortfall in silver further reduced peasants' ability to earn enough to pay land taxes. Peasants normally sold their small surpluses in local markets for copper coins. Their land taxes, however, were payable in silver which increased three times in value compared to copper as silver became scarcer. Inflation in the cost of silver even rendered many peasants with larger than average farms unable to buy enough to pay their taxes; many lost their land, swelling a resentful rural underclass and ushering in the beginnings of social instability. Peasant unrest finally exploded in the rebellion of one of China's secret societies, the White Lotus, in 1796, a revolt that took three years to quell.

The White Lotus had a long duration. Like many Chinese secret societies, it was closely connected with religion, especially a Buddhist belief in the coming of Maitreya, a sort of Buddhist messiah. Organized as a secret society in 1133 with a grand master, blood oaths, secret passwords, an elaborate ritual, nocturnal sessions and an underground organization, it first entered the political sphere by helping to secure the throne for the Mongol dynasty. Later it served as a focal point for dissatisfaction with Mongol rule, and its rebellion in 1322 was a factor in the establishment of the succeeding Ming dynasty. Apparently content under the native Chinese rule of the Ming, it reappears under the Manchu dynasty, another period of foreign rule in China. It rebelled several times in the late 1700s weakening the alien Manchu dynasty. Its history of sporadic rebellions extended over more than 500 years.

With the deterioration of the balance of trade and inability to collect land taxes, the Manchus would eventually be gripped in a financial crisis and unable to finance a serious military response to aggressive Western demands beginning in the 1830s. The crisis was not yet visible, though, at the end of Qianlong's reign. China was still one of the richest lands in the world and looked back on thousands of years of advanced civilization, philosophy, painting, calligraphy, poetry, technology, historical literature, metallurgical techniques, medical discoveries, and an efficient civil service.

Unfortunately, China had turned inward after the voyages of Zheng He during the early Ming dynasty. China remained ignorant of Europe's improvements in military technology. Able emperors that they were, Kangxi, Yongzheng, and Qianlong had one common failing–a lack of interest in developments in far-off parts of the world. Their eyes had been fixed on the Mongols as the major threat to China, and to them the Europeans were just another group of barbarians. That failing would ultimately be catastrophic for China.

## 3. Cultural Advances

As part of their effort to mollify the Literati, the alien Manchu emperors, especially Kangxi, provided much employment for Chinese degree holders in cultural endeavors. A monumental dictionary with over 44,000 characters of the Chinese script was compiled as well a vast encyclopedia and a huge collection of Chinese literature. Some highly original novels were written, including *The Dream of the Red Chamber*, the last of the "Four Great Classical Novels," which occupy the same place in Chinese letters that Shakespeare's plays hold in English literature. Some good poetry was produced. Painting tended to copy earlier styles, but was often of high quality. Porcelain, on the other hand, continued to exhibit originality and reached a peak of excellence under the early Manchus.

Wealthy Europeans, especially in France, eagerly sought Chinese porcelains to decorate their manors, creating what came to be called "chinoiseries." European *philosophes* of the Age of Enlightenment also admired Confucianism as a society based on human reason. European evaluation of Chinese culture was quite positive in the 18th century. That was soon to change.

Unfortunately, the Qing era was as unfruitful in technological progress as the preceding Ming era. That Europe was in the early stages of an industrial revolution and had already undergone a scientific revolution boded ill for the Chinese. Especially damaging was China's failure to move beyond the *ad hoc* technology of the tinkerer to science. The failure is related to China's world view, to its three major creeds. One condition precedent to modern science is a curiosity about Nature. Were Confucianists, Buddhists, or Daoists curious about Nature?

Confucianism, despite its enormous contributions to traditional Chinese civilization, was incompatible with the scientific spirit. Almost uniquely among the creeds of the world, Confucianism concentrated exclusively on humans and their social relations. For the Confucianist, although Nature existed, it was of little importance. A quotation from *The Analects* shows the attitude of Confucius himself:

> Fan Ch'ih requested to be taught agriculture, The Master said, "I am not so good for that as an old farmer." He requested also to be taught horticulture, and was answered, "I am not so good for that as an old gardener." Fan Ch'ih having gone out, the Master said, "A small man, indeed, is Fan Ch'ih! If a superior man love propriety, the people will not dare not to be reverent. If he loves righteousness, the people will not dare not to submit to his example. If he loves good faith, the people will not dare not to be sincere. Now, when these things obtain, the people from all quarters will come to him, bearing their children on their backs; what need has he of a knowledge of agriculture?"[25]

While such an attitude may be conducive to good government and harmonious social relations, Confucianism was not a path to modern science. It served as a restraint on Chinese science.[26]

Whoever truly believed what Buddhism taught had no incentive to investigate Nature. Buddhism denied that life was worth living. Such an attitude is profoundly anti-scientific, for an interest in investigating Man's environment implies that life is, indeed, worth living. One whose ultimate desire is to escape from the pain and suffering of the world is unlikely to have an affirmative, enthusiastic curiosity about it.

---

[25] *The Analects of Confucius*, James Legge (translator), Part 13.

[26] Neo-Confucianiasm, in contrast, involved much metaphysical abstraction and might have led to science, but the conservatism of the Ming and Qing dynasties after the Mongol conquest seems to have deterred such a development.

In Daoism there is an interest in Nature. A quotation from Zhuangzi, a major Daoist philosopher, rather amusingly brings out the Daoist attitude toward Nature in an imaginary conversation between himself and a Confucianist:

> Tungkuo ShunTzu said to Zhuangzi, "Where is this so-called Dao?" Zhuangzi answered "Everywhere." The other said, "You must specify an instance of it."
>
> Zhuangzi replied, "It is here in these ants." Tungkuo replied, "That must be its lowest manifestation, surely." Zhuangzi said, "No, it is in these weeds." The other said, "What about a lower example?"
>
> Zhuangzi said, "It is in this earthenware tile."
>
> "Surely brick and tile must be its lowest place?" "No, it is here in this dung also." To this Tungkuo gave no reply.[27]

While Confucianism was too concerned with human social relations to give birth to science, Daoism was *too accepting of nature* to do so. The Daoist was to lead a life of primitive simplicity in contemplation of the Dao, the way of Nature. The Daoist had no need to *understand* Nature scientifically.

Unlike the Confucianist, the men of the modern West were interested in Nature as well as social relations. Unlike the Daoist, they were interested in social relations as well as Nature. For them Nature was *a gift of God for human exploitation* in the construction of

---

27 Joseph Needham, Science and Civilisation in China, Cambridge University Press, Volume 2, p.47 (1991)

their own society. The exploiters of Nature needed to investigate how Nature worked.

Another reason for China's failure to advance to science-based technology was its failure to advance much beyond algebra, which is not a sufficient basis alone for modern science. Shortly after China's last great algebraic innovations in the Song era, men of the West in the 16th and 17th centuries began that series of mathematical innovations that in less than 500 years created modern industrial society. John Napier invented logarithms in 1614 making possible modern astronomy, and Isaac Newton and Gottfried Wilhelm von Leibnitz independently in 1665 and 1684 invented the infinitesimal calculus, the basic mathematical tool of modern biology, chemistry, physics and all related disciplines. Thanks to their enormous intellectual achievements and those of others the West moved from a position of inferiority, an insignificant peninsula of the great Eurasian landmass to a scientific superiority that has compelled a substantial Westernization of the rest of the world in the last 200 years.

# 5. *The Stability of Confucian Civilization*

For almost 2,000 years Confucian civilization and culture enjoyed a remarkable stability, a longevity and brilliance rarely matched in human history. China was a land of prosperity, technological ingenuity, cultural refinement, and mild rule–marred, though, by male domination of women, especially through its last several hundred years. The Chinese considered their country the Middle Kingdom, the center of the civilized world, ruled by the "Son of Heaven." All other lands were but tribute states. The Chinese graciously received and accorded the valuable privilege of trade to those who bore gifts to the Emperor and recognized China as the fount of civilization radiating in all directions–the Middle Kingdom surrounded by the "Barbarians of the Four Corners." When King George III of England sent a mission to Beijing in 1793 to request the establishment of diplomatic relations, Emperor Qianlong responded in the same way he would have responded to any "barbarian" nomads on China's borders:

> As to your entreaty to send one of your nationals to be accredited to my Celestial Court...this request is contrary to all usage of my dynasty and cannot possibly be entertained....It behooves you, O King, to respect my sentiments and to display even greater devotion and

> loyalty in the future, so that, by perpetual submission to our Throne, you may secure peace and prosperity for your country hereafter.[28]

Although earlier chapters have discussed most of the factors individually contributing to China's millennia-long cultural stability, it remains to see how those factors supported one another in an integrated whole. Chinese civilization had far fewer loose ends than other civilizations.

Ten major causes of the stability of Chinese civilization are the following:

Confucianism
The political system
Actions of Shi Huangdi, and Han Wudi
Territorial unity
Geography (human and physical)
Intensive agriculture
Written Chinese
Prosperity
Technology
Social Structure (Literati)

**Han Wudi's** adoption of **Confucianism** shaped the **political system** in several ways. By limiting the role of the emperors mostly to water management and defense, functions with precedents in the past, it minimized the need for large central revenues and helped maintain local **prosperity** by keeping taxes low. Ironically, **Han**

[28] Qian Long: Letter to George III (1793), Modern History Sourcebook, Fordham University

**Wudi** also minimized the need for imperial taxes by establishing iron and salt monopolies, innovations without precedents in the past. **Confucianism** also **politically** allowed local resolution of local problems (by the **Literati,** especially from the Song dynasty on) in an era when inadequate transportation and communication made decentralized decision making preferable. It promulgated a moral code with reciprocal rights and duties binding even the emperors. It conceived of society as a hierarchy–a large family in which all knew their place with the emperor at the top. Should the emperor not govern his family well and mildly, it allowed his **political** overthrow under the doctrine of the Mandate of Heaven and legitimated the rule of the succeeding dynasty.

The **political system**, in turn, shored up **Confucianism** in several ways. From an early date the imperial government overcame the problem of nepotism in a society based on family relations by 1) never posting officials to their home provinces and by rotating them to a new province every three years and 2) sending inspectors from the Censorate periodically to check on activities of local officials.. China, consequently, had competent, educated secular officials over 1,000 years before Europe. The civil service examination system reinforced **Confucianism** by making long, profound study of that philosophy a requirement for entry into the government to some extent from the Tang dynasty but especially from the Song dynasty on.

**Confucianism** reinforced **agriculture** through the moral requirement that filial sons should always obey their fathers, ensuring family solidarity and survival in a land of labor-intensive agriculture. **Agriculture**, in turn, reinforced **Confucianism** by preserving prosperity through technological innovations and the introduction of new crops and new techniques in the face of increasing population. In addition, the intensive nature of Chinese **agriculture**, farming by hand, also led to higher yields on available land. The resulting surplus contributed to farm **prosperity** and fostered considerable urbanization. These improvements in **agriculture** contributed to keeping the **Literati**, the guardians of **Confucianism**, at the top of the **social structure**. China was an agricultural civilization. As long as agriculture progressed, the social structure remained intact.

China's human **geography** also reinforced **Confucianism**. China's only aggressive neighbors, the nomads, were at a lower level of culture. Other civilizations were isolated from China by mountains and deserts. Even when the nomads defeated the Chinese militarily and occupied large areas of China, they normally adopted Chinese culture. Confucianism's sway over China, consequently, was little challenged by foreign ideas. The one exception was otherworldly Buddhism, which practical-minded Confucianists brought under control in the Tang dynasty. China's physical **geography** also contributed to China's **prosperity**. The Yellow, Yangzi, and other rivers permitted extensive irrigation and abundant yields on the arable land owned by Chinese farmers and landlords.

**Shi Huangdi's** conquests of all the other remaining contenders at the end of the Period of the Warring States from 230 to 222 recreated the **territorial unity** of the Chinese people after five centuries of division. Cruel as it was, **Shi Huangdi's** decision to build the original Great Wall of China helped overcome the **geographical** problem of warring nomads' easy access to the north China plain and gave considerable protection to the culture built on **Confucianism**. The mountainous **geography** of south China, on the other hand, gave **Confucianism** a safe haven even when the nomads could breach the Great Wall. The terrain of south China was unsuitable for the nomads' cavalry. The one exception to the safe haven was the Mongols' dogged 45-year conquest of all China.

The Chinese **written language** helped maintain China's stability by overcoming negative aspects of China's human **geography**. With different, mutually incomprehensible languages and dialects at the beginning of the imperial era, **Shi Huangdi's** standardization of written Chinese characters allowed empire-wide communication and helped maintain China's **territorial unity**.

**Technology also** contributed to China's **prosperity.** A few of the many technological advances that contributed to general **prosperity** were paper, printing, paper money, use of coal as fuel, steel making, stirrups, porcelain, clocks, and many medical discoveries.. The breast strap harness for horses, deep drilling, planting crops in rows, rotation of crops, pest control, and advanced water management techniques are a few of the many technological advances that strengthened Chinese **agriculture.**

Which of the factors in China's stability were the most important? The most important were the **prosperity** of a **technologically** advanced **agricultural** land **geographically** isolated from contact with other civilizations and **territorially unified** by its **written language** with **Confucian** philosophy morally undergirding both its **social structure** and **political system**. In short, Chinese civilization was a cultural Rubik's Cube–an amazing fit. *Nine of the ten factors listed at the beginning of this chapter are contained in this one-sentence summary* (all except the actions of the two emperors), illustrating the impossibility of separating the nine. China's complex culture was an integrated whole. That fact explains the longevity, power, and splendor of China, a leading civilization in the world for almost two millennia.

The power and splendor were not to last. From about 1775, confronted by population growth and a little later by aggressive Western nations, China moved to a position of unimaginable impotence. The reader–and statesman, for that matter–who wishes to understand contemporary China must taken into account the residual Chinese memory of its longevity, power, and splendor, of its historic position as the Middle Kingdom, the center of the civilized world. The reader and statesman must also take into account the residual deep resentment felt by the Chinese for its humiliation by the Western powers. Chinese attitudes in the 21st Century will owe much to past centuries.

The next chapter will begin a consideration of China's passage from unrivaled power to utter helplessness in a mere 125 years.

# 6. *The Late Qing Dynasty*

## (1796 to 1912)

The first few decades of the 19th century in China bear a surface appearance of relative calm. Both at home and abroad, however, forces were at work that would eventually lead to the collapse of the Confucian order. The early Manchu emperors finally spawned weak heirs, and the dynastic cycle slowly drew to a close. It was a great misfortune for China that no one of the caliber of Qianlong or Kangxi occupied the Dragon Throne during the 19th century when weak rule was aggravated by a unique series of problems: excessive population growth, widespread addiction to opium, and the impact of Western soldiers, merchants, and missionaries. That China faced these problems under feeble rulers in the 19th century rather than a hundred years earlier is one of history's outstanding examples of bad timing.

Internally, faced with a need to alleviate peasant distress by heroic measures of flood control, famine relief, etc., the imperial authorities became ever less capable of acting boldly. The two immediate successors of the Qianlong Emperor were men of modest ability. They inherited a government whose finances had been compromised by Heshen's corruption and by a shifting balance of trade. Without a firm hand in control, nepotism and squeeze increased markedly, and the government was lax in keeping corruption within tolerable limits. Under the Daoguang Emperor (1821-50), especially, there was a tendency for provincial officials to tolerate corruption and secret society activities. Political wisdom dictated silence about local problems rather than honest reports of the truth. The dynastic cycle began to close.

Externally, Europe had plunged into the Industrial Revolution. In a few decades China gradually fell from a position of equal or near-equal power with the West to one of undeniable inferiority. The close of the dynastic cycle accelerated the trend just as Europe surged forward with an impressive burst of energy. As the nations of the West flexed their muscles in an era of colonialism, it was inevitable that friction would occur with the Chinese.

## A. Population Growth

China has not always been an overpopulated land. As late as the beginning of the Manchu dynasty, China's population was relatively stable and modest. Some censuses show a vast difference from the China of the 19th century:

| Date | Population |
|---|---|
| 1741 | 143,000 000 |
| 1774 | 221,000,000 |
| 1804 | 304,000,000 |
| 1851 | 432,000,000 |

Until about 1775 several factors allowed food production to keep pace with the increasing number of new mouths. The introduction of food crops from the New World had made possible an expansion of agriculture. A shift from the practice of allowing fields to lie fallow every other year to one of crop rotation, had also greatly increased the amount of arable land under cultivation at any one time.

The early Manchu emperors also helped maximize production. Kangxi initiated a long period of repair of neglected dikes and irrigation works. Fewer lives were lost to the floods that periodically ravaged China; water-borne diseases, such as cholera, typhoid fever, and parasites took a lesser toll; and better and more extensive irrigation reduced the impact of China's periodic droughts. Moreover, the increased food supply during much of the early Qing era led to better nutrition, healthier young women better able to bear the sons so necessary for ancestor worship, and an increase in female fertility. More population also led to an increase in farm labor to produce more food.

Kangxi issued an important edict in 1740 urging peasants to bring all uncultivated arable land into production. In mountainous south China, peasants laboriously terraced the hillsides ever higher, increasing the quantity of rice produced though significantly reducing the productivity of farm labor. To the normal labor of planting while walking backwards, of cultivating, and of harvesting were added the labor to create the terraces and then year after year trudging up and down steep hillsides with tools, seedlings, and harvests.

Of equal importance in the surge of population was the long period of internal peace under the early Manchu emperors. Internal strife–rebellions of the secret societies and the warfare accompanying the close of dynastic cycles–commonly led to declines in population. The long period of internal peace under the early Qing emperors had the opposite effect.

By 1775, the population began to outstrip the available food supply.[29] Internally, population pressure grew. The number of new mouths to feed outstripped the amount of new land brought into production. With smaller land holdings, peasants were at the mercy of village moneylenders, and increased competition for loans led to soaring interest rates. Many families were compelled to sell their land to the great Literati landlords. The economic gap between rich and poor steadily widened and created a substantial class of landless agricultural laborers. Life became more onerous, and many were undernourished. Secret society rebellions spread throughout the land. Heavier taxation to defray the cost of their suppression caused peasants to suffer even more. While none of the rebellions threatened to topple the dynasty, they foretold the massive Taiping rebellion in 1850, which almost ended Manchu rule in the middle of the century. With the Qing dynasty also facing a fiscal crisis, the days of the dynasty seemed limited.

## B. The Opium War (1839 to 1842)

Throughout the early period of Western trade with China, the European nations were at a continuous disadvantage. While demand for Chinese goods ran high at home, demand for Western goods on the Chinese market was initially negligible. Ships

[29] Recent research has challenged the old belief that until some time in the reign of the Qianlong Emperor China was the most prosperous country in the world. Whether or not the *per capita* gross domestic product of Western nations exceeded that of China, however, does not refute the view that China was still at a high level for an agricultural civilization up until around 1775.

returned to Europe laden with Chinese goods, but, all too often, the voyage out was in empty ships.

Western merchants sought products for the Chinese market. The first they found was opium from the poppy fields of India. By the end of Qianlong's reign, the Chinese were buying only 500 tons annually, but the trade grew dramatically in the 1830s. By 1899, according to the official Maritime Customs Reports, China had imported the astounding total of approximately 800,000,000 lbs. of opium in a century when the Chinese began growing substantial quantities of their own.

The Chinese imperial court in the early 19th century was concerned about the increase in the importation of opium from India. The British, on the other hand, found it a profitable item of trade, accounting for about half their cargoes arriving in Guangzhou. A ban on the trade by the Jiaqing Emperor (1796 to 1821) proved ineffective. Usually local officials in Guangzhou were willing for a price to turn a blind eye to importation of the drug. When such local connivance was not forthcoming, opium could be smuggled in through Hong Kong and Macao. Under these circumstances the Daoguang emperor committed the grave error of legalizing the trade in 1836. Imports shot up and many Chinese embarked in all earnestness on an experiment in self-poisoning that was to endure for decades. Within two years the Emperor reversed his position and sent Commissioner Lin Zexu to Guangzhou to suppress the trade.

Events at Guangzhou (formerly "Canton") in the 1830s led to the first war between China and a nation of the West. The Qianlong emperor in 1757 had limited trade with foreign ships to the single port of Guangzhou ("Canton"). In many ways the Guangzhou System was as unequal (in favor of the Chinese) as the later series of treaties that the West imposed upon the Middle Kingdom. One principal irritant in trade relations was the unpredictable application of tariff regulations to foreign goods. Although duties were theoretically established at fixed rates by the imperial court, they were interpreted and applied in such a manner that the Western merchant could never be sure how much additional duty the Guangzhou authorities would exact from him for their own benefit. The Chinese authorities also imposed vexatious social restrictions on foreign merchants forbidding them, among other things, to go on boat excursions in Guangzhou's environs except on three specific days each month, to engage more than a limited number of Chinese servants, and to enter the walls of Guangzhou itself. Such restrictions in Chinese eyes were entirely consonant with their view that Europeans were merely "ocean barbarians," not fundamentally different from Mongols and Tibetans.

Another problem was that the Chinese side of the Guangzhou trade was monopolized by the co-hong, an association of local merchants who had informal government approval. Until 1833 the British, who conducted the bulk of the Guangzhou trade, also operated as a monopoly, for the crown had previously granted sole trading rights with China to the English East India Company. After 1833, though, when the Company's monopoly was abolished, individual British merchants found their economic bargaining power substantially weaker than that of the cohong.

The abolition of the English East India Company's monopoly in 1833 was a critical event in Chinese history. A representative of the Crown assumed the functions of the Company's chief agent in protecting British trade interests. While the Company as a private trading organization was willing to tolerate the discriminations of the Guangzhou system for the sake of profits, the British government quickly showed itself unwilling to accept such treatment. The first superintendent of trade, Lord Napier, arrived in Macao with instructions to correspond directly with the local governor-general. Simultaneously the latter ordered Napier to wait in Macao until a passport authorizing him to proceed to Guangzhou came from Beijing. Napier refused to receive the Governor-General's communication on the ground that he could not as a representative of the British Crown accept an order from a foreign government. The Governor-General, in turn, refused Napier's letter on the grounds that precedent required its submission to the cohong and that it was in the form of a letter between equals. The British concept of the equality of nations under international law conflicted with the Chinese concept of the proper and inherent superiority of China to all "barbarians." Subsequent events, including a cessation of trade by the cohong, led the two nations perilously close to war, but Napier's sudden death temporarily averted hostilities.

In 1839 a clash began between two of the strongest personalities of the 19th century: Charles Elliott, the fourth British superintendent of trade, and the imperial commissioner, Lin Zexu. Elliott's two immediate predecessors had followed a policy of tolerating the Guangzhou system and limited their activities to keeping London informed of events on the South China coast. British merchants, chafing under the system, raised a storm in London with calls for a reversion to Napier's aggressive methods. Elliott arrived to assume his duties with the implied consent of the British foreign secretary to use force, if necessary, to resolve the grievances of the merchants and to obtain an extension of trade to other Chinese ports. Elliott was a man to whom the use of force was not an uncongenial exercise. Lin, like Elliott, was not one to back away from a fight.

Each side had grievances. The British had objections to how the trade was conducted; the Chinese had objections to what was being traded. Lin made the first move. Only eight days after his arrival in Guangzhou he assembled the British merchants, informed them that all their opium would be confiscated and demanded that they sign a pledge not to engage in the trade in the future. Shortly afterwards, Chinese guards appeared at the trading stations, Chinese servants were prevented from entering, and the merchants were held virtual prisoners. After a few days the merchants offered to surrender more than 1,000 chests of opium. Lin, aware that a far greater quantity was held in storage ships outside the port, refused their offer.

Elliott arrived on the scene and issued official government receipts to the merchants for all of their opium, over 20,000 chests. With this single stoke, he transformed the dispute into a confrontation between the Chinese and the British governments. He then surrendered the opium to Lin, who ordered it mixed with salt and lime and dumped into the river. Lin's success was less than total, however, for Elliott remained adamant that British merchants not sign the pledge to refrain from the pernicious trade in the future.

With the dispute stalemated, a complication arose when an unidentified British sailor killed a Chinese in a drunken brawl. Although Elliott ordered a navy courtmartial for five sailors who had participated in the brawl, Lin was not satisfied. Unhappy with the light fines (£20 to £50) and light sentences meted out (3 to 6 months in English jails), he insisted that the men be tried in a Chinese court. Elliott, however, was aware of the Chinese courts' use of torture and feared that under the Chinese practice of group responsibility all five might be made to pay the penalty for the crime of the actual murderer. Exasperated by Elliott's refusal to surrender the five, Lin cut off all supplies of food and fuel to the British.

The British remained on their ships until reinforcements arrived whereupon Elliott arranged a show of force by the fleet. As the British ships moved closer to Guangzhou, Chinese batteries opened fire. In the ensuing engagement, three Chinese vessels were sunk. Lin reported the loss to the throne, and an imperial decree formally declared the cessation of all trade with Britain. The Opium War had begun.

The war lasted three years and two major agreements were reached between the British and the Chinese. After Britain's initial victories the Chuanbi (Chuenpee) Convention of January, 1841, was negotiated between Elliott and Qishan, who had replaced the disgraced Lin Zexu. The Convention required the Chinese:

1. To cede the island of Hong Kong to the British;
2. To pay an indemnity of 6,000,000 Chinese silver dollars.

Unfortunately, both Beijing and London repudiated the Convention. Beijing thought Qishan had gone too far, and London believed Elliott had not gone far enough. Their governments recalled both, and hostilities resumed.

After further clashes around Guangzhou and a shortlived truce, Sir Henry Pottinger arrived in Macao and immediately ordered the fleet north where a mere 10,000 British troops scored an impressive series of victories including the seizure of cities well up the Yangzi River (formerly "Yangtze"). A year later in 1842 the Treaty of Nanjing was signed. Stunned by having lost a war to "barbarians," the

Chinese had little choice but to accept the terms being forced on them. As later amended, the treaty required China:

1. To pay indemnities of $21 million Chinese silver dollars of which $6 million was for the opium destroyed by Commissioner Lin;
2. To cede Hong Kong to Britain in perpetuity;
3. To open the ports of Fuzhou, Xiamen, Ningbo and Shanghai to British trade;
4. To permit extraterritorial jurisdiction over British subjects by British courts in criminal cases;
5. To establish a moderate uniform tariff on British goods (eventually set at 5 per cent ad valorem);
6. To grant equally to the British any future treaty concession to any other foreign nation – the most-favored nation clause.

The Treaty was silent about opium. The British took the position that China might legalize or prohibit the trade as it wished but that it was its sole responsibility to enforce any ban.

The Treaty of Nanjing was the first of a series of "unequal treaties" to which the West would subject China in the future. The provisions of the Treaty that would eventually prove most damaging to the Chinese were the last three.

The most-favored-nation clause was perhaps the most astute diplomatic "gimmick" of the century. All ultimately shared whatever could be extracted from China by anyone. The Chinese, however, had a tradition of equal treatment of all "barbarians" and naively accepted the clause.

The extraterritoriality provision was a serious infringement of Chinese sovereignty. For long, the British were conscientious in conducting judicial business in China, but decisions of their judges in favor of the Chinese stirred indignation among British merchants. Eventually the provision operated to give foreigners virtual immunity from the law; in any criminal proceeding, they could generally count on their own courts to render favorable verdicts. Not until too late did the Chinese realize the grave implications of extraterritoriality. In granting it to the British in the aftermath of the Opium War, they were merely applying a precedent of the Song dynasty that required Arab traders on the south coast to regulate their own affairs.

Most damaging of all was China's loss of full control over her own tariffs. Trade in the 1840s was still quite small, though, and the Chinese were blissfully ignorant that by the century's end the industrial revolution in the West would flood the archaic Middle Kingdom with cheap, machine-made goods wrecking the traditional agricultural economy forever.

In the next few years the Manchus concluded similar unequal treaties with the United States, France, Norway and Sweden. The treaty with the United States was historically the most damaging. It extended extraterritorial jurisdiction to civil, as well as criminal cases. Under the most-favored-nation clause, this jurisdiction automatically accrued to other Western treaty powers.

Comments from two contemporary observers indicate attitudes toward the opium trade in the decades after the Opium War. In a light vein, the special correspondent in China of the London Times reported to his readers in 1857 that the sale of opium was as common in all the cities of China as the sale of hotcross buns on Good Friday in the streets of London. Seen from Chinese eyes, on the other hand, the matter was not so frivolous. Following is a selection from the memoirs, written in 1893, of Li Hongzhang, China's elder statesman of the closing decades of the 19th century:

> "...every well-read and intelligent Britisher or Oriental, is aware of the unhappy and disgraceful fact that but for Great Britain there would not be a picul of opium sold in China today....
>
> "I know that, because of this money-grasping, trade-compelling feature of England's dealings with my country, millions of wretched people of China have been made more miserable; stalwart men and women have been made paupers, vagrants, and the lowest of criminals; and hundreds of thousands of the weaker ones of my race–mainly among the women–have been sent to suicide graves.
>
> "And all this because otherwise British trade might not flourish in Chinese ports.
>
> "All this because gold and territory are greater in the eyes of the British Government than the rights and bodies of a weak people....
>
> "Yes! Yes! Yes! We Chinese have been laughed and sneered at in the streets of London itself, and have been called 'pig-tailed Opium Eaters,' when for years and years it is the Government of these same Londoners which has been responsible for the millions of human wrecks throughout the length and breadth of the Middle Kingdom . . . .

> "Yes, in all my years, in my studies, in the army, during the wars and the famines, in all my political and business life, I have studied and combated this devouring evil; and the more I know and see and learn of it the greater does England's crime become in my eyes. England–proud and mighty and rich England–England with her great armies and navies and great men–is shamed and covered with ignominy because of the crimes of her Indian poppy."[30]

The drug poisoned Sino-Western relations for decades. It was a major cause of the resentment still felt by the Chinese today for Western mistreatment of China in the late Qing period. The attractiveness to the Literati of learning from the West must have seemed slight indeed. Just when China needed all its strength, a substantial proportion–estimated by Li Hongzhang at 10 per cent of the adult population–lay dazed in a stupor, unable to contribute effectively to family, village or country.

So far, China's experience with drugs is unique. Widespread drug addiction, though, is not irremediable. The most successful aspect of the belated Manchu Reform Movement in the opening decade of the 20th century was an attack upon this social evil. By policies of heavy taxation of opium, the negotiation of a series of treaties calling for annual decreases in importation, and control of smuggling, the Manchu government turned the corner. Unfortunately, opium smoking increased in the period between 1916 and the Communist victory in its civil war with the Nationalists in 1949. Thereafter, Chairman Mao Zedong successfully ordered a

---

30 Memoirs of Li Hung Chang [Li Hongzhang], Houghton Mifflin Company, pp. 280-291 passim (1913)

crackdown on the evil, executing drug suppliers, sending millions of addicts to rehabilitation, and outlawing production of poppies.

## C. The Taiping Rebellion (1850 to 1864)

. By 1850, as a result of population pressures and the decay of the dynasty whose prestige had suffered in the debacle of the Opium War, China was ripe for a major peasant rebellion. The Manchus were losing the Mandate of Heaven.

The Taiping was a heretical Christian sect. Its founder, Hong Xiuquan, was an unsuccessful candidate at the civil service examinations who in a dream induced by illness had a vision of Jehovah. Concluding that he was the younger brother of Jesus Christ, Hong unfurled the banner of revolt in 1850, declared himself king of the Heavenly Kingdom of the Taiping ("Great Peace"), and plunged China into a fourteen-year convulsion.

His version of Christianity included the community of goods, the destruction of idols, the equality of men and women, and the primacy of individual wishes in selecting a marriage partner. He also advocated many needed reforms: land redistribution, modernization of China by building railways and factories, simplification of the Chinese script, and abolition of foot binding, infanticide and household slavery. He viewed China not as the Middle Kingdom but as one nation among equals.

The rebellion began when a battalion of local militia in Guangxi province, sent to track down a notorious bandit, attempted to extort money from some Taiping charcoal workers. Hong and several of his principal subordinates decided to revolt and assembled some 10,000 armed members.

Although the Manchus sent troops to suppress the insurrection, it gathered strength from the dissatisfied peasantry. Most of the battles were won by the Taiping, who gradually worked their way north. By 1853 the rebels, 3,500,000 strong, took control of the Yangzi (Yangtze) valley and established their capital at Nanjing (Nanking). Manchu military weakness contributed greatly to their success in those early years. The Taiping's own failure to organize efficient administrations in the 7 of 18 provinces that had fallen to their arms augured their later defeat.

The Taiping obtained some sympathy in the early years from Westerners. Hong's conversion to Christianity and his plans to create a modern economy marked him as an attractive alternative to the tradition-bound, difficult officials of the Manchu court. Such sympathy eroded as Westerners learned more about his claim to be the younger brother of Jesus and as the Taiping began to prove politically inept. Nepotism became as serious a problem for the rebels as for the Manchus, and internal dissension arose as subordinate kings vied for power while Hong whiled away his time with his concubines. Most serious of all, the Taiping failed to implement their reform program. Peasant support might have helped them to bring down the Manchus, but they held to the towns and cities, and their program of land redistribution became a dead letter. The Taiping had few men of real talent and were deficient in the arts of government. Their sole success lay in the military realm. Not until a hundred years later was another Chinese revolutionary, Mao Zedong, to avoid the mistakes of the Taiping and rise to power on an alliance of peasants and intellectuals.

The Taiping's military advance crested in 1854 when the Manchus repulsed a northern expedition. Afterwards fighting was largely confined to the Yangzi ("Yangtze") valley. A trend developed of Manchu reliance on local militias that would ultimately weaken the dynasty. China's Manchu commanders with few exceptions had proved themselves incapable of defeating the Taiping, and as early as January 1853 the Emperor asked Zeng Guofan to organize the militia of Hunan province in the Yangzi valley. Zeng had returned to his native Hunan in 1852 to observe the customary three-year mourning period after the death of his mother, an expression of filial piety. Zeng accepted the commission but immediately decided to build an authentic army rather than a local militia: "My humble idea is to train 10,000 . . . . whose pains and itches will be of common concern to one another, and who will even rush together into fire or into a pond of boiling water . . . . In retreat they will exert their strength until death to rescue all of their comrades."[31] With such esprit de corps was born the first of China's crack provincial armies, the Hunan Army of Zeng Guofan. These "Hunan braves," not the imperial Manchu troops, were ultimately the conquerors of the Taiping rebels.[32] The rebellion lasted 14 years, and estimates of deaths from combat, executions, and starvation range

[31] Li Chien-nung, *The Political History of China, 1840-1928*, Stanford University Press (1956), pp. 66-7

[32] The Manchus also received the help of a curious group of Western mercenaries, the "Ever-Victorious Army." Some of the leaders of the Ever-Victorious Army are of incidental interest in and of themselves. The final leader was Charles George Gordon, a strange mystical young British officer, better known in history as Chinese Gordon. Some twenty years later he met his death in the defense of Khartoum in the Anglo-Egyptian Sudan against a fanatic Muslim group of "whirling dervishes" whose leader, the Madhi, in a manner reminiscent of Gordon's previous Chinese adversary, believed himself to be a prophesied redeemer of Islam who would rule the world briefly before the Day of Judgment. An earlier leader of the Ever-Victorious Army, H. S. Burgevine, a former English instructor at the University of North Carolina, was one of only two United States citizens who ever made a bid to rule a foreign nation. Burgevine actively plotted to overthrow the Manchus and make himself the Emperor of China. His mysterious death has never been explained. The only other American who ever tried to seize control of a foreign nation was William Walker, a military adventurer who established an ephemeral dictatorship in Nicaragua in the 1850's.

from 20,000,000 to 100,000,000. If the latter estimate is correct, the Taiping Rebellion was the bloodiest war in world history.

Military power having passed to local Chinese commanders, the Manchus occupied the Dragon Throne not by virtue of superior force but only by Confucian loyalty to the Emperor of provincial leaders like Zeng Guofan and his two protégés, Li Hongzhang and Zuo Zongtang. This decentralization of power set the stage for the warlord period of the early 20th century when provincial leaders shattered the unity of China and gained virtual independence.

## D. The Arrow War (1856 to 1860)

Even while the Manchus were embroiled with the Taiping rebels, storm clouds were gathering on the international scene. The British wished to renegotiate the Treaty of Nanjing. Both the merchants and the home government were disappointed with it. The merchants had not reaped the fortunes anticipated from the opening of additional ports to trade and, somewhat unrealistically, dreamed of the profits to be garnered in trade with the interior. The editorials of their newspaper The *North China Herald* frequently read like chapters from *Alice in Wonderland*. Her Majesty's government, on the other hand, quite realistically believed that Beijing was attempting to evade its obligation to treat Britain as an equal.

Officials of the treaty port provinces handled most Chinese foreign affairs. Although relations were relatively amicable in the fast-growing port of Shanghai, they were strained at Guangzhou. The Chinese still refused to allow foreigners to enter the city walls, and provincial officials ignored representatives of Western nations. Since the officials were always too busy to talk, diplomats might wait years for an interview, and even if they obtained one, the Chinese tried to play the "barbarians" off against each other in traditional fashion.

It was a tragedy for China that her statesmen did not try to learn more about the rest of the world during this period. The Chinese not only denied themselves an opportunity for greater knowledge of their new adversaries but also neglected specific problems. No steps were taken, for instance, to put an end to the coolie trade. Chinese peasants, frequently drugged and kidnapped, were shipped like so many cattle to work under inhuman conditions in the fields of Latin America.

Perhaps China's statesmen may be forgiven for their failure to learn more about the West. They had had experience with the Khitan, the Jurchen, and the Mongols, barbarians who were stronger militarily but culturally inferior to the Chinese. Unfortunately, the Westerners in China were far from the most refined representatives of their countries–just aggressive drug dealers. What was the point in seeking knowledge about people whose conduct was immoral and whose culture seemed inferior to that of China in every *known* respect except military technology?

Two incidents occurred which precipitated China's second war with the West. In early 1856, Chinese authorities executed a French Catholic missionary, Auguste Chapdelaine, and some of his converts as rebels. The French government then joined the British in seeking a thorough revision of existing treaties. Napoleon III saw an opportunity to become the defender of the Catholic Church. In late 1856 the Arrow Affair began. Although Chinese-owned, the Arrow, a boat plying the waters between Hong Kong and Guangzhou, was of British registry and flew the British flag. The dispute following its seizure by Guangzhou authorities on charges of piracy precipitated the war. The British viewed the Arrow as a British vessel; the

Imperial Commissioner in Guangzhou just as stubbornly viewed it as a Chinese vessel and refused all amends. Eventually the British and French forces took Guangzhou and sailing north destroyed the forts guarding the entrance to Tianjin, uncomfortably close to Beijing.

Under military compulsion, the Chinese signed the Treaties of Tianjin in 1858. The major points provided that:

1. Britain and France were to have the right to maintain resident ministers in Beijing;
2. Several additional ports were opened to trade including three islands on the Yangzi River;
3. British and French citizens could travel in the interior under special passports;
4. Missionaries were permitted access to all regions of the interior;
5. The Chinese were to pay an indemnity of 4,000,000 taels of silver.

The treaties provided that they were not effective until ratified at Beijing. The anger and humiliation of the war party in the capital produced little but foot dragging, and when the Western fleets returned a year later, hostilities resumed.

An initial victory by Chinese shore batteries over the fleets merely brought naval reinforcements. In 1860 after defeating the finest of the imperial troops, an allied expedition entered Beijing itself. The Xianfeng Emperor and the war party fled westward.

Precipitated over a trivial incident and used as an excuse to extort concessions from China, the Arrow War is, like the Opium War, another source of resentment and extreme nationalism emanating from some present-day Chinese military and civilian officials.

## E. The Beginnings of Modernization

The years following the Arrow War were calm as both sides moved toward more moderate positions. A new government was established under the leadership of Prince Gong, an advocate of friendly relations with the West and of steps toward modernization of his country.

By 1860, the treaty powers had come to the conclusion that their interests lay in supporting the Manchus. Even while the British were advancing on Beijing in the north, British troops were fighting alongside the Manchus in the Yangzi valley to repel a Taiping attack on Shanghai. The treaty powers have been accused of supporting the Manchus in the 1860s because they could easily manipulate the weak Manchus to their own advantage. While there is much truth in the statement, their envoys in Beijing during this decade were sensitive to China's problems. Men like Britain's Rutherford Alcock, Francis Wade, and Sir Robert Hart and the United States' Anson Burlingame often viewed themselves as intermediaries between their own governments and the Chinese; among Westerners they are probably the best friends China ever had..

Prince Gong's government, supported by Zeng Guofan and other provincial leaders, succeeded for about a decade in giving China the type of vigorous government it had not had since the heyday of the Qianlong Emperor nearly a century earlier. Their efforts temporarily abated the close of the dynastic cycle. Historian Mary Clabaugh Wright has characterized the accomplishments of Prince Gong and his colleagues as the "last stand of Chinese conservatism,"[33] not the blind, overconfident conservatism of the decades from 1840 to 1860 but an attempt to revitalize China by the application of traditional Confucian principles without fear of adopting Western methods where necessary. It was China's modern tragedy that the attempt finally ended in failure.

Prince Gong embarked upon a nationwide program of developing talent. Libraries and schools were rebuilt throughout the area devastated by the Taiping. The Confucian classics were reprinted and widely distributed. The civil service examinations were broadened to include practical questions. In one examination with 17 questions, 5 dealt with military matters, 4 with criminal law and the reduction of crime, 1 dealt with how to reduce extravagance, and only 7 with the Confucian Classics. For over a decade the Literati responded to Prince Gong's program and there was an increased flow of able men into government.

Despite the still-traditional flavor of Prince Gong's government, he and his colleagues were more active economically than was historically normal. Steps were taken to repair the havoc wrought by the Taiping. Dikes were repaired, land was reclaimed, refugees and repentant rebels were resettled, taxes were reduced, seed and animals were provided to the peasants, additional rebellions by the Nianfei and the Muslims were suppressed, parts of Mongolia and Manchuria were opened to emigration, and the government was active in famine relief. Zeng Guofan, Zuo Zongtang and other provincial leaders played key roles in these programs.

While China's new leaders were revitalizing the Confucian order (for the last time) the government also began to take a few

---

[33] Mary Clabaugh Wright, The Last Stand of Chinese Conservatism: The T'ung-Chih Restoration, 1862-1874, Stanford University Press (1957)

halting steps toward Westernization. The government implemented Commissioner Lin's advice, ignored throughout the two preceding decades, to purchase and manufacture Western weapons. Under the aegis of Li Hongzhang and Zuo Zongtang, respectively, an arsenal was built in Shanghai and a shipyard in Fuzhou. An Interpreters College opened in Beijing, and its curriculum soon expanded to include Western science and mathematics. Beyond those subjects, China's leaders were hardly aware of anything else of value in Western culture.

Equally important, the government managed to establish the Zongli Yamen, a near approach to a modern ministry of foreign affairs. Those who took this half step toward modernization, though, had difficulty in staffing the new organization. A great majority of the nation's Literati considered foreigners "devils" and anyone who associated with foreigners "devils' slaves." They viewed the Zongli Yamen as a medium through which the hated foreigners could penetrate China. Many Literati considered appointment to the Zongli Yamen a disgrace and a stain on their honor. Wo Jen, a leading conservative, "shed tears of shame" when the Emperor appointed him to the Zongli Yamen.

Despite Literati disdain the personnel of the Zongli Yamen became adroit in supporting China's position by appeals to Western concepts of international law. Their skill in using these concepts enabled them to establish that the treaties represented maximum Western rights in China rather than minimum rights as in previous decades.

Prince Gong's government also expanded the Customs Service under the direction of Sir Robert Hart. The centralization of these important organizations was out of keeping with the historical tendency to rely heavily on provincial officials; a degree of coordination was achieved that was almost "unChinese."

As long as China remained geographically isolated, the conservative majority of Literati were able to take it for granted that China was the center of civilization and dismiss the rest of the world as mere barbarians. The intrusion of the West in the 19$^{th}$ century made this dismissal untenable. Suddenly Confucian civilization no longer seemed to be working. Yet, the Chinese could not simply jettison their 4,000-year-old culture and westernize. China's intellectuals, whether conservative or liberal, felt psychologically compelled to preserve a continuity with its long past; they felt a need to maintain much specifically Chinese in whatever the future might hold for them.

Influential men in Prince Gong's government formulated a new theory and practice called "Self-Strengthening" that supposedly provided for *both necessary westernization and cultural continuity.* One of the earliest officials to develop the theory was Feng Guifen, who served as a subordinate to both Commissioner Lin Zexu and Li Hongzhang. In the first of two important essays written around 1860, Feng noted that China had few sources of knowledge about the West. Fewer than 100 Western books had been translated into Chinese. He advocated establishment of translation offices in which brilliant Chinese students would be taught both by Westerners in languages and Chinese in the Confucian classics and history. Chinese ethics and Confucian teachings were to serve as a foundation supplemented by Westerner methods to obtain strength and prosperity. Finally, he noted the great importance of mathematics: "All Western knowledge is derived from mathematics."

In the second essay, Feng argued that the only thing China needed to learn from the "barbarians" was technology for producing ships and guns. He urged the establishment of shipyards and arsenals staffed by hired Westerners. He advocated awarding the imperial *jinshi* degree to those Chinese students who learned to produce weapons better than those of the barbarians. He noted that the best scholars in China had wasted too much time on eight-legged essays. Finally, he rejected the idea of merely purchasing modern arms from Western nations. Such a course would not restore China's strength and redeem it from former humiliations.

The theoretical basis of self-strengthening did not become completely explicit until 1898 when Zhang Zhidong formulated the slogan "Zhongxue Wei Ti, Xixue Wei Yong" (Chinese learning for the fundamental principles, Western learning for the practical application). The distinction between fundamental principles (Ti) and practical application (Yong) is, however, already implicit in Feng's essays. He is arguing that the Chinese could adopt Western science and manufacturing techniques where necessary because Confucianism could control them. There are several points of interest in the two essays:

1. Feng shows the tendency typical of his day to believe that the Yong for which Western learning was necessary was primarily military; forty years later the scope of Western Yong also encompassed railroads, telegraphs, textile mills, etc.;
2. Feng realizes that behind Western arms lie Western science and mathematics. As yet he only dimly perceives that behind science and mathematics lies Western civilization, a whole complex of ideas and institutions;

3. Feng is beginning to recognize the conflict between an education in the Confucian classics and an education in Western subjects. He is, nonetheless, as a dedicated Confucianist, psychologically incapable of drawing the inevitable conclusion; China was to wait an additional 45 years till the Manchus finally abolished the civil service examinations with their heavy emphasis on Confucianism.
4. Feng is concerned about the social standing of students of Western learning. In passing he implies what others made explicit, that those who learn Western techniques would by traditional Confucian criteria be classified with the lowly artisans. His unheeded suggestion that these men be awarded the very degrees coveted by the Literati was an attempt to assign them a higher social prestige. After all, what intelligent student faced with two equally demanding and time-consuming courses of study is likely to choose the lesser path? The Confucian social scale was a factor hardly conducive to attracting able men to Western learning.

Feng deserves credit for being one of the first of his generation in a position of political influence to advocate moving beyond the position of the majority of the Literati. His was one of the first attempts to formulate a theoretical path whereby China could introduce some Western reforms and still preserve a cultural continuity. It is, however, painfully obvious in retrospect that the Ti-Yong distinction was a blind alley.

The Ti and Yong of a civilization are intertwined and cannot be compartmentalized. The introduction of Western Yong would be followed, step by step, by Western Ti. The Chinese would be sucked into a process of cultural changes from initial adoption of Western arms to machinery to technology to science, to new educational curricula appropriate to an industrial society, to changes in political institutions, to a republic rather than an empire. As railroads, telegraphs and factories were built, together with all the changes to support them, what would really be the value of an education in the Confucian classics? What would really be the value of a class of cultivated, literary amateurs at the apex of power? Self-Strengthening was no way to preserve Chinese Ti intact.

Wo Jen, who had "shed tears of shame" when appointed to the Zongli Yamen, and a majority of the Literati were unwilling to take even Feng Guifen"s half-way steps to modernization. In response, the Self-Strengtheners sought to use history to shore up their theory.

If it could be shown that there was precedent for Western techniques in Chinese history, Self-Strengthening would not represent a substantial break with China's past. The Ti-Yong advocates argued that the adoption of Western Yong was not a threat to Chinese Ti; and that Western Yong was not really Western anyway since precedents for Western science and techniques could be found in Chinese history. They pointed to Chinese mathematics and such practical inventions as the seismograph and the magnetic compass as Chinese pedigrees for Western science. Scouring Chinese history, they found almost forgotten writings that contained the seeds of Western science. Early Moist works, for instance, contained many principles of mechanics and optics.

The historical counterattack by the more intelligent conservatives was obvious. The effort to find roots for Western science in Chinese history was too labored. The precedents indicated by the Self-Strengtheners were not in the mainstream of Chinese history. The conservatives offered a radically different interpretation of Chinese history. Contrary to proving that Western

Yong was really Chinese, they contended the examples cited by the Self-Strengtheners proved that the Chinese had considered the possibility of a scientific Ti and had rejected it. Wo Jen argued that propriety and righteousness were the core of Chinese Ti that had sustained a harmonious society in China for millennia, and that mathematics could not raise the nation from weakness to strength. Wo Jen's view of Chinese history seems irrefutable. Confucian civilization was something quite different from scientific civilization, and the attempt to say that science was merely Yong, (and maybe Chinese Yong at that) was but self-deception. Irrefutable or not, the conservative position was beside the point. Pressure by the Western soldier and the Western merchant was undermining Confucianism. The problem was not to arrive at the truth (which the conservatives did) but to find a way to fit western civilization into the Chinese landscape (which the Self-Strengtheners at least tried to do even if they had to torture the truth).

By 1870 China had recaptured some measure of her historical greatness but afterwards the trend reversed, both domestically and internationally. Two key events served to destroy the confidence in each other that the Western envoys and the Zongli Yamen officials had so painstakingly developed in the 1860s: the rejection of the Alcock Convention of 1869 and the Tianjin Massacre of 1870. The former was the first and last effort for a long time to achieve an equal treaty between China and a Western power. In negotiating a revision of prior treaties, the British envoy, Rutherford Alcock, showed himself willing to make concessions to the Chinese on points of vital concern. He agreed, for instance, that the Chinese should have a consul in Hong Kong to help quell smuggling and that the duty on opium should be increased. The Chinese, in turn, agreed to eliminate most internal transit taxes (a patent evasion of the 5 per cent tariff rates), to allow temporary residence of British citizens in the interior, and to adopt a written code of commercial law. Alcock hoped that such a code would eventually eliminate the need for extraterritoriality. Unfortunately, the British merchants residing in China thought that the proper function of Her Majesty's envoy was to extract the maximum concessions possible from the Chinese rather than to treat China as an equal in the family of nations. Their letters home demanded that the whole interior be opened to trade, that they have the right to operate steamships on all internal waterways, that no duties be increased, etc. After a few months of such pressure, the home government, against its own better judgment, gave way and declined to ratify the Convention. Indignation among the Chinese ran high; they had assumed that Alcock was empowered to reach an agreement with them. For the rest of the century they consistently viewed Western proposals with suspicion.

Just one month before the British destroyed Chinese confidence in the West by rejecting the Convention, there occurred the event that destroyed Western confidence in the Chinese: the Tianjin Massacre. By 1870 the activities of missionaries in the provinces had created substantial ill feeling among the Chinese. Among other impolitic actions, the Catholic fathers in Tianjin had razed a Confucian temple to make room for a new cathedral, and the French government had opened a consulate in an imperial villa. The well-meaning Sisters of St. Vincent de Paul, who ran an orphanage, exacerbated local feeling most. Concerned lest some orphans be neglected, the Sisters had offered a small reward for each child brought to them. Ugly rumors of kidnapping and cannibalism spread. Various Chinese began to demand an inspection of all mission premises. Under these circumstances, the French Consul Henri Fontanier, after an earlier confrontation with an angry district magistrate, reached an agreement with the ranking imperial official in the area, to permit an inspection (at some future date). The following morning, however, Fontanier was notified that the magistrate and other lesser officials–apparently on their own initiative–were at the cathedral door insisting upon immediate inspection. Losing complete control, Fontanier burst into the magistrate's office, struck him with a sword, fired two shots, smashed furniture, and shouted obscenities. While this scene of folly was transpiring, an angry crowd gathered outside. Still infuriated, Fontanier rushed into the crowd wielding his sword. Then, when the magistrate moved toward him, he fired again accidentally killing a Chinese bystander. The crowd disemboweled Fontanier and another French official on the spot and proceeded in a rampage to burn the cathedral, the consulate, and the orphanage and to mutilate and murder twelve Catholic nuns and priests, several foreign residents, and a number of Chinese converts.

Almost simultaneously, storm clouds began to gather as the quality of government resumed its decline. Death removed Zeng Guofan from the scene, and other key figures in the efforts of the 1860s were unwilling or unable to oppose the machinations of the Dowager Empress Cixi. This remarkable woman, condemned by most historians as a blind reactionary, was originally the favorite concubine of the dissolute Xianfeng Emperor. She became one of three regents for her infant son when he succeeded to the Dragon Throne in 1862. Her coregents were Ci'an, the childless widow of the Emperor, and Prince Gong. From the very beginning of the Regency, Cixi grasped for power. She relied heavily on the support of the palace eunuchs, the males best positioned to influence the intellectual development of a child emperor. Men who had not been castrated were not allowed into the imperial living quarters.

Empress Dowager Cixi, ca. 1890

When her son reached maturity, Cixi encouraged him in debauchery lest power slip from her own hands. She also shrewdly invoked the filial duties of a son to his mother to interfere with state affairs. When the young emperor died in 1874, she placed the infant son of her sister on the throne and continued to increase her power; by 1881, it was virtually absolute. She was the *de facto* ruler of China until her death in 1908.

In all her acts Cixi proved herself a master of intrigue. While invoking Confucian filial piety to secure the obedience of her son, she eventually destroyed the Confucian tone of government so carefully cultivated by Prince Gong and his colleagues. Corruption increased and the quality of government deteriorated. The dynastic cycle began to close again.

In the next two decades the government became increasingly incompetent, the Western powers extracted additional unequal treaties, France seized China's tributary states in IndoChina, Russia temporarily occupied parts of the Northwest, and Japan seized the Ryukyu Islands and briefly invaded Taiwan. The Chinese experienced setbacks in all areas except in industry, transportation and communications. Even though Literati objections slowed progress considerably, by the mid-1890s China had finally begun to build railroads, telegraphs, modern mines, and factories.

## F. The Sino-Japanese War (1894 to 1895)

Trouble had been brewing for years between China and Japan over influence on Korea. Although the latter was traditionally one of China's tributary states, the Japanese were in an expansionist mood. Having made a decision (in contrast to the Chinese) to learn Western ways, they became as imperialist as any Western nation.

Korea was a logical spot for the aggressive Japanese to seek their first foothold on the mainland of Asia. The straits separating the two lands are only a hundred miles wide. Politically, Korea was afflicted by the problem shared by all East Asian nations during the century–the challenge of the Western Impact. Various shifting factions in Korea advocated solutions ranging from total isolation (an exaggerated version of China's response) to Westernization (an imitation of Japan's response).

At first the isolationists controlled the "Hermit Kingdom" and attempted to exclude the Japanese entirely. A naval incident in

Korean waters, however, created a pretext in 1876 for compelling the Korean government to permit trade relations. The Chinese stood idly by during this first instance of Japan's application of force to solve the "Korean problem."

By 1882, the pro-Chinese conservatives in Korea had lost power to the pro-Japanese progressive faction. The conservatives then incited the Korean army to mutiny against the progressives, whose embezzlement of funds had left the soldiers hungry and underpaid. The Japanese legation was attacked, and Japan immediately sent troops. This time the Chinese reacted by dispatching several thousand soldiers under the command of Yuan Shikai, a protégé of Li Hongzhang. The leader of the Korean conservatives was punished and war was averted, but the peace treaty ominously permitted Japan for the first time to station soldiers in Korea to protect the Japanese legation.

By 1884, the dominant Korean progressives had fragmented into two rival factions. Fishing in troubled waters, the Japanese Minister to Korea incited the out-group to attempt a *coup d'état*. The in-group responded to a wave of assassinations by appealing to Yuan Shikai for help. The Chinese defeated the outnumbered Japanese, and both sides rushed reinforcements. Again, however, a peace treaty in which the Koreans agreed to pay indemnities to Japan averted major hostilities. A year later Japan's Ito Hirobumi and China's Li Hongzhang attempted to settle differences in Korea definitively. By the Treaty of Tianjin, both countries agreed to withdraw troops from Korea, recognized each other's interests in Korea, and pledged to notify the other in advance of any intention to send troops back. Hirobumi and Li also discussed the problem of reforming China in the course of their conversations. Ten years later when they met again to negotiate the end of the Sino-Japanese War, Hirobumi reminded Li of their exchange of views and asked why progress in China had been so slow. Li's answer that affairs in his country had been confined by tradition summed up China's problems in the 19th century.

For several years after the Treaty of Tianjin, Japan contented itself with its treaty privileges in Korea. Its only aggressive act was to infiltrate Korea with a group of young militarists organized as the Heavenly Inspired Heroic Corps. In general calm prevailed.

In 1894, the ultraconservative Korean Tonghak party triggered a war between China and Japan by rebelling. Various Japanese officials quickly approached both Li Hongzhang and Yuan Shikai with a request that China send troops to quell the disturbance. The Chinese decided to send 1,500 soldiers and notified Japan accordingly. Shortly thereafter Li, much to his surprise, received official notification that Japan was sending 7,000 troops. Worried about Japanese intentions, the Chinese lost valuable time by seeking foreign mediation. The Japanese refused all mediation, continued to build up their military strength in Korea, and seized control of the Korean court. By the time China realized war was inevitable and sent her own reinforcements, the Japanese had occupied all strategic military points. War was formally declared on August 1, 1894, but the results of the campaign within Korea itself were a foregone conclusion. What was unexpected, though, were successful Japanese invasions of southern Manchuria and the Liaodong peninsula and a crushing defeat inflicted on a numerically superior Chinese fleet. The armament of the Chinese ships and the training of her sailors were inferior to Japanese armament and training. Cixi had spent 20 million ounces of silver intended for the navy on a summer palace outside Beijing.

With Japanese arms everywhere victorious, Li Hongzhang traveled to Japan and in April 1895 signed the humiliating Treaty of Shimonoseki. The Chinese recognized the full independence of Korea (formally annexed by Japan in 1910), ceded Taiwan, the Pescadores Islands, and Manchuria's Liaodong peninsula to Japan, paid a heavy monetary indemnity, and agreed to grant Japan Western-style "unequal rights" in China.

Japan's victory in the Sino-Japanese War is attributable to its early decision to copy Western military technology and expansionism. Its reaction to the Western Impact stands in startling contrast to that of the Chinese. The very stability of Chinese civilization, an advantage to China for over two millennia, was an impediment in the $19^{th}$ century to China's transition to a modern society. The Japanese, in contrast, rapidly "Westernized:"

1868: Establishment of the first vernacular newspaper.

1869: First telegraph line built.

1870: Work began on a modern civil code along French lines, eventually adopted along with a German-style commercial code in 1899.

1871: Establishment of a Ministry of Education, followed a year later by compulsory education.

1871: Modern postal system instituted.

1872: First railroad built.

1872: System of national banks established.

1872: Universal military training instituted. Army established along French (later German) lines. Separate Navy Department established on the British model.

1873: Work began on a modern penal and criminal code on the French model, eventually adopted in 1882.

1876: First Japanese gunboat of modern design launched.

1878: Prefectural Assemblies established.

1881: First of several modern political parties organized.

1882: Central Bank of Japan established.

1889: Proclamation of a constitution, primarily on the German model.

1890: National Assembly convenes.

1898: First labor union formed by railway workers.

Innumerable Japanese were sent overseas to bring back knowledge of German medicine, U. S. business methods, etc. As Edwin O. Reischauer put it so well, "The world was one vast schoolroom for them, and they entered it determined to learn only the best in each field."[34]

[34] Edwin O. Reischauer, Japan, Past and Present, Alfred A. Knppf (1964), p. 123

The factors that propelled Japan ahead while China stood still are many. Three of the most important are the following:

1. A military class controlled Japan politically and socially. When Commodore Matthew Perry, U.S.N., sailed into Edo (Tokyo) Bay in 1853 with a squadron of American ships equipped with the first naval guns designed to fire explosive shells, not only were the Japanese military able to recognize the threat of Western arms but also saw in them an opportunity entirely consonant with their own training, interests, and instincts. The Literati of China, on the other hand, were primarily interested in philosophy and the preservation of Confucian civilization and saw Westernization as an instrument of their own destruction as a class. Few were the Literati who could bring themselves, like Kao Song Tao, China's first minister to England in the 1870s, to admit that "Confucius and Mencius have deceived us . . . . the present barbarians are different from former barbarians; they also have two thousand years of civilization."
2. For centuries, Japan had borrowed much Chinese culture, e.g. the Chinese written script, Chinese architecture, Zen Buddhism, the tea ceremony, painting, poetry, landscape gardening, and flower arrangement. The Japanese were highly conscious of their role as borrowers and cognizant of the profitable possibilities of borrowing. The Chinese, on the other hand, conceived of themselves strictly as teachers, not students, exporters, not importers of culture–the Middle Kingdom, the center of civilization.

3. Japan by the mid 19th century had a deeply developed sense of nationalism entirely consonant with the Western view of world organization. As cultural borrowers, Japan had long been overshadowed by China, and the Japanese were fully conscious of their differences from the Chinese. Loyalty in Japan was loyalty to a particular ruling house, to a particular race, to a particular group of islands, not, as in China, to a particular way of life. Whatever might contribute to the strength of the Japanese nation seemed beneficial even if it required substantial changes in the Japanese way of life.

The significance of the Sino-Japanese War is both external and internal. Internally, the defeat inflicted by a people whom the Chinese Emperor in his declaration of war had haughtily called "dwarfs" opened the eyes of an increasing number of Literati to the crisis posed by industrial technology. The Sino-Japanese War was an enormous psychological shock for the Chinese and quickened the pace of change. It was one thing to be defeated by a Western power, quite another to be defeated by the "dwarfs."

Externally, although the alarmed Western powers forced Japan to return the Liaodong peninsula to China, the Japanese example touched off a scramble for spheres of influence in China. Where the Western powers had previously been content to obtain "rights" in China, Germany and Russia now sought territorial acquisitions, and the future existence of China as an independent state was called into question. The threatened dismemberment of China into foreign colonies stimulated U.S. Secretary of State John Hay to announce the Open Door Policy. In notes sent to Britain, Germany and Russia in 1899, Hay called for equal commercial opportunity for all in

China and refused to recognize the developing spheres of influence. Although unwilling to seek its own sphere, the United States was determined not to be excluded from the profitable China trade. The Open Door Policy has sometimes been touted as proof that the United States was China's only true friend among the Western powers. While such a conclusion seems generally unwarranted, the United States record in China during the 19th century does seem comparatively "clean" when weighed against the deeds of the European nations.

## G. Economic Changes

The impact of the Western merchant (and the industrialist who stood behind him) on traditional China was slower than that of the soldier. In the military arena where China was suffering so visibly in comparison to the West, ideas progressed rapidly after the humiliating defeat in the Arrow War. By 1861 the government of Prince Gong saw the necessity of purchasing Western arms; by 1865 with the establishment of an arsenal in Shanghai the Chinese took the further step of manufacturing Western arms. Without really comprehending what lay behind the Western soldier, China was willing within 20 years after the Opium War to imitate him.

In the economic arena where a rededication by Prince Gong's government to Confucian principles alleviated China's woes temporarily, there was no compulsion to make changes in the structure of Chinese society. Modernization economically would have required the elevation of Chinese merchants from the status of parasites to that of the leading class in society. The creation of a modern military force was one thing, the Literati could control a modern army; but the creation of a Western-style industrial economy in which the commercial classes held the real power in society was quite another proposition entirely.

Despite early hopes of British merchants that the textile mills of England would be kept busy forever if each Chinese only added one inch to his shirt tail, foreign trade remained minor compared to domestic production until the 1890s, and Literati rice bowls remained full.

During the three decades after the Arrow War, while Western nations were building thousands of factories, the Chinese cautiously experimented with a few, and they had little comprehension of industrial organization or of the usefulness of modern transportation and communications networks.

The history of railroads in China is illustrative.. Although the officials of the Zongli Yamen urged the construction of railroads as early as 1866, conservative officials succeeded in blocking the project on the ground that railroads would make foreign invasion of the interior easier. It was left to foreigners to build the first railroad in China in 1876, running approximately 12 miles from Shanghai to Wusong. Built without official authorization, the project quickly evoked fears that hens would cease to lay eggs, cattle would be disturbed in grazing, and the air would be poisoned by black smoke. The provincial governor negotiated the purchase of the line and destroyed it. Not until five years later was another train seen in China when the Chinese themselves built a short line in the north to connect an inland coal mine with shipping facilities.

At about the same time, the Chinese began to build their first textile mills. Machine textile production was a key factor in upsetting agrarian economies throughout the world in the $19^{th}$ century. When not occupied with crops during the sowing and harvesting seasons, farmers of all traditional agrarian countries produced their own tools, utensils and, especially, cloth, activities that provided for household needs and produced small but important surpluses for sale in the market towns. Such cottage industry in China was not limited to peasants, for Literati fortunes were equally tied to agriculture. Even the ladies of Feng Guifen's household spun and wove, partly to satisfy family needs and partly in good Confucian fashion to set a proper example for the peasantry.

It became increasingly difficult for Chinese peasants to compete with Western machine-made cloth of higher quality and lower price. The resultant partial unemployment of the peasants and their loss of income had severe consequences. By the 1900s the process was almost complete. The traditional economy stood in ruins.

## H. The Final Years of the Qing Dynasty

### 1. Kang Youwei and the Reform Movement

In 1895, a young *jinshi* scholar named Kang Youwei rose to prominence. A fresh and original thinker, Kang, like the Self-Strengtheners, plunged back into the byways of Chinese history and found commentaries that had been neglected for centuries. Heavily over-interpreting these "true" commentaries, he concluded that Confucius, far from being one of history's greatest conservatives, was a rather utopian progressive. Had later generations not misinterpreted the Master, Chinese civilization would already be on the path of reform and progress and still be true to the Master. Disregarding millennia of institutionalization of the "orthodox" view, Kang went back to the "early church," shades of Martin Luther!

Although Kang's interpretation of Chinese history salved his Confucian conscience, its flaws were as obvious to the conservatives as were the defects of the Self-Strengtheners' earlier scientific interpretation of Chinese history. Confucius had simply made too many conservative statements to be labeled a progressive. What Confucius had meant to say mattered little; Confucian civilization had been constructed on how a hundred generations of orthodox Literati had interpreted him. Kang might save Confucius, but the conservatives were interested in saving Confucian civilization. In reality, Kang was trying to change Chinese Ti. Again, even though the conservatives were right and Kang was wrong, their intellectual victory was hollow. Kang tried to save a link between "modern" China and Confucian China; the conservatives stood still, historically right but sociologically, economically, and politically wrong.

Determined to reform China, Kang led hundreds of young scholars in addressing a petition to the Guangxu Emperor, Cixi's nephew, who now occupied the throne in his own right under watchful eye of Cixi. Convinced by the Japanese example that China must change, Kang was not deterred by the failure of his petition to reach the Emperor. He assembled a group of talented disciples, including Liang Qichao, who became a prominent journalist, educator, and philosopher–ultimately an advocate of democracy–for the next 30 years. The reformers were active throughout China in opening study clubs and newspapers for the propagation of their ideas. Kang also carefully cultivated some of the more open-minded Literati around the throne.

After seven petitions, the Emperor summoned Kang for an imperial audience. The young reformer and the still-younger Emperor liked each other from the start. Gradually, Kang's influence increased until by June 1898 he had access to the Emperor practically at will. In that month the famous Hundred Days of the Reform Movement commenced. Convinced by memorials submitted by allies of Kang in the imperial government, the Guangxu Emperor issued a series of decrees for the reform of China. The scope of the decrees was breathtaking, covering reforms of the examination system and the organization of government, including the military and police, as well as wide-ranging changes in commerce, agriculture, medicine, education, and study abroad. Never before had an emperor ordered such sweeping changes in Chinese society, except Wang Mang almost 2,000 years earlier during the Han dynasty.

Unfortunately, Kang attempted too much, too fast, and, like Wang Mang, failed to reform China. The conservative Literati felt threatened by the reforms and objected fiercely. Aware of the distaste of Cixi for Westernization, the reformers sought the support of Yuan Shikai, the leader of China's finest military force, the Beiyang Army, to isolate the Dowager Empress in a *coup d'état*. In the first of his acts of treachery Yuan revealed their plot to her. Kang and Liang managed to escape Cixi's crackdown, but six of their colleagues were executed. The Emperor himself spent the remaining ten years of his life a prisoner in the palace. Cixi again exercised overt control, and China entered a period of strong reaction. Within a month all the reform edicts were rescinded with the exception of one establishing Beijing University.

## 2. The Boxer Rebellion of 1900

During the next two years, the province of Shandong in north China saw increasing peasant discontent. A secret society, the

Society of Righteous, Harmonious Fists (or "Boxers") became the focal point for peasant grievances. An outgrowth of an older Daoist-flavored secret society, the Boxers grew rapidly in strength under the protection of a xenophobic governor of the province. The Society expanded from a little over a thousand members to hundreds of thousands in a single year. Fueling its growth were the cumulative effects of drought and flood, the increasingly severe economic pinch of competition from machine-made goods, and Germany's seizure of Jiaozhou Bay in the province.

Historically, Chinese peasants in China rebelled against the ruling dynasty. The Boxers, though, found a new scapegoat for their woes: the foreigner, especially the foreign missionary. In truth, the Chinese did have a legitimate grievance against the missions. All too many missionaries had attempted to protect their Chinese converts from the jurisdiction of local officials, an attempt to extend extraterritoriality to a segment of the native population. Many criminals had converted in an effort to escape prosecution.

The Boxers revived and broadcast many anti-Christian rumors prevalent ever since the Arrow War had led to missionary penetration of the interior. One such belief was that mission hospitals extracted a drug from the eyes of Chinese orphans, a drug so powerful that whoever took it would be instantly converted to Christianity.

At first the imperial court was cautious in dealing with the Boxers. No dynasty had ever encouraged peasant disorders. Yuan Shikai, appointed governor of Shandong, suppressed the society and drove its adherents across the border into neighboring Hebei, the province in which Beijing was located.

Cixi concluded that the court could manipulate the Boxers to expel the hated foreigners from China. The upshot was a spree of murder in the summer of 1900. The Boxers killed over 200 missionaries and other foreigners along with thousands of Chinese converts–"traitors"–throughout north China. They assassinated the German minister and laid siege for 55 days to the Legation Quarter in Beijing. At the height of their rampage, Cixi, against the advice of many high officials, committed the incredible folly of declaring war against the militarily superior Western powers. A joint British-French-Japanese-German-Italian-American-Russian expedition raised the siege of the Legation Quarter as Cixi and her court fled west. The ensuing Boxer Protocol, among other provisions, imposed an indemnity of $333,000,000 on the Manchu government, a sum in excess of the government's annual revenue. The indemnity not only directly furthered the cause of revolution by requiring heavier taxation of the peasantry but also indirectly. Both Britain and the United States used the funds for the education of Chinese students. Exposed to Western ways, many of these students became strong opponents of the traditional order.

The Boxers' rage against the missionaries was misplaced. The missionaries were no threat to the Chinese. They had already failed in their primary aim, the creation of Christian China. By 1900 the number of Christians barely exceeded half a million in the most populous country in the world.

Doctrinally, the missionaries labored under serious handicaps. First, in contrast to Mencius's view that Man was by nature good, the missionaries offered the doctrine of Original Sin, which most Chinese found gloomy and depressing. Second, in contrast to the Confucian hierarchy of the "Five Relationships," the missionaries preached the equality of all men in the eyes of God, a message that the Chinese viewed as tending to undermine an orderly society. Finally, the missionaries aggressively claimed exclusive

Truth for their creed and attributed Error to the native religions. Such a concept was alien to Chinese thought. Few could see any contradiction between Christianity and ancestor worship, but the missionaries insisted on choosing the one or the other. Such intransigence required the convert to turn his back on nearly 4,000 years of native religious experience, a denial of the national heritage that all too few were willing to make.

In practical matters, too, the missionaries failed to interest most Chinese in Christianity. Protestants, often fundamentalists, brought with them numerous prejudices from the home country. Since drink and tobacco were evils and the stage was licentious, they forbade their Chinese converts to drink wine, smoke, or attend performances of Chinese drama, prohibitions which the Chinese found as meaningless as the peculiar Muslim ban on eating pork. The Catholics stressed the creation of Christian families; they sought no economic or social progress for the Chinese, only the continuous birth of children to be educated in the faith. They seemed to most Chinese to be interested only in introducing a new superstition without any benefit to the people.

Many Chinese also saw missionary zeal as substantially identical to the aggressiveness of the Western soldier and Western merchant. The missionary may have thought he came merely to preach his creed; the Chinese viewed him as the religious representative of Western culture. The missionaries' claims were not considered in a vacuum: how could "dope peddlers" backed by gunboats presume to teach the Chinese the fundamentals of morality? Even in native hands, Christianity seemed to lead only to social woe. Was not the Taiping Rebellion the "first fruit" of missionary endeavor? In their effort to convert the Chinese, the missionaries offered a sad lesson in how to achieve little while attempting much.

## 3. The Manchu Reform Movement

After the Boxer debacle, not even the reactionary court could maintain China's stand pat position. All attempts to ward off the Western powers had failed, and Cixi, albeit half-heartedly and insincerely, instituted many of the reforms advocated by Kang Youwei during the Hundred Days. The venerable examinations, China's key cultural and political institution, with roots going back over 2,000 years, were abolished; the Six Boards were replaced by ten ministries organized along Western lines; education was reformed; and steps were taken to end the opium evil. The Manchus also sent commissions abroad to study foreign constitutions. Although they recommended a rather unimaginative copy of the Japanese constitution (under which, significantly, the Emperor remained virtually all-powerful), the mere consideration of a constitution was a giant step for the reactionary old Dowager Empress. In 1906, only two years before her death, an imperial decree promised constitutional government by 1917. A Central Legislative Council, half-elected and half-appointed, met for the first time as early as 1910.

These reforms could not save the dynasty–too little, too late. They only succeeded in whetting the desire of the Chinese for broader reforms. A revolutionary psychology began to grip the land.

## 4. The Revolutionaries

Central to the revolution of 1911 to 1912 and the collapse of the Confucian order was Sun Yatsen (formerly "Sun Yat-sen"). The future "father of his country" was born in 1866 in south China, where he imbibed the legend of Hong Xiuquan of the recent Taiping Rebellion. After an uneventful boyhood helping with the family crops, he moved to Hawaii at the invitation of an older brother, a successful rancher there. Sun spent three years in a missionary school and came into contact with Western ideas. By 1883, he had settled in Hong Kong where he pursued a Western education eventually becoming a physician. By the age of nineteen he had already resolved to overthrow the Manchu dynasty.

In 1894 imperial armies had crushed a revolt in Guangzhou by his Revive China Society. China was ripe for reform but not yet for revolution. Sun acquired a scurrilous reputation just as Kang Youwei's star began to rise. For the next few years Sun traveled throughout the world enlisting support, financial and otherwise, from overseas Chinese and from returning students whose contact with Western ways made them sympathetic to a revolution. By the opening years of the 20th century he resided in Japan.

In China itself, another important group, mostly Hunanese students led by Huang Xing, Song Jiaoren, and Wang Jingwei plotted uprisings in five cities in 1904. After discovery of the plot, the conspirators fled to Japan. There, together with Sun, they formed a new organization, the Revolutionary League. In the first issue of the League's newspaper, Sun expounded his ideas, the Three Principles of Nationalism, Democracy–preceded by three years of military government and six years of tutelage under a provisional constitution–and the People's Livelihood. Disconcertingly vague

(Sun was no great ideologist), they constituted the principal aims of the revolutionaries. This new umbrella group of anti-Manchu Chinese induced leaders of some of China's ever-present secret societies to launch local insurrections and sought members among the increasing flood of Chinese students into Japan. Revolutionary sentiment also increased among other groups. Zhang Binglin, for instance, organized the anti-Manchu Chinese Education Society in Shanghai in 1902.

Zhang Binglin was the next major Chinese intellectual to reinterpret history in defense of Chinese civilization. His thought was curiously ambiguous: like Wo Jen he was dedicated to maintaining the purity of Confucian civilization; like Sun Yatsen, he was a revolutionary advocate of overturning the Manchu dynasty. The reason for China's weakness, he argued, was the historic distortion of Confucian civilization by the alien Manchu conquerors. Such a position is untenable. Far from distorting Confucian civilization the Manchus were among its most ardent supporters. They had learned well what the Mongol conquerors had not, that the Chinese would accept foreign rule easily if, but only if, the alien conquerors accepted Chinese civilization. The Chinese were not devoted to a nation or a race but to a way of life. Zhang's attack on the Manchu dynasty was hardly consistent with his dedication to the purity of Confucianism, for the throne was an integral part of the system. Was Zhang naive? Not really, for Zhang seems to have realized by the first decade of the 20th century that the conservative defense of Confucianism was futile. He seems more interested in finding a scapegoat than in saving the Confucian civilization he loved. At heart Zhang was a defeatist. He served as an intellectual bridge to the nationalists, men who also wanted to oust the Manchus but who had other ideas, men who wanted to end

Confucian civilization just as much as Zhang sentimentally wished to preserve it.

After several abortive uprisings by Sun Yatsen's Revolutionary League, a successful revolt finally began in 1911. Ironically, there were many revolutionaries among the Manchu military forces. Modernization of the army had led to a desire for political modernization as well. About 2,000 of Sun's sympathizers among imperial troops in the city of Wuhan planned a revolt in mid-October and invited Huang Xing to take command. The conspirators accidentally detonated some explosives prematurely, and local Manchu officials got wind of the plot. In an atmosphere of crisis the insurrection began on October 10 (always thereafter China's national holiday). Since Huang Xing had not yet arrived in Wuhan, the rebels turned to an imperial officer, Li Yuanhong, who reluctantly assumed command. A combination of his skill and the flight of Manchu civil and still-loyal military officials gave control of the city to the rebels, who formed a revolutionary government. Most provinces of China quickly declared their independence from the Manchus.

By this time Cixi had died shortly after poisoning the Guangxu Emperor, and the imperial government was headed by incompetent regents for the child emperor Puyi. Alarmed by the outbreak of revolution, the regents sought to counter it as early as October 14. They ordered Yuan Shikai to suppress the "bandits," setting the stage for the next of Yuan's acts of treachery. At first Yuan attempted to decline his new duties; but, after repeated urging from Beijing, agreed to suppress the rebellion upon the following conditions:

1. A parliament be opened the next year;
2. A responsible cabinet be organized;

3. Amnesty be granted to the revolutionaries;
4. The revolutionary party be accorded full legal recognition;
5. Yuan be given complete control over all armed forces;
6. Adequate military funds be supplied.

Yuan had no intention of suppressing the revolution; such a course of action would have strengthened the Manchus, not Yuan personally. Instead, he sought to further his own ambitions by playing the role of middleman between the two sides. A suspicious Manchu court yielded slowly to the demands of the "indispensable" Yuan while he applied both carrot and stick to the various revolutionary groups.

One setback in Yuan's drive for power was the arrival of Sun Yatsen in China on December 25. Sun had received word of the revolution in a hotel room in Denver, Colorado, where he was seeking support among Chinese-Americans. By now the revolutionists recognized that Sun alone, as elder statesman among the revolutionaries, had sufficient prestige to unite their various factions. On December 29, 1911 they elected him Provisional President of China and Li Yuanhong Vice-President.

Yuan Shikai through his Beiyang Army, however, controlled the military power in China. Wisely or foolishly, Sun on January 15, 1912, offered to step aside after the Manchus abdicated in favor of Yuan if he declared his support of the revolution. Yuan thereupon brought sufficient pressure on the befuddled imperial court that the Manchus formally abdicated on February 12. Yuan's second act of betrayal, this time of the hapless Manchus, thrust him to the pinnacle of power in the land. On February 15, 1912, the revolutionaries in Nanjing formally elected him Provisional President of China.

# *7. The Early Republic*

## (1912 to 1949)

After Yuan Shikai assumed office as Provisional President of China in early 1912, Sun Yatsen's Revolutionary League transformed itself into a political party, the Guomindang, to compete in a national election for a provisional assembly on a platform of Sun's Three Principles–nationalism, democracy, and the people's livelihood. The new assembly would write a constitution for the new republic. A clear victor in the election, the Guomindang chose Song Jiaoren as its candidate for premier. Before the new assembly had met for the first time, though, Song fell to an assassin's bullet in a Shanghai railroad station. Though definitive proof is lacking, Yuan was surely responsible. When the assembly finally met in April of 1913, Yuan's supporters offered 1,000 pounds sterling to Guomindang deputies to quit the party. With 2,000 years of autocracy behind them and no direct experience of parliamentary democracy, all too many of the Guomindang deputies accepted the proffered bribes. Those who refused soon found themselves doggedly harassed by the police. Yuan then revoked their credentials and, since a quorum was lacking, dissolved the assembly. Sun Yatsen fled back to Japan with hundreds of his followers.

Next Yuan concocted a constitution in 1914 heavily weighted in favor of presidential power. The president could serve an unlimited number of ten-year terms and even name his own successor. Yuan's betrayal of the fledgling republic–his third betrayal of those who trusted him–was the most egregious of all.

Yuan decided to take the dragon throne for himself as the founding emperor of a new dynasty, and soon restored many of the rituals performed by emperors of the old Confucian order. He might well have succeeded in his plans but for the outbreak of World War I in August of 1914. Japan, copying Western-style imperialism, quickly declared war on Germany and seized Germany's territorial concession on China's Shandong peninsula. In January of 1915, the Japanese presented Yuan with the infamous Twenty-one Demands, envisaging China's conversion to a semi-colony of Japan. China was to confirm Japan's gains in Shandong, grant concessions for railroads, grant special privileges and concessions in Manchuria, and employ Japanese advisors in financial, political, military, and police matters. Word of Japan's demands leaked out and infuriated the Chinese intellectuals and businessmen who supported Sun's call for nationalism, democracy, and the people's livelihood. The Western nations, preoccupied with war in Europe, made no effort to restrain their Japanese ally.

Yuan Shikai

Sun Yatsen

Yuan, in need of funds available from Japan, convinced the Japanese to drop some of the Twenty-one Demands but ultimately yielded to the threat of superior military force and his own need for Japanese financing. In December of 1915, Yuan accepted the call of a puppet "National Congress" to assume the throne the following spring. Within days Yunnan province, at the urging of Liang Qichao, declared its independence from the government in Beijing. By March 1916, generals commanding the military in other provinces took similar steps. Yuan dropped his plan to establish a new dynasty and died in June (of natural causes?).

For the next 11 years, China fragmented. Military strongmen (or "warlords") ruled the provinces, sometimes a single province, sometimes two or more, sometimes a handful of counties or villages. Even within these areas, the militarists' control was usually not complete, for their subordinate commanders often harbored ambitions of their own. All told, over 110 individuals are identifiable as the highest military authority at various times in one or another of China's provinces.

Four major wars were fought after 1920 between shifting alliances of warlords in north China. By then armaments included machine guns, armored vehicles, heavy artillery, and even a few airplanes. All in all, the peasant conscripts of these warlord armies suffered an estimated 2,000,000 deaths, and an untold number of peasant families, fleeing the fighting, became impoverished refugees.

Whoever temporarily dominated the capital of Beijing maintained the fiction of a central government. That fiction gave at least a superficial appearance of legitimacy to military usurpations. Six men served as President, and 17 served as Prime Minister in 11 very unstable years.

Some significant changes occurred despite China's instability. The war in Europe from 1914 to 1918 disrupted Europe's export trade to China, and considerable industrialization took place in China to replace imported goods no longer available, particularly textiles. Most new factories sprang up in the port cities where the Western powers had previously obtained territorial concessions. The Western presence protected those cities and the new industries from incursions by the warlords.

Intellectuals increasingly viewed Confucianism as a dead weight and sought new paths for China. For some time, most looked upon liberal democracy as the solution to the country's ills. It was the apparent source of power that had permitted the West to repeatedly humiliate China. Other new ideas also began to reach China, including anarchism, socialism, and equal rights for women, all of which originated in the West. Liberal democracy had competitors in the realm of ideas.

The Bolshevik revolution in Russia in 1918 suddenly made revolutionary socialism increasingly attractive. Karl Marx had said that in their struggle with capitalists, workers would someday spontaneously revolt and seize power. The revolution, however, would occur only when the time was ripe and only after the bourgeoisie had fully realized a capitalist society. Vladimir Lenin had significantly amended Marxism: Workers did not need to wait for some future "ripe" moment but should actively promote revolution. Events in Russia seemed to confirm his views. Russia was still at best a semi-capitalist, semi-feudal land in which workers were a small minority. Yet Bolshevik activism had launched a revolution. The oppressors of Russia's common people were being defeated on the battlefield, and an egalitarian society was in the offing. Facts seemed to verify theory for once. A Marxist study group was formed at Beijing University in 1918, including a young assistant librarian, Mao Zedong, and Chinese scholars began translating the works of Marx and Lenin into Chinese.

A year later events led to what some scholars consider the birth of modern Chinese nationalism. At the Paris Peace Conference after World War I, the allied powers, contrary to the expectations of Chinese public opinion, confirmed Japan as the legitimate successor to Germany's territorial concession on the Shantung peninsula. At the urging of the allied powers, China had declared war on Germany and Austria in 1917, and thousands of Chinese had gone to France as laborers in the allied war effort or as students–many of whom eventually became convinced Marxists. Yet the allies, having previously made secret pledges to Japan, ignored China's territorial rights.

When news of the allies' decision reached China, some 3,000 students on May 4, 1919 took to the streets at Beijing's Tiananmen Square in angry protest. They proceeded to the home of the pro-Japanese Foreign Minister of the warlord government then controlling Beijing and burned it down. Police intervened throughout the various events, arresting many and beating some. For the next month protests, strikes against foreign enterprises, and boycotts of Japanese goods roiled China's cities. No longer would Chinese nationalism be directed against the presence in China of "foreign devils" as in the 19$^{th}$ century or against the alien Manchu rulers of China as in the run-up to the revolution of 1911. After May 4, 1919, Chinese nationalism would be directed against imperialism, both Western and Japanese.

The intellectuals of China, in a contemporaneous step referred to as the New Culture Movement, also called for a general rejection of their antique culture. Confucianism had served an agricultural

China well for over 2,000 years but no longer functioned in a modern, industrializing world.

Hu Shi and other leaders of the New Culture Movement realized that China would remain weak unless education was more widespread. A major stumbling block was classical Chinese writing, unchanged for thousands of years. Spoken Chinese, on the other hand, had changed radically just as modern English had changed from the language of *Beowulf* and *The Canterbury Tales*. Learning to read classical writing was so time-consuming that no more than 5 per cent or so of the population had the leisure to learn the meanings of characters that no longer corresponded to the meanings of the same characters in modern times. New ideas, such as equal rights and democracy, could not spread easily if people couldn't read. Hu Shi and his colleagues began a campaign to publish newspapers, magazines, and books using written characters that reflected the spoken language. Their efforts succeeded, and the next two decades were an impressive era of Chinese literature in the new style. Works by Lu Xun and Shu Qinchun, for instance, are available in English translation. Later the Communists in the 1950s and 1960s further advanced the prospect of greater public literacy by a movement to simplify the writing of Chinese characters. 當, for instance, became 当 in simplified form. Thereafter, it was easier to write Chinese as well as to read it.

By 1921, Sun Yatsen, having returned from Japan with his Guomindang followers, had formed the Chinese National Military Government in Guangzhou ("Canton"). Sun had concluded that his provisional government failed in 1913 because he had lacked a strong army to defend the republic. The Military Government's authority, though, extended to only part of Guangdong province in the far south of China and that only because of the sympathy of a local warlord.

Twelve members of various Marxist study groups formed the Chinese Communist Party (hereafter referred to as "CCP") in Shanghai in 1921. A representative of the Comintern, the Soviet Union's organization to promote world communism, assisted the founding members. Though the CCP soon expanded to some 300-odd members, it was even less significant in war-lord-dominated national affairs than Sun Yatsen's political party.

The Comintern sent representatives to advise both the Guomindang and the Communists. Moscow believed that there were not enough workers in China to achieve a revolution led by the proletariat. The better course was to assist the bourgeois revolution of Sun Yatsen and to form an alliance between the Guomindang (hereafter called "Nationalists") and the Communists. In the meantime, the CCP could concentrate on building membership and await the moment to launch its own revolution.

The Comintern representatives met with resistance to the idea of a merger between the two groups from both sides. Some Communist leaders were reluctant to support a bourgeois society as a replacement, even a temporary replacement, of the old Confucian society. Sun Yatsen, an advocate of western liberalism, simply distrusted the Communists.

In 1923, Sun, eager to solve his military weakness with aid from the Soviet Union, agreed to allow Communists to join the Nationalists but only as individuals. Upon orders from Moscow, the Chinese Communists, despite misgivings, fell into line. Although this first united front was an uneasy alliance, both sides had several goals in common. Communists and Nationalists alike opposed imperialists, warlords, and the large landlords of rural areas who oppressed the peasantry.

The young Mao Zedong joined the Nationalists and became head of the Nationalists' Peasant Bureau, a post in which his observation of rural conditions eventually led him to base his hopes on revolution by rural peasants, not by urban workers–a Marxist heresy. Another young Communist, Zhou Enlai, served as deputy to the head of the Whampoa Military Academy, established with Moscow's help and led by a young officer, Chiang K'ai Shek, who opposed communism. Sun had appointed Chiang because he had demonstrated great loyalty, a character trait that would not be to his advantage in the Nationalists' final showdown with the Communists in the late 1940s.

Communists and Nationalists alike were active during the next three years. The former gained many new converts and, working in the larger cities where warlords were absent, succeeded in organizing labor unions. The latter prepared for an eventual Northern Expedition to reunite China under a Nationalist government. Whampoa graduated some 7,000 cadets over the next three years to lead some 85,000 peasant conscripts. Though a relatively small force compared to warlord armies, this Nationalist army was better armed and better trained thanks to Moscow's help.

The death of Sun Yatsen in 1925 led to a protracted struggle for succession to the Nationalist leadership between the right-wing led by Chiang K'ai Shek and the left-wing led by Wang Jingwei. Chiang emerged victorious.

In 1926 Chiang felt strong enough to launch the Northern Expedition. Within six months, he had broken out of Guangdong and controlled seven southern provinces. His stunning success was attributable to many factors. First, some warlords did not initially take the Nationalists, previously confined to a small area in far-south China, seriously. Second, the peasant armies faced by Chiang K'ai Shek, although many times larger in size, were comparatively ill trained, poorly equipped and undisciplined. Chiang faced opponents exhausted by years of fighting. Moreover, not all the peasant soldiers proved loyal to their respective warlords, for Communists had preceded the Nationalist army and induced many to lay down their arms and join the CCP. Third, Chiang offered to incorporate several warlord armies into his own. After hard bargaining by which the defectors retained a degree of independence even within the Nationalist army, six warlords and many more field commanders switched sides. While this additional military strength facilitated a more rapid reunification of China in the 1920s, Chiang's lack of total control over the ex-warlords in his army would in the late 1940s contribute to his defeat by the Communists.

Reinforced by warlord defections, Chiang advanced to the outskirts of Shanghai in central China, China's most industrialized city where the Communists had succeeded in organizing most workers. The Shanghai General Labor Federation paralyzed the city with a general strike to facilitate the entry of Chiang's troops. What ensued was an unexpected massacre of communists and union members by the Nationalists and by Shanghai's Green Gang, a criminal network of tens of thousands, whose support Chiang had arranged clandestinely in advance. Similar suppression soon took place in other cities in central and south China where the Communists had been active in organizing workers. Chiang meanwhile announced the formation of a Nationalist government in Nanjing ("Nanking") with himself at its head. The left wing of the party, led by Wang Jingwei, fell in line behind China's new dictator

Generalissimo Chiang K'ai Shek. The years of military government preceding true democracy contemplated in Sun Yatsen's Three Principles (nationalism, democracy, and the people's livelihood) had begun.

The Communist Party, sharply reduced from strength of some 60,000, was in a state of near collapse. Some members abandoned the party. Some went underground. Others fled to Moscow, and still others, including Mao Zedong, fled to south central China, where they eventually established the Jiangxi Soviet Republic in the mountains of that province. The Soviet initially controlled only a few hundred square miles with a force of a few thousand soldiers, the large majority of whom had no rifles.

Chiang K'ai Shek moved north from Shanghai to defeat the warlords still resisting and complete a unification of all China under his government. On June 3, 1927, Zhang Zuolin, the strongest of his remaining opponents, decided to withdraw to his stronghold, Manchuria. The next day Japanese militarists blew up Zhang's train. They sought to create a crisis that would discredit the new civilian government in Tokyo as "weak" and unwilling to add Manchuria to Japan's previous acquisitions of Korea and Taiwan. For the moment, though, the civilian government held firm and remained in power. Six months later, Zhang Zuolin's son and successor, Zhang Xueliang, went over to the Nationalists, and the Warlord era ended.

In his new capital at Nanjing ("Nanking") Chiang K'ai Shek appeared to all foreign observers to have achieved permanent victory. The warlords had surrendered or joined the Nationalists; the left wing of the Nationalists had fallen in line; and the Communists were in disarray.

Support for Chiang's right-wing regime came mostly from the urban middle classes and rural landlords who remained Confucian in outlook, unaffected by the May 4th Movement. For the next year Chiang organized his government and paid little attention to the Communist remnants. His apparent victories, though, masked his greatest weakness. Other than his opposition to both the imperialists and the Communists, Chiang had no real vision of a future for his country. Eight years later he would launch the New Life Movement, which was mostly a revival of the old Confucian virtues. While urging the Chinese to virtue in their personal lives to strengthen the country, the New Life Movement was silent about economic and political matters. Land reform and citizens' participation in government received short shrift. Chiang's lack of vision stood in stark contrast to that of Mao Zedong.

While Chiang consolidated his grip on power, the Communists, underground in various cities, followed the Comintern's lead and organized working-class revolts. The Nationalists quickly and ruthlessly suppressed them. Communists who survived these Autumn Harvest Uprisings then fled to the Jiangxi Soviet Republic, where they wrested leadership from Mao Zedong, or to other smaller rural areas held by Communists elsewhere in China

Although leadership of the Jiangxi Soviet was in the hands of men who followed Moscow's directions, the views of Mao Zedong began to gain credibility in the rural setting of the Jiangxi Soviet. Mao believed that the revolution would happen only when China's hundreds of millions of suffering peasants arose in fury against their landlord oppressors. The defeats of urban workers in the Autumn Harvest Uprisings raised Mao's prestige in the party and made his ideas suddenly more attractive, though he was still not yet the party's leader. Perhaps peasants, not workers, were the key.

Mao began to think about how peasants could prevail militarily against a better-armed foe. The first task was to win the overwhelming loyalty and support of local populations. Communists should treat them fairly and persuade them patiently. Both officers and common soldiers should share the burdens of the common people. Both should work along side the peasants whether in menial farm tasks or as teachers, administrators, or in other useful positions.

Mao formulated eight rules of "do's" and "don'ts" for common soldiers: 1) speak courteously; 2) pay fairly for purchases; 3) pay for damaged property; 4) return borrowed items; 5) don't abuse people verbally or physically; 6) don't damage crops; 7) don't take liberties with women; and 8) don't mistreat captives.

Of greatest importance in winning the loyalty of the peasants was land reform. The strong growth of population since the late 18th century had reduced the size of peasant farms, most rented from wealthy landlords, to a bare subsistence level and also created a large contingent of landless peasants. The Communists in the Jiangxi Soviet undertook one of the bloodiest anti-landlord programs of land redistribution in Chinese history. Despite some excesses against small landlords, the program won the support of the Soviet's peasants.

Mao believed that this support by the people would give the Communists an advantage in intelligence concerning Chiang K'ai Shek's troop movements and deny corresponding intelligence to Chiang's forces. It would also provide Mao's guerrilla armies with soldiers more motivated than those they opposed.

As for military strategy, Mao was well-versed in Chinese history and drew heavily on the military theories of Sun Wu from the

Period of the Warring States (481 to 221 B.C.E.) Sun Wu had said, "Avoid what is strong; strike what is weak."

Mao concluded that a guerrilla commander's field of battle was largely behind the enemy's lines attacking lines of communication and supply, rear bases, and small detached units. He should not directly confront the enemy in conventional warfare without a superiority of at least 5 to 1 at the time of engagement.

Sun Wu had also said, "Make an uproar in the east. Strike in the west." Deception, surprise, and rapid mobility were keys to defeating a stronger enemy. The guerrilla commander should make the enemy believe that he would strike at one point and then strike at a different place important to the enemy but left lightly defended, a place where the enemy did not expect an attack. Captured enemy weapons, ammunition and equipment would strengthen the guerrilla forces for an eventual direct assault on an enemy reduced to defending its rear and immobilized.

While Mao and his comrades experimented in the tiny Jiangxi Soviet with refining his techniques for winning over the peasants, Chiang K'ai Shek organized and consolidated his government in the new capital Nanjing. The port cities continued to see the building of factories, schools, and hospitals.

With the warlords and the Communists both defeated, the Japanese military became concerned that a strengthened and reunified China under the Nationalists might thwart their ambition to take control of Manchuria. The Nationalists' capture and execution of four Japanese spies in June 1931 in Manchuria lent a sense of urgency to the militarists. On September 18, they detonated bombs on a railroad track outside the city of Mukden (now named Shenyang). Confusion ensued, Chinese and Japanese troops exchanged fire, and the Japanese occupied Mukden. The

400,000 Chinese troops of Zhang Xueliang in the area outnumbered the Japanese substantially. When Zhang sought instructions from Chiang K'ai Shek, though, he was ordered to offer no resistance. Zhang moved his troops south of the Great Wall, and the Japanese took control of Manchuria. In 1932 they set up a puppet state called Manchukuo with Puyi, the young child who had inherited the dragon throne in 1908, as emperor. The Japanese takeover was the beginning of World War II.

Illustrating Chiang K'ai Shek's tenuous control over the warlords who had adhered to his cause were two Chinese generals in Manchuria: one defected to the Japanese; the other offered substantial but ultimately unsuccessful resistance despite Chiang K'ai Shek's instructions to the contrary. Although Chiang recognized the danger from Japan, his first priority was to complete his defeat of the Communists–a decision that lost him considerable public support even in the prosperous cities. To the public, the concept of nationalism meant opposing foreign aggression, not engaging in a civil war.

China's appeal to the League of Nations in early 1932 elicited strong words and nothing else. The League declared Japan an aggressor and demanded the return of Manchuria to China; but, contrary to the League's Covenant, neither sanctions nor military action were requested of member states. The demise of that toothless organization lay only a few years in the future.

From 1930 to 1933, Chiang K'ai Shek undertook four "bandit suppression campaigns" against the Communists in the Jiangxi Soviet, even while the Japanese made periodic incursions into north China. "Bandits" was Chiang's favorite derogatory term for the Communists.

Although the Nationalist armies numbered in the hundreds of thousands, they failed to dislodge the more mobile Communists operating in a mountainous area. Zhu De, the Communist field commander, was adept in applying Mao Zedong's tactics. Over the years with peasant support the Soviet had gradually expanded from a few hundred square miles to 12,000, an area about the size of the state of Maryland. About 100,000 peasants served in the Communist army.

For the fifth "bandit suppression campaign" in 1933, Chiang on the advice of his German military advisor, the famed strategist Hans von Seeckt, devised a new plan of attack. Roads were built encircling the Soviet along with a network of airfields. Some 700,000 Nationalist troops then built concentric rings of interconnected blockhouses slowly squeezing the Communist troops into a smaller and smaller area and reducing the Soviet from 12,000 square miles to 1,500.

With defeat looming, Communists had no choice but to break out. On October 15, 100,000 soldiers and party officials accompanied by 35 women broke through von Seeckt's ring in two places to the southwest. Thus began their legendary Long March, covering some 6,000–undoubtedly exaggerated–zigzag miles under frequent attack by Nationalist and provincial forces, bandits, remaining warlords, or hostile tribesmen. They crossed raging rivers, snow-covered mountains, and an area of interminable swamp on the Sichuan-Gansu border. Many died en route from battle or disease; others simply abandoned the cause. The Long March was the greatest retreat in all history. Xenophon's embattled retreat from Persia to Greece was but 1,700 miles, and the retreat of Napoleon's army from Moscow to France only 1,500 miles. Heroic as the Long March was, however, the participants did not endear themselves to the peasants whose crops they commandeered as they lived off the land. After thirteen months, 20,000 survivors of China's great modern epic finally joined up with 10,000 fellow Communists living in caves near the town of Yan'an in northern Shaanxi province.

One important event en route was a leadership conference in January 1935, at which Mao Zedong took over leadership as Chairman of the Chinese Communist Party from Bo Gu, one of the Communists favored by Moscow. Until his death in 1976, Mao would remain paramount leader of the Chinese Communist Party.

Still convinced that he could not succeed against the Japanese imperialists until he had eliminated the Communists, Chiang K'ai Shek ordered Zhang Xueliang, commander of the best army group in China, to attack Yan'an. Rallies shortly before by thousands of students demanding resistance to Japan, as well as adverse press criticism, did not deter Chiang from his stubborn intent to wipe out his internal enemy first. The Japanese by this time had occupied various points in northern provinces and even penetrated Hebei province south of the Great Wall. What they were unable to accomplish by the Twenty-one Demands of two decades earlier, they intended to achieve by military aggression.

Unfortunately for Chiang, Zhang Xueliang was of the same mind as the demonstrating students. Ever since the Japanese takeover of Manchuria, Zhang had nursed a desire for revenge against those who had expelled him from his homeland, the vast region that his warlord father had once ruled unchallenged.

Zhang Xueliang's refusal to obey the Generalissimo's orders set in motion a series of events known as the "Xi'an incident," a turning point in Chinese history. On December 12, 1936, an enraged Chiang K'ai Shek flew to the city of Xi'an, about 100 miles south of Yan'an, to confront his defiant general. Upon his arrival, Zhang

Xueliang and his supporters arrested Chiang and demanded that he form a new United Front with the Communists and begin armed resistance to the Japanese. When the news reached Yan'an, Mao and others among the elated Communist leadership wanted an immediate execution of Chiang. In the end, the Soviet Union had the last word. Moscow learned that Chiang's long-term rival, Wang Jingwei, had just stopped in Berlin to confer with Hitler before returning to China in apparent hopes of becoming the new leader of the Nationalist government. Stalin was apprehensive that a Nationalist government formed by Wang Jingwei might establish closer relations with both Germany and Japan, leaving the Soviet Union vulnerable to external threats on three sides. Stalin's fears concerning Wang's ambitions were not unfounded, for Wang two years later headed a pro-Japanese puppet government in the area of China occupied by Japan after its full-scale invasion in 1937. To prevent the prospect of a third unfriendly power along the borders of the Soviet Union, Stalin ordered Mao to seek a friendly solution with Chiang. A Communist delegation headed by Zhou Enlai went to Xi'an to negotiate a second United Front. Chiang's wife, Soong Mayling, also flew to Xi'an to urge her husband to seek peace with the Communists. Chiang, angry that he had been within "five minutes" of finishing off his weakened internal foe, held out for 12 days before agreeing in principle to a new United Front. The 30,000-man Communist remnant in Yan'an had escaped probable annihilation by the narrowest margin, and the modern history of China was set on a new course.

Six months later, war broke out between China and Japan. After an initial clash at the Marco Polo Bridge, a few miles west of Beijing, the Japanese invaded China in full force in July 1937. Taking Shanghai was a principal goal. Some 50,000 Japanese troops stationed at the Japanese concession in that city were joined by reinforcements proceeding by rail from the north. The Nationalists suffered a devastating defeat, losing more than half of their best troops to their better-armed foe. Chinese battle deaths exceeded 250,000.

After occupying Shanghai and several cities on the north China plain, the Japanese moved on China's capital, Nanjing. After three weeks of resistance and 70,000 dead, the Nationalist general in charge of the defense abandoned the city, and an extraordinary rampage of atrocities ensued: the Rape of Nanjing ("Nanking"). Japanese troops ran wild in an orgy of decapitations, disembowelments, live burials, mutilations, and other atrocities. Estimates of Chinese women and girls, raped and then murdered, range from 20,000 to 60,000, of total deaths from 90,000 to 300,000. The carnage continued for six weeks. Looting and arson left the Chinese capital in ruins.

As Japanese troops advanced westward up the Yangzi River delta in the summer of 1938, the Nationalists made a stand at the city of Hankou, only to lose most of their air force and suffer another 200,000 casualties. Chiang K'ai Shek then moved his remaining forces far west to a new wartime capital at Chongqing in Sichuan. The Japanese decided not to overextend their supply lines by pursuing, and the war quieted down for several years with both the Japanese and the Nationalists maintaining their positions, occasionally attacking or defending but not engaging in all-out war. From twelve major battles in 1937, the number steadily dwindled to three per year in 1943 to 1945. Stalemated, the Nationalists and Japanese both settled in.

By the end of 1938, the Japanese controlled the cities of most of eastern China. By day at least they also controlled the roads and railroads connecting them. Chiang K'ai Shek controlled west and southwest China and a few pockets in the southeast.

Even with the great majority of the Chinese population under Japanese occupation, Chiang still considered the Communists his principal enemy. He believed that the United States would eventually enter a coming conflagration and defeat Japan, freeing the Nationalist armies to destroy the Communists. With different goals from those of the U.S. military establishment, represented in China by Lieutenant General Joseph Stillwell, Chiang sat tight except for defense all through the World War II. Stillwell constantly urged Chiang to no avail to supposedly shorten the war by engaging the Japanese.

Historians are often critical of Chiang for his inactivity during the long years of the war. The criticisms seem unfounded for many reasons. First, the Nationalists were no match for the Japanese, especially since an army on the offensive usually needs superiority over the defense–five to one according to Mao Zedong. Active offense by the Nationalists would have only led to hundreds of thousands or millions more casualties. During the war, mostly in the early years, they suffered over 3,000,000 casualties. Second, the Nationalists had lost much of their equipment in battle. Landlocked in western China, they received only a trickle of American supplies over the 715-mile Burma Road, not enough to undertake a sustained effort to defeat the Japanese. The U.S. did manage, though, to train and equip many Nationalist divisions in Burma for a campaign to prevent the Japanese from blocking the Burma Road. Those American-trained divisions, the best fighting force in the Nationalist army, returned to China at the end of World War II. Third, even though the Nationalists were inactive, their presence in China tied down the majority of Japan's army throughout the war and drained 35 per cent of total Japanese expenditures–clearly substantial contributions to the allied cause and more important than those of his Communist adversaries. Chiang had faults and made poor decisions that ultimately doomed the Nationalist cause, but his inactivity against the Japanese was not a mistake. He correctly calculated that the United States would defeat Japan in any event and turned a deaf ear to American diplomats and generals who urged him to attack the Japanese forces energetically. Why, indeed, sacrifice an army that he would need after the war when that sacrifice would accomplish little?

Ironically, the Japanese invasion was a key factor in the eventual takeover of China by the Communists. No longer did the Communists face a stubborn Chiang K'ai Shek determined to destroy them. Instead, operating behind Japanese lines in north China, safe from the Nationalists, they had the support of the local populace everywhere. They could practice and refine all of Mao Zedong's prescriptions for guerrilla warfare and for gaining the support of the populace. By resisting the Japanese while the Nationalists did little, they were regarded as the true champions of Chinese nationalism, leaving Chiang K'ai Shek bereft of his previous one remaining ideological advantage. By modest social programs and land reform in the countryside, the Communists gained the loyalty of the peasants. That loyalty after the war would provide the CCP with hundreds of thousands of recruits willing to fight for their cause. Party membership had increased to 1.2 million by the end of the war.

Shortly before Japan's surrender to the allies, the Soviet Union invaded Manchuria under the Yalta agreement with its wartime allies. That agreement included a promise by the Soviet Union to withdraw three months after the Japanese capitulation and to recognize the Nationalists' authority over Manchuria. Chiang K'ai Shek knew that he could not move his armies quickly enough from southwestern China to control Manchuria by the time the Soviet Union withdrew. He obtained Moscow's agreement to delay the evacuation.

The Communists were in a much more favorable position. They had been operating behind Japanese lines in Manchuria throughout the war, and their forces in north China were close enough to send reinforcements before Chiang's were likely to arrive. The Communists during the Moscow's continuing occupation of Manchuria began to move their troops into the rural areas. They also profited from hundreds of thousands of captured Japanese rifles turned over to them by the departing Soviet Union.

Chiang would have been wise simply to move into north China and consolidate his position there before moving beyond the Great Wall. Over-confident, he made the key military mistake of the impending civil war. He sought and obtained Washington's agreement to transport his troops by sea and by air to Manchuria, including his best troops, the divisions the United States had trained and armed in Burma. Upon arrival in Manchuria, the Nationalists occupied the major cities.

Communist forces, newly named the People's Liberation Army (the "PLA"), applied Mao Zedong's theories on guerrilla warfare and constantly disrupted Nationalist supply lines in Manchuria as General George C. Marshall tried fruitlessly to convince the two sides to negotiate a common plan for postwar China.

By the time Marshall left China after 13 months, the Nationalists were besieged and immobilized in the Manchurian cities they occupied, and the PLA was ready to make direct assaults. Nationalist losses of some 150,000 of their best troops in the guerrilla phase had weakened them. Communist losses were made up–and more–by new peasant recruits. Marshall's mission was doomed from the start, as neither Chiang K'ai Shek nor Mao Zedong wanted anything less than complete submission by the other.

By June 1947, the Nationalists in Manchuria were surrounded in a small triangle–a mere one percent of Manchuria. By November, the 800,000 troops of the PLA led by Lin Biao, had crushed their enemy, and the Communists took control of Manchuria. Altogether, the Nationalists lost 470,000 men in Manchuria, despite a 2 to 1 superiority over the Communists in troops in China as a whole and the possession of superior weapons. Simultaneously, the PLA defeated the Nationalists in Shandong province in north China, a lesser but important victory that cost Chiang 100,000 killed or wounded in eight days.

These losses quickly led to a general demoralization of the Nationalist forces as both sides prepared for a showdown near the city of Xuzhou in northern Jiangsu province. Two Nationalist divisions defected at the outset, an ominous sign. The battle pitted 400,000 Nationalists with tanks, heavy artillery and armored cars against 550,000 troops of the PLA. Known as the Battle of Huaihai, the fighting raged for three months from October 1948 to January 1949. The Nationalists suffered 200,000 casualties, and thousands more defected to the enemy. The PLA also captured much equipment, reducing the Nationalists' advantage in armaments.

Meanwhile, Lin Biao's men moved south from Manchuria and together with the Communist North China Army attacked the Beijing-Tianjin area in a pincers movement. A month later the Nationalist commander surrendered with 200,000 of his men. Many Nationalist commanders were aging former warlords who had joined the National cause in the 1920s but whose loyalty and willingness to obey orders were tenuous.

By January 1949, in various battles the Nationalists had lost 1,500,000 of their 3,700,000 men. In April, the PLA crossed the Yangtze River and took Nanjing, forcing the National government to flee to Guangzhou (Canton). On October 1, 1949, Mao Zedong proclaimed the establishment of the People's Republic of China. In December, Chiang K'ai Shek and most of his remaining troops fled to safety on the island of Taiwan.

Besides his military blunder in sending his best troops to Manchuria, Chiang made mistakes on the civilian side. One was allowing inflation to get out of control. Inflation began as early as 1928 as deficit financing was required for military expenditures–some 80 per cent of the budget over the years. By 1937, inflation reached 29 per cent annually. During most of the war, starved for revenues from the rich coastal provinces occupied by the Japanese, Chiang turned to the printing press, and inflation exceeded 100 per cent. By 1948, during a six-month period, prices rose an astounding 85,000 times, affecting army morale and alienating industrialists, the middle class, and urban intellectuals alike. Another mistake was failure to control corruption. Nationalist generals and officials liberating the coastal areas confiscated all the Japanese property and factories they could lay their hands on. They also routinely auctioned off supplies earmarked for civilian relief. The most flagrant corruption, though, came from forcing civilians to convert the currency of the puppet Japanese government to the Nationalist currency at about half its true value. The resultant economic distress allowed the generals and other officials to buy vast amounts of residential and commercial property at fire-sale prices. The severe inflation completed the financial ruin of huge numbers of middle class civilians who soon looked upon the Nationalists more as conquerors than liberators. Chiang K'ai Shek, himself personally honest but overwhelmed by his tasks, railed against the corruption but never took vigorous steps to stop it. He had too much residual loyalty to the aging warlord generals who had facilitated his victory in the 1920s.

# 8. *The People's Republic of China: The Mao Zedong Era*

## (1949 to 1976)

The new People's Republic of China (the "PRC") was the first unified Chinese government in decades and the first to govern a country at peace–advantages that the Nationalists had never enjoyed. Still, Communist rule began under many unfavorable circumstances. The new leaders were revolutionaries and guerrilla fighters without experience in creating or managing a modern industrial economy. Worse yet, China's economy had suffered greatly during the long war with Japan. Industrial production limped along at 56 per cent of the prewar peak, and agriculture was little better at about 70 per cent or so. The Nationalist currency was still widely used and inflation raged. The thorny task of changing attitudes, especially those held for over 2,000 years by land-hungry peasants, and creating a socialist culture lay ahead.

Compounding the difficulties was a military challenge little more than a year after the People's Republic was born when the People's Liberation Army was still engaged in wiping out Nationalist pockets and bringing the country under control.

Communist North Korea, with the approval of both Mao and Stalin, invaded South Korea in the late spring of 1950 and quickly drove almost to the very bottom of the peninsula. A brilliant encircling move by General Douglas McArthur, commander of the opposing United Nations forces, though, sent the North Koreans in headlong retreat. Rather than simply chasing the invaders back to North Korea, McArthur pursued them across the border between the two Koreas, disregarding an earlier Chinese warning that China would fight to prevent a conquest of North Korea. He also ignored a directive by President Harry S. Truman not to enlarge the war.

In late October, some 270,000 Chinese "volunteers" crossed the Yalu River from Manchuria into North Korea and engaged the United Nations forces. General Peng Dehuai, applying the ancient tactics of Sun Wu, executed his own set of brilliant maneuvers. After hard-fought initial engagements drove the U.N. forces back, Peng retreated into mountainous areas. McArthur mistakenly interpreted Peng's retreat as a sign of weakness and overextended his forces in pursuit. In November Peng turned south again and struck heavy blows at McArthur's forces causing a U.N. retreat all the way back into South Korea. Afterwards, the war settled into a stalemate along the pre-war border for almost another two years before a truce was signed. Recent estimates put battle deaths by all sides at 1.2 million. The Chinese and North Korean forces that sought to neutralize U.N. advantages in better equipment by resorting to "human-sea" tactics had the greater share.

The war was a distraction from all the aforementioned problems that the new People's Republic faced, as well as a financial burden. It did, however, stimulate a sense of pride in the Chinese that they had stood off armies led by the world's most powerful country. It also helped maintain border security in the future. During the

Vietnam War, the United States informed China that it would not repeat McArthur's error by sending ground forces into North Vietnam, and the two nations remained at peace with each other.

Surprisingly, the new inexperienced rulers of China accomplished much in the first few years of the People's Republic. To their credit, they balanced the budget by 1950 with new taxes of various sorts. In the same year, they also brought inflation under control with a new People's Currency and the weekly indexing of wages to the cost of five basic commodities, rice, oil, coal, flour, and cotton cloth. Workers consequently maintained a relatively stable purchasing power regardless of currency fluctuations. Bank and savings deposits were similarly indexed.

With the help of the Soviet Union, which granted $300,000,000 in credit and sent some 400,000 scientists and technicians to China, industrial production by 1952 was 77.5 per cent higher than the 1949 level. Ironically, capital outlays budgeted for agriculture over the next few years were a mere 7.6 per cent, a paltry reward for the peasants who had spilled their blood to give Mao his revolution. Expenditures for industrial construction alone were budgeted at 58.2 per cent. Mao was turning to Karl Marx's model of basing the transition to socialism on the industrial proletariat and to Vladimir Lenin's concentration on heavy industry in particular. The role of the peasants was to provide food for the cities and to finance industry by producing grain for export.

Politically, the Chinese Communist Party organized a government that functioned reasonably well. Mao held the chairmanship of all the leading branches, including the National People's Congress, the Politburo, the Central Secretariat, and the Military Council. The Constitution of 1954 mandated the "Thought of Mao Zedong" as the official ideology of the PRC. Mao was turning to the Soviet model of creating a cult of personality around himself as paramount leader.

One early step on the road to a socialist culture was the Marriage Law, an audacious step to overturn Confucian family relationships that had endured for thousands of years. The age-old practice of arranged marriages was forbidden. Women like men could petition for divorce. Most importantly, when land was redistributed, women had equal ownership with their husbands. Without this economic stake in the economy all rights given to women would have proven meaningless.

Most significantly, the Communists took steps to overturn the social relations of rural China by redistributing land. The Agrarian Reform Law of 1950 divided the rural population into five categories: great landlords (roughly 5 per cent of the rural population), rich peasants (10 per cent) who rented out some land and were money lenders but worked themselves in the fields, middle peasants (20 per cent) with adequate land of their own, poor peasants who rented at least some land, and the landless.

The methods of redistribution were psychologically brilliant and often brutal. Communist "work teams" would go to villages and seek out the peasants most aggrieved by the existing social structure. Over weeks or sometimes months the teams would understand all economic relations in the village. Then after slowly whipping up anger at the exploiters of the people, they would hold mass "struggle sessions" at which the peasants would denounce the landlords, humiliate them, force them to confess to various crimes, and often beat or kill them. Mao Zedong as early as 1948 had thought that many millions of great landlords and rich peasants might have to be destroyed to change the social structure of rural China. He wanted the peasants, not his work teams, to take the initiative in meting out punishments; they would be more committed to the revolution if they were the ones who made the decisions of life and death. The work teams were mere psychological facilitators. Estimates of executions range up to 28,000,000 (more than 5 per cent of the rural population) though 3,000,000 or so seems a more plausible figure (less than 1 per cent). Mao himself believed that only (!) 800,000 died–beaten to death on the spot or saved for public execution. Mao liked to compare himself as the creator of a new China to Shi Huangdi, the unifier of China in 221 B.C.E., who was equally careless of human life.

Altogether, some 115,000,000 acres (170,000 square miles) of arable land were redistributed to poor and landless peasants. Brutal as it was, the land reform broke the power of the descendants of the old Literati families for good. The popularity of the CCP rose to new heights, and party membership increased. The whole process had identified tens of thousands of politically motivated peasants, many of whom would join the CCP and serve in local cadres in the coming years. Ironically, though, having satisfied the hunger of hundreds of millions of poor peasants for *land of their own*, the CCP would eventually drop in popularity a few years later when it created first collective farms and then communes, taking the land away from its new owners.

The Communists also undertook a campaign to change the culture of the cities, again by brutal methods. Some 700,000 "rightists" were executed in the early 1950s–former Nationalist officials, oppressive capitalists, and outspoken dissenting intellectuals. Most intellectuals, though, were merely subjected to brainwashing in endless public sessions goading them to confess all their "polluted" thoughts, a humiliating loss of "face." Such sessions were psychologically intended to break down the resistance of the intellectuals to the new regime. Avoiding loss of "face" had been a significant must of their culture for many centuries.

These campaigns were followed shortly by two others: the 3-Antis Campaign against corruption, waste, and bureaucratic arrogance and complacency and the 5-Antis Campaign against bribery, tax evasion, embezzlement, theft of state property, and theft of state secrets. The former, directed mostly against lower-level cadres, was relatively mild. The latter, targeting the private economic sector, was harsher in punishments. It also encouraged spying and informing on others in neighborhoods, offices, and factories. Even parents were not safe from denunciation as "rightists" by their children. These practices would long endure.

The death of Josef Stalin and the succession of Nikita Khrushchev to power in the Soviet Union in 1953 gave a boost to Chinese industrial development. Where Stalin had lent the PRC money repayable in part by shipments of grain, Khrushchev made outright grants to China to fund 150 major new industrial projects. The Chinese leaders soon decided that the transition to socialism could be accelerated. By the end of 1956, the State took over ownership of all private companies. Because their skills were still critical, former managers were allowed to remain as salaried employees of the State.

Khrushchev's next impact on Chinese politics came in 1956 when he denounced the many crimes of Stalin and his fostering of a cult of personality before the 20th Congress of the Communist Party of the U.S.S.R.. Shortly afterwards, some of Mao's old comrades, including Zhou Enlai, Liu Shaoqi, and Deng Xiaoping, picked up on the latter theme and eliminated all reference to the "Thought of Mao Zedong" from the PRC Constitution. A supreme egotist, Mao thereafter nursed a grudge against Khrushchev. His war of words with Khrushchev and his successors would greatly increase within a few years as the Soviets sought to liberalize their version of communism modestly and to find a *modus vivendi* with the United States in a world threatened by nuclear self-destruction. Soviet "revisionism" of Marxist-Leninist doctrine was anathema to Mao, who wanted continuing revolution throughout the world and was willing to accept 100 million Chinese deaths in nuclear war to defeat the imperialists. Ironically, Mao, in basing the military phase of the Chinese revolution on peasants rather than workers, was himself a foremost revisionist of Marxist-Leninist doctrine. He had read little of Karl Marx. His main understanding of Marxism had come from Josef Stalin's *History of the Communist Party of the Soviet Union (Bolsheviks), Short Course*. To Mao, correct doctrine was what Mao said it was.

From about 1953 to early 1958, the CCP reorganized Chinese agriculture. By a series of three steps, subject to trial and error, they sought to convert the peasants to socialism and to increase agricultural production substantially. China had some 30,000,000 more people to feed than in the pre-war period, yet farm output was still below pre-war levels. Increased yields could also provide capital for industrial expansion and repayment of Stalin's loans.

The first step involved the creation of small work teams. Six to eight families comprised a team, sharing tools and draft animals and helping each other in planting and harvesting. Each family continued to own its land and, after making delivery of a mandatory quota of grain to the government, could consume the produce or sell the excess in local markets, as they wished. The combination of continued private ownership and mutual help in farming was quite successful. Crop yields went up, the peasants were pleased, and the CCP gained in popularity.

The second step was the voluntary creation of farm co-operatives of twenty to thirty families. Although theoretically each family retained ownership of its own land, in practice the land belonged to the co-op. All compensation came only from the co-op according to a set formula. Half of a family's compensation was based on the amount of land and other assets contributed to the co-op–a lingering aspect of peasant private property rights. The other half was based on the amount of work contributed to the enterprise–a half step to agricultural socialism.

The scheme soon ran into difficulties. Much of the produce derived from the land of the better-off peasants was allocated to the poorer peasants. To maintain their standard of living, the better-off peasants, thus, had to contribute more labor than they were accustomed to. Because participation was voluntary, the better off had no incentive to join–though many did at least temporarily.

The poorer peasants, on the other hand, had every incentive to join and share in the higher yield of crops derived from better land, tools, and draft animals than their own. As the better-off peasants held back, poorer peasants eagerly joined the new co-ops. Swamped by the poor, the better-off peasants who had initially joined began to withdraw.

The scheme was a modest success as agricultural production rose slightly. The larger size of the co-ops allowed some efficiencies of scale, and, from an ideological point of view, further accustomed the poorer peasants to working as a group, each contributing to the common good–another small lesson in socialism.

Mao Zedong, though, was not pleased that better-off peasants were dropping out of the co-ops and that farm production was increasing so slowly. Impatient to realize socialism's promise of an egalitarian society, he thought that the CCP was playing into the hands of "rightists" by going too slow. Agriculture, moreover, was not yielding funds for industrial expansion.

Mao claimed that the masses were enthusiastically demanding further steps along the socialist path. He demanded the acceleration by two full years of the planned third step in the process of changing Chinese agriculture, the organization of large collective farms of 100 to 200 families–about the size of the average village. By the end of 1956, local cadres of the CCP forced almost all peasants, better off and poor alike, into collective farms. The aspect of private property that had lingered on in the co-ops was eliminated. All compensation would be based only on the amount of work done by each family. All land except tiny garden plots for family use became the property of the collective farm.

Mao's agricultural acceleration on the path to socialism had mixed results. Positively, the size of the new units, from 500 to 1,000 people, allowed for more efficiencies of scale, new agricultural techniques, the introduction of small-scale mechanization, and better use of fertilizers. Negatively, the mandatory inclusion of the better-off, perhaps 25 per cent of the rural population, stimulated much resentment over their forced "impoverishment." More problematic was the "free rider problem." Keeping track of the amount of work contributed by each individual in a unit the size of the collective farms was difficult. Some were able to go through the motions rather than exert themselves to the fullest in the interest of the common good. Human nature began to place obstacles on the road to socialism. Still, production did increase initially. At the same time, thanks in part to Soviet aid, industrial production also rose.

Encouraged by the early success, Mao Zedong concluded that the difficult task of converting conservative farmers to socialism could be achieved much more rapidly than previously foreseen. He adopted an idea of Zhou Enlai and sought to enlist the skills of China's uneasy non-Communist intellectuals–scientists, writers, artists, and professionals–to aid in the task of building socialism. They were invited to air their grievances openly: "Let a Hundred Flowers Bloom. Let a Hundred Schools of Thought Contend." Allowing a dialogue with the CCP would help to convince them of the errors in their own thinking. Then with guidance from the CCP, they would realize the merits of socialism and lend their help in the task of creating a new type of society.

Because the intellectuals at first were not forthcoming, the CCP held a series of open forums in early 1957 to reassure them that they could safely state their complaints–complaints far harsher than Mao was expecting. Not long afterwards wall posters highly critical of the government–even of Mao himself–also began to appear in Beijing. Enraged that the Hundred Flowers scheme was backfiring, Mao put his foot down and started an Anti-Rightist Rectification Campaign in which hundreds of thousands of intellectuals were subjected to "struggle sessions" and various punishments, including beatings, loss of jobs, and exile to rural areas for farm work. The outcome of the Hundred Flowers scheme helped to further radicalize Mao's thinking: the masses alone sufficed to create a classless society; the intellectuals were not needed.

In early 1958, the National People's Congress called for a "Great Leap Forward" by China's masses. That same year, the government also instituted the *hukou* system of household registration which required citizens to obtain permission to change their place of residence, in effect, binding peasants to the land or at least to their localities.

Some agricultural communes–vast collective farms with tens of thousands of members–had already appeared independently at local initiative, and Mao called them "a good idea." He seems to have been influenced by a utopian work of Kang Youwei from the Qing Dynasty. Mao, like many of his CCP comrades, was knowledgeable about Chinese history.

The CCP's controlled press publicized Mao's approval of communes, and local cadres all over China began to merge collective farms into communes with an average of 25,000 people. The communes owned all property. A new scheme of compensation aggravated the "free rider" problem. Unlike the collective farms where compensation for the able-bodied depended entirely on the amount of their work, only 30 per cent in the communes was based on work. The remaining 70 per cent was distributed solely on the basis of the needed caloric intake of men, women, and children. It apparently did not occur to most of the CCP's leaders that more peasants would be tempted to take it easy once food was guaranteed. "To each according to his need..." was guaranteed; "From each according to his ability..." had no guarantee other than individual choice. While keeping track of each individual's work effort was difficult in the collective farms, it was almost impossible in the vastly larger communes.

The communes took over local administrative functions and had their own hospitals, schools, and child care. Members of the commune usually continued to reside in the houses they had previously occupied, though widows and the elderly often lived in communal lodgings. Communal dormitories for all were the ultimate goal, but it was impossible to provide new shelter for the inhabitants of hundreds of thousands of villages within a short period of time. The building of common dining facilities proceeded more quickly. Mao even envisaged industrial self-sufficiency, including steel production, for the agricultural communes. Some urban communes centered on particular factories also sprang up but were organized differently from the farming communes.

In rural districts, local cadres massed huge numbers of peasants to build reservoirs, irrigation canals, and roads. As many as 10,000 men were transported to distant areas to work for weeks or months on end with periodic visits home. The women stayed behind to work in the fields. Unfortunately, Mao's disdain for the intellectuals led to errors in blueprints, specifications of materials, surveying, and the like. Mere approximations and the guesses of amateurs often took the place of careful technological planning. Some of the reservoirs and irrigation canals functioned well for many years, but others were poorly built and soon abandoned. The waste of manpower and economic resources in failed projects, though, were offset somewhat by benefits in the future provided by successful projects.

Other errors included faulty farming techniques. Decisions were often made by a centralized cadre that failed to take into account local conditions and local knowledge–one-size-fits-all farming. Worse yet were innovations often mandated from higher authorities ignorant of good agricultural practices. An attempt to increase yields by interplanting crops in the same field, for example, made harvesting more difficult. Planting crops closer together allowed for an easier spread of diseases. Fertilizers were applied to the most productive fields while many that would have profited more from adequate applications were left fallow. Another widespread "innovation" called for planting rice twice as deep and twice as close–twelve inches deep and six apart–as previously, resulting in loss of the entire crop. Since sparrows ate grain, the cadres organized campaigns to eliminate them and established quotas for their eradication. Millions of women, children, and the elderly stood in fields clanging pots and pans to frighten the birds into flight and to prevent them from coming back down. When the sparrows finally fell to earth in exhaustion, the peasants destroyed them. The destruction of tens of millions of birds accomplished little other than wasting manpower. Sparrows also eat insects, and insects simply proliferated.

The most notorious "innovation" in the countryside was the drive to increase steel production by building some 600,000 small clay kilns to operate day and night. Forests were denuded to supply fuel for the kilns, and household items were sacrificed to supply necessary scrap iron–pots, pans, metal tools, and even woks. Total output in 1958 was about 3,000,000 tons of mostly worthless low-grade steel. Mao Zedong and the other CCP leaders had not consulted the intellectuals–engineers and scientists–who could have told them that high-quality steel could only be produced in giant modern steel mills. After the movement got underway, Mao actually visited a modern steel plant in Shenyang. Although told by the experts that backyard steel production was doomed to fail, he allowed production of largely worthless steel to continue because he was reluctant to dampen the peasants' enthusiasm. Ideological faith that the masses could overcome all on the road to socialism had trumped careful planning and technological expertise. Again, huge amounts of manpower were wasted. Afterwards, the PRC finally called a halt to rural industrialization.

Initially, the peasants greeted the communes' promise of a better life with enthusiasm. Their hard work and good weather in the first half of 1958 yielded a better-than-average crop, and, ironically, created yet another serious problem. Local cadres wished to impress their superiors and exaggerated their results. Provincial cadres often added their own exaggerations so that when production statistics reached the highest levels of the PRC, fantasy replaced fact. The reported output on the farms was more than double the actual output. Competitions between communes also led to inflated predictions of future output. By August, the leaders of the CCP were elated with the agricultural success and substantially raised future quotas for mandatory deliveries of grain to the government.

The last half of the year dashed the euphoria, as the next crop was much smaller. Hunger began to stalk the countryside.

Many factors contributed to millions of ultimate deaths. Bad weather played a major role, but was by no means the sole cause. Too many men needed for the harvest were off building roads and waterworks or smelting worthless steel while crops rotted in the fields. The peasants had to send a larger part of that smaller crop to the cities to satisfy the increased quotas. Local cadres were often brutal in enforcing the quotas, for their advancement in the Party was at stake. Not all of the reduced production went to feed either city dwellers or peasants, for Mao was still exporting (!!!) grain to the Soviet Union to repay China's loans from Stalin. Finally, previous decimation of the landlord class had deprived the peasants of much experienced leadership.

As word of rural famine filtered slowly back to Beijing, Defense Minister Peng Dehuai on his own initiative toured several provinces and concluded that the inflated figures reaching the leadership were inaccurate. In late summer 1959 at a leadership conference in Lushan, Peng strongly criticized Mao Zedong for the famine. Mao's power over his colleagues, though, was such that no one else in the top leadership backed Peng in calling for an end to the unrealistic grain quotas. Zhou Enlai, Liu Shaoqi, and Zhu De all remained silent. Peng was dismissed and Lin Biao took his post. Lin, as dogmatic an ideologue as Mao himself, afterwards abolished formal ranks in the army in the interest of egalitarianism. The Lushan Conference changed internal politics within the CCP. Previously the party leaders had been free to speak their minds; then, when Mao made his decision, all fell in line, a cultural holdover from the Confucian era when court officials could freely argue until the emperors made their decisions. After Lushan, simply speaking in opposition to Mao could be dangerous.

Mao, on the one hand, continued to believe that the masses could accomplish anything. The trouble, he thought, was sabotage by peasants who were hiding grain. Searches of peasants' residences by local cadres for hidden grain were soon common. On the other hand, in a contradictory vein, he thought that the masses were still enthusiastic about the Great Leap Forward.

The Great Leap and bad weather continued until 1961. In many areas, people ate the bark of trees or sacrificed some of their children–usually the girls–to save the others. Demographic studies estimate that deaths from starvation and weakened resistance to disease ranged from 18 million to 42 million, figures far greater than the estimated 5.5 to 8 million rich peasants who were executed or starved to death–murdered–by Josef Stalin from 1929-33. Additionally, China's industrial development suffered a setback when Khrushchev, alarmed at the erratic events in Mao's China, decided to withdraw all Soviet technicians with their tools and blueprints. Harsh polemics from both camps thereafter increased substantially

After the Lushan Conference, Mao withdrew from day-to-day management of the government and concerned himself with overall policy as Chairman of the Communist Party. Liu Shaoqi, as President of the PRC, and Deng Xiaoping, as head of the Central Secretariat, set about quietly to correct the grossest errors of the

Great Leap Forward. Both were pragmatists who preferred science, technology, accurate statistics, and careful planning to a utopian faith in class struggle by largely uneducated masses. Liu and Deng were patriots concerned for the progress of their country primarily and socialists secondarily. Mao was willing to sacrifice progress rather than retreat from socialism.

By a series of steps–without fanfare so as not to upset the egotistical Mao–Liu and Deng drastically reduced the size of basic farming units to 20 or 30 families with each family accountable for its own production. Peasants once again owned small private garden plots, and the "free rider" problem faded. Small markets again flourished, and the rural economy gradually recovered. Commenting on the restoration of certain elements of capitalism in China, Deng said, "It doesn't matter if a cat is white or black so long as it catches mice."

By 1964, Mao was increasingly furious with Liu and Deng about shunting class struggle aside for pragmatic reforms. He also recognized that his reputation as the infallible leader of the revolution was tarnished and took steps to restore it before launching an attack on Liu and Deng, who were taking "the capitalist road." In 1965, Defense Minister Lin Biao initiated a movement to "Study the Thought of Chairman Mao" in the armed forces. Lin personally collected various sayings of Mao in "The Little Red Book," printed in 350 million copies by 1968. After the loyalty of the army was assured by constant readings of the Little Red Book and study sessions, the movement was extended to the schools to whip up the enthusiasm of the most idealistic generation.

An opening occurred to start a Great Proletarian Cultural Revolution ("Cultural Revolution") when Nie Yuanzi, a philosophy professor at Beijing University, put up a wall poster protesting the school's rules prohibiting student mass meetings and political wall posters. After a few days of struggle between Nie and her followers and the university administration, Mao publically praised Nie as a Marxist-Leninist heroine, a green light for radical student activity. All over China students formed radical organizations. Mao then followed up by pointing to unnamed power holders following the "capitalist road" as the main targets for the students. He thought the CCP's own bureaucracy was becoming a new elite class more interested in preserving its own position on top of society than in creating a truly egalitarian one. Between August and November of 1966, Mao addressed 11 million students in eight rallies. Free transportation was provided for students not only to attend Mao's rallies but also to travel anywhere they wanted in China to challenge the bureaucracy's capitalist roaders.

Mao's radical wife Jiang Qing was soon appointed to lead the cultural subgroup of the new Central Cultural Revolution Group. She and three leftist supporters from Shanghai, the "Gang of Four," controlled the press and directed propaganda against Liu, Deng, and their supporters. The activities of Jiang Qing and her supporters fueled the Cultural Revolution.

What happened in the next two years was extremely complex and well beyond Mao's intention merely to root out supporters of Liu and Deng from the government and party. The students split into two factions each based on a different theory. The "Red Guards," mostly teen-aged middle school students, were often children themselves of CCP cadre. They targeted fellow students and others from bourgeois, rich-peasant, and landlord families. Those students from better-educated families had kindled the Red Guards' resentment because they were admitted to universities in disproportionate numbers. Test scores were taken into account in enrollment as well as the political factors that favored cadre offspring. The "Revolutionary Red Guards," the second faction, were mostly of college age and often children of families targeted by the "Red Guards." They accused the latter of simply defending their rightist bureaucratic parents. Arguing that the correctness of one's politics was more important than one's family background, they were often more radical than the Red Guards. They also tended to adhere more closely than the Red Guards to Mao's aim to cleanse the bureaucracy of his opponents.

Initial attacks were mostly directed against the students' teachers and school administrators, who were humiliated, and often beaten, sometimes to death. Afterwards, clashes between the two groups became common. Protected by Mao's order to the People's Liberation Army not to interfere with the students, the students stole military equipment openly from army bases to use against each other, resulting in hundreds of deaths or executions. In the city of Wuzhou in eastern Guangxi Province, for instance, rival factions armed with machine guns and light artillery fought a pitched battle resulting in the destruction of some 2,000 buildings and leaving 40,000 residents homeless. Although the Maoists had made clear their preference for verbal struggle, violence quickly pervaded the entire movement.

Lesser disturbances included destruction of old books, paintings, temples, historical relics, and the like as part of a simultaneous campaign against the "four olds:" old ideas, old culture, old customs, and old habits. Attacks on anyone in Western dress were common.

In urban areas, the two groups disrupted factory production despite worker resistance. For at least two years, China made no industrial progress. Radicals even ousted the government of

Shanghai and established a short-lived Municipal Revolutionary Committee in its place.

Mao achieved his goal. Liu, Deng, and thousands of other supposed capitalist roaders were dismissed from government. Liu soon died in a prison hospital from medical neglect. Deng was lucky that Premier Zhou Enlai sent him off to the far south where he was less exposed to danger. Sharing the life of ordinary workers, Deng was "reeducated" by working in an engine factory.

Finally Mao decided to call a halt to the chaos spread by the millions of young radicals roaming the country and wreaking havoc. On September 5, 1968, he ordered the People's Liberation Army to put a stop to the movement. From that moment, the PLA has been the ultimate arbiter of Chinese policy and has used its power to insist on military modernization.

Encountering frequent student resistance, the army added to the slaughter but brought the situation under control although the Cultural Revolution continued to a modest degree in the countryside until Mao's death in 1976. Government in the rural areas was often brought to a standstill by power struggles among local cadres that merely reflected petty rivalries, and many peasants faced starvation when fanatics coerced them to stop such capitalist practices as raising pigs, ducks and chickens for private sale.

A reasonable estimate of deaths as a result of the Cultural Revolution is 400,000. The national government was weakened. The role of the PLA in Chinese society was expanded to a dangerous degree. The cult of the individual reached new heights, as Mao became almost a godlike figure. Exhibition halls devoted to Mao's career were built throughout the country, and school children began the day by chanting, "May Chairman Mao live ten thousand times ten thousand years." Industrial production was also seriously curtailed during the Cultural Revolution.

The effect of the Cultural Revolution on the Chinese education system went far beyond the loss of two years while students roamed the country instead of studying. The quality of teaching was substantially reduced for many years because huge numbers of qualified teachers were eliminated from the system. After suppression of the movement by the PLA, countless students were sent to the rural areas to learn about the problems of the peasants. They and many intellectuals and cadres who had resisted the Cultural Revolution ended up spending many embittered years doing menial work in the countryside. Almost an entire generation received an inadequate education. Nonetheless, Mao was pleased with the Cultural Revolution. It, at least temporarily, eliminated those who opposed him, "capitalist roaders" like Liu and Deng, from positions of power. Deng's talents, though, were such that he was eventually given a new post, only to be dismissed again in the early 1970s. The Cultural Revolution was also consistent with Mao's ideological belief that mass mobilizations–rather than careful planning and technological expertise–were the road to socialism. He even stated at the Twelfth Plenum of the CCP in 1969 that a similar movement would be necessary every 10 to 15 years to rekindle the enthusiasm of the young and to eliminate future bureaucratization.

Despite the chaos of the Cultural Revolution, at least one program benefited the suffering Chinese people: a new system to bring better medicine to the rural areas. Chinese medicine had become bureaucratized, and health care was available mostly to city dwellers. Once the PLA had stabilized the political situation, "barefoot doctors," personnel with rudimentary training, brought basic care to the peasants, and many urban doctors were sent to the countryside.

After withdrawal of the Soviet technicians from China in 1960, Mao's quarrel with the Soviet Union over revisionism, the damping down of efforts to create world revolution, intensified. In 1964, China exploded its first atomic bomb, and Leonid Brezhnev, the new leader of the Soviet Union, sought better relations with China. Mao rejected the overture angrily; he stepped up polemics against the Soviet "heretics." In 1966-7 during the Cultural Revolution, students by the thousands demonstrated against revisionism outside the Soviet embassy. Armed clashes along the 4,000-mile border between the two countries broke out. Most upsetting to the Chinese was the Soviet military intervention in Czechoslovakia in 1968 and announcement of the doctrine of conditional sovereignty. Brezhnev asserted a right of the Soviet Union to intervene militarily in nations with Communist regimes under certain circumstances, a position that the Chinese found unacceptably threatening. As border clashes continued, the U.S.S.R. deployed 1,000,000 troops along the border and aimed hundreds of nuclear missiles at Chinese targets.

Moscow even asked the United States to endorse a "hypothetical" Soviet attack on China's nuclear bomb facilities. President Richard Nixon firmly rejected the proposal. Nixon was convinced that the world would be better off if China joined the family of nations. He also believed that friendly relations with China was in the national interest of the United States and would help contain the Soviet Union. He had secret contacts with the Chinese that led to his visit to China in 1971. Mao's belief that the "imperialist" U.S.S.R. was planning an attack had provided an opening for Zhou Enlai to persuade Mao to seek regular diplomatic relations with the "imperialist" United States.

In the United States conservative supporters of the Nationalist regime on Taiwan were strongly opposed to recognition of "Red China." In China the leftists, including Lin Biao, author of *The Little Red Book*, and Mao's wife Jiang Qing, who controlled propaganda and the press, were equally opposed to friendly relations with "Imperialists." The fierce opposition to full diplomatic relations in both countries was ultimately overcome.

Nixon's "opening to China" was a turning point for the Chinese. Ending relative isolation led to greater Chinese access to Western technology and increased trade relations with the rest of the world–preliminary steps to the "Chinese economic miracle" to come. Full diplomatic relations between both countries did not come about, though, until the presidency of Jimmy Carter.

Backyard steel furnaces

Liu Shaoqi, President of the PRC

Red Guards on cover of an elementary school textbook

# *9. The Deng Xiaoping Era*

## (1976 to mid-1990s)

When Mao died in 1976, he was briefly succeeded by his chosen successor Hua Guofeng, an undistinguished politician, whose effective grip on power lasted only two years before Deng Xiaoping became China's leader.

The Party leaders who had survived the Cultural Revolution wanted to prevent any future leftist repetition of Mao's policies. They moved quickly to arrest the Gang of Four, convicted a few years later for crimes committed during the Cultural Revolution, including the murder of 34,375 people. A court condemned two to death–later commuted to life in prison–and the others to prison terms. Lin Biao, the leftist Defense Minister, had already died in 1971 in a mysterious plane crash in Mongolia after plotting to overthrow the government.

A major meeting of China's top leadership in 1978 buried many of Mao's ideas and policies. Henceforth, class struggle would no longer be the overriding priority of the PRC, and mass mobilization campaigns, such as the Great Leap Forward and the Cultural Revolution, would be shunned. From then on, there would be much less ideological indoctrination in China's schools on class struggle and more emphasis on science and math. Many leaders dismissed by Mao and his leftist allies were rehabilitated, including Peng Dehuai and Liu Shaoqi (both posthumously) and Deng Xiaoping, appointed Vice Premier.

Improvement of the economy was to be the central concern of the leadership, and there great progress was made. Collective leadership, "socialist democracy," and "socialist legality" were to be strengthened. Some quite modest reforms were achieved in both areas over the years, including better protection for private property, the right of a defendant to counsel and an open trial, and a degree of greater judicial independence. Competitive elections between candidates approved by the CCP were allowed at local levels. One of the CCP's several revisions of China's constitution even recognized "human rights," defined as rights to food, shelter, and medical care rather than rights to free speech, freedom of assembly, and freedom of religion so prized in the West–a socioeconomic rather than a political view of "rights." Despite minor reforms, though, the Leninist structure of a dictatorship of the proletariat remained intact.

Deng Xiaoping was the last important leader of the generation of the May 4th Movement. His official position was Vice-Premier, but the Party soon named him "Paramount Leader." As the leader of the so-called Second Generation in command–a mix between elderly revolutionaries and younger technocrats–Deng would lead China at least nominally until his death in 1997. The economic development of China, discussed below, was first in his priorities and any transition to socialism only secondary.

Ironically, Deng, one of the political victims of the Cultural Revolution, profited from it in advancing his goals. It strengthened the public's fear of disorder, allowing Deng to maintain the power of the CCP. The horror of that slaughter also made the Chinese public cynical about Marxism, permitting Deng to embark on a new path. Nationalism, bringing the Chinese nation back to its elevated position in the world before the humiliations of the Western Impact, became the new dominant ideology, one that Deng could agree with wholeheartedly. The elderly Deng also profited from the Chinese norm of deferring to the judgment of elders. Both fear of disorder and deference to elders had been elements of Chinese culture for thousands of years.

Throughout the late 1970s, the Chinese slowly dismantled the cultural straight jacket imposed by the Gang of Four's ideology. Traditional Chinese opera, totally suppressed by the Gang of Four in favor of eight new operas preaching class struggle, was again performed. The brilliant poems of the great Tang dynasty poets Li Bo and Du Fu were no longer denigrated as feudal relics. The music of Western classical composers and such hobbies as stamp collecting and flower arrangement were no longer maligned as bourgeois decadence. Women began to dress in Western fashions and use cosmetics. The unisex baggy clothing of the Mao era began to disappear. Official publications over and over criticized the Gang of Four explicitly–and Mao implicitly. Members of an incipient Democracy Movement concurred by placing posters critical of the Gang of Four on walls in Beijing.

A major meeting of China's top leadership in 1981 finally evaluated the leadership and contributions of Mao Zedong after consideration by a committee for 15 months. Deng Xiaoping had previously warned that Mao could be criticized but that his overall reputation was to be preserved. The legitimacy of the CCP was at stake. If Mao's role in his last 20 years was entirely negative, one might ask why the CCP had allowed him to wreak havoc on the nation and why the Party should remain in power. An eruption of discontent might even topple the CCP. Besides, after years of creating an almost sacred image of Mao, the CCP would also lose credibility among those who had believed the propaganda–another possible source of trouble for the Party. The 35,000-word evaluation praised Mao for his "brilliant" early contributions to the revolution but criticized him especially for his "leftist errors" during the Cultural Revolution–a "devastating setback." Concluding that his contributions far exceeded his errors, the assessment theoretically preserved the Party's legitimacy. In the popular view, the evaluation meant that Mao was 70 percent correct and 30 percent wrong.

Historians are much more critical in assessing Mao's impact on China. All concede that he was brilliant in adapting Marxist-Leninism to a nation with few proletarians but hundreds of millions of peasants. He was the greatest theoretician and practitioner of guerrilla warfare in the 20th century. He was a leader of tenacity, achieving victory in the revolution after a grueling struggle against both Nationalists and Japanese invaders for more than 20 years. His greatest impact was in changing forever the social structure of China by breaking the centuries-old iron grip of the rural landlords on the peasants. He also largely eliminated the problem of opium smoking in China and outlawed foot binding once and for all.

His mistakes were, however, as great as his achievements. Politically, Mao intimidated the collective leadership of the CCP, silenced criticism of his policies, and established one-man rule–a rule by one man who made unwise decisions. Morally, his cavalier sacrifice of an estimated 18 to 42 million lives in the Great Leap Forward was reprehensible.

Economically, after a brief period of pragmatism in the earliest years of the PRC, Mao lost touch with reality. His utopian belief in mass mobilization and continual revolution kept the country in turmoil and hindered economic progress for 20 years. China's gross domestic product (GDP) grew at only 4 percent annually during the Mao era, a growth rate barely able to keep up with China's burgeoning population growth. His isolation of China compounded the error by preventing the country from acquiring technological skills being developed in the West and Japan.

One is tempted to say that, had Chiang K'ai Shek not been prevented by the "Xi'an incident" from eliminating the Communists, China would be as prosperous today as it is under the CCP and perhaps at least a little less authoritarian. Chiang favored a market economy from the beginning. China would not have needed to wait until the Deng Xiaoping era and beyond to achieve an "economic miracle." A speculative thought but one worth thinking about.

Especially damaging was Mao's disdain for birth control. To him more children meant more socialists to work for the common good. Not until the 1970s did he wake up and put his immense authority behind a campaign for voluntary birth control. By then, the population of China had increased by an additional 260 million even as his economic ignorance, failure to consult experts, ideological fanaticism, and one-man rule had prevented the country from producing the wherewithal to support the swollen population at a significantly increased standard of living. Only after his death did China adopt a policy of limiting each family to one child–a belated effort to correct Mao's limited vision concerning the consequences of overpopulation.

In summary, had Mao died in the early 1950s, he would have had an unblemished reputation as an extraordinary revolutionary leader.

China would, however, have been better off without him thereafter. Seventy percent correct and thirty percent wrong is a substantial over-evaluation

One of the first important developments of the Deng Xiaoping era was an effort to bring population under control by limiting families to one child. Over the years the policy has reduced population growth from 2.2 percent annually in the 20 years from 1950 to 1970 to less than 0.5 percent at present. The achievement is remarkable in that the death rate declined by half simultaneously. Unfortunately, however, the policy continued too long and will create problems in the future.

Rural couples can have a second child if the first is female, because male children are more useful farm workers. Urban couples have no such privilege if the first-born is a girl. They are more likely to accept nature's choice, however, despite a longstanding preference for sons carried over from the Confucian era. Children of neither sex are economic assets in cities. Urban couples who have more than one child may simply pay a "fine" for a second, accidental child–really a "fee" in the case of planned children. The "fine" or "fee" for a couple with an income equivalent to $27,000 a year is $64,000. Exceptions to the one-child policy are also made for couples whose first born is intellectually challenged or physically handicapped, for couples who have twins, for ethnic minorities (6 percent of the population), for Chinese living overseas, and for inhabitants of Hong Kong and Macau. Another exception reflects the inadequacy of China's social safety net. As in the Confucian era, most Chinese are still dependent in their old age for family support. Consequently, couples both of whom are only children themselves may have a second child because they would have no siblings, nephews, or nieces to help out in their declining years, and their single child would be supporting two parents on one income.

The one-child policy has several advantages, The need to consult physicians about birth control methods has apparently led to some improvement in women's health overall. Those couples who receive their "one-child certificate" are rewarded with bonuses and other benefits. The limit on family size has reduced strain on family budgets and allowed for more savings and investment, a plus for the Chinese economy.

The policy also has disadvantages. The longstanding Confucian preference for boys has led to much selective abortion of female fetuses and to female infanticide creating a gender imbalance by 2000 of 117 male babies to 100 female. Consequently, traffickers frequently kidnap or lure women from surrounding countries and sell them to Chinese men wanting wives. The psychological impact of the one-child policy on Chinese women has also apparently added to the strains usual in societies undergoing rapid change–in China's case twice and in two diametrically opposed directions, socialism and capitalism. China is the only country in the world that has a higher suicide rate by women than men. Some critics of the one-child policy also believe that the one-child policy was unnecessary in the first place. They argue that urban women who are better educated and those who participate in the work force are less desirous of having many children anyway–as is the case in developed countries.

Some pluses are offset by minuses. Economically, as fewer new workers enter the labor market than retire from it, higher wages for Chinese workers will enlarge the middle class and lead to a better life for many–two pluses, one for the nation and one for its citizens. As a consequence, however, China will lose its advantage as a low-cost labor market and experience higher inflation–two minuses.[35]

A modest change in the one-child policy in December, 2013, is discussed briefly in the chapter on "Deng's Successors (mid-1990s to 2014)" It will have little economic significance for another 15 to 20 years.

Never as strong politically as Mao Zedong, Deng Xiaoping faced opposition from the right or the left or both. On the issue of political liberalization, he faced resistance on the left from students and intellectuals who sought greater democracy and civil rights and from Party leaders on the right who insisted, to the contrary, that the CCP remain in complete political control of the nation. Deng himself appears to have had a degree of sympathy with both objectives. He was eventually forced to choose between them in 1989 when radical pro-democracy students occupied Beijing's Tiananmen Square, site of many of Beijing's most important landmarks, including the Mausoleum of Chairman Mao and the Gate of Heavenly Peace, entrance to the Forbidden City.

On economic issues, Deng faced resistance from hard-line leaders who wanted only limited market reforms. Unconcerned with whether the cat was white or black as long as it caught mice, Deng saw substantial market reforms as the key to modernizing Chinese agriculture and industry. He justified his moves away from central planning and state ownership toward a freer market as a primary stage of socialism. Marx had viewed capitalism as a necessary historical stage before the proletariat's

[35] Accurate economic predictions are especially difficult to make for China. The one-child policy, which has lasted three decades, is without precedent and, consequently, is unusually vulnerable to the law of unintended consequences. Any forecasts by economic experts beyond the medium term should be taken with caution.

revolt and the birth of socialism. An impatient Mao had tried to short circuit the process. A patient Deng was willing to tolerate a degree of capitalism provided it led to socialism at some future time. Ironically, in this respect, Deng was a more orthodox Marxist than Mao. Ironically also, Deng's market reforms were a reversion toward a more traditional concept of economic life, for Confucius and Mencius had advised emperors to let the people make most decisions for themselves. Capitalism with its restraints on government is more compatible with Confucianism than is centralized Marxism.

Political problems began in early 1979 when the media began to criticize China's legal and political system. The courts were receiving thousands of petitions for redress of wrongs suffered from illegal persecutions during the Cultural Revolution. With Deng's approval, the government quickly passed laws that narrowed the vague definition of "counterrevolutionary activities" and restricted arbitrary actions by the police. A code of criminal procedure mandated speedy trials, the right to counsel by defendants, and the right to face one's accusers. By the following year the number of petitions seeking redress exceeded 1,000,000, and an ever-increasing number overwhelmed the courts, which had reversed fewer than 300,000 cases. The slow pace of investigation by the courts led to some violence and much protest.

Hard-line party elders wanted a crackdown, but Deng's two liberal protégés, Party Chairman Hu Yaobang and Premier Zhao Ziyang, favored the petitioners' right to protest. While Deng waivered, Wei Jingsheng, a leader of the Democracy Movement, in a celebrated wall poster severely, unwisely, and insolently excoriated Deng as a dictator and pushed him into the hard-line camp. Deng then declared strict limits on political speech, in essence that only speech upholding socialism and the leadership of the CCP's "democratic dictatorship" was permissible. Wei Jingsheng was tried–without the safeguards of the new criminal code–and sentenced to prison for 15 years. Protests died down.

Even though he insisted that the CCP remain in power, Deng was not a hard-liner on reforming the government. When the workers of Poland formed the Solidarity union in the summer of 1980 and demanded workers' rights, Deng's liberal protégés, Hu Yaobang and Zhao Ziyang, urged allowing workers to choose their own labor representatives. They also urged internal reform of the government by 1) separating the making and executing of policy from the CCP, which would then only verify that the government was following the Party's guidelines; 2) establishing term limits and mandatory retirement ages for high officials; and 3) ending the practice of officials' holding more than one post. When events in Poland began to threaten the rule of the Polish Communist Party, however, Deng withdrew his support of the reforms and said that martial law would be invoked if necessary to preserve stability in China. A brief campaign by hard-liners against bourgeois decadence followed, targeting Western fashions, popular music, cosmetics, movies, appliances, and motorcycles, but was unsuccessful in weaning citizens away from such "spiritual pollution."

Citizen protest was relatively low key for the next few years, as economic change took center stage in China. Fixed capital formation in the Deng Xiaoping era and after continuously amounted to some 30 to 40 percent of China's Gross Domestic Product (GDP), a compound rate of investment matched nowhere else in the world.

Major changes also occurred in agriculture. From 1979 to 1984, a new system reintroducing material incentives for hard work, the household responsibility system, spread to 98 percent of the agricultural population. The communes leased a plot of land to each farm household, which, in turn, contracted to supply a certain quantity of crops at prices 20 percent higher on average than those paid in 1978. Surplus crops belonged to the household, and rural free markets again flourished. Initial leases were for a year. By 1984 leases were for 15 years and eventually for up to 99 years. Leases became inheritable and were transferable to another family when illness prevented working the land. With these steps down the "capitalist road," the communes had no economic role but still provided some health care and primary education for which they received fees. Crop and livestock production rose 50 percent in the first five years and household income more than tripled in the first 10. Despite solving the free rider problem by reintroducing incentives, though, the system had some drawbacks. Because peasants were only lessees rather than owners of their land, they could not mortgage it in order to invest in it nor sell it in order to move to an urban area and start a new life. Lack of collective endeavor led to some neglect of irrigation systems. Moreover, the small size of individual plots, usually no more than an acre and a half, led to a decrease in mechanized farming. Small plots were once again cultivated with substantial hand labor as in the Confucian era, and yields per acre increased. China now feeds 20 percent of the world's population with less than 10 percent of the arable land.

Within a few years, grain production had reached its highest potential yield under the new system. Due to a surplus, the government then lowered the price it paid for grain. Consequently, peasants converted much land to more valuable crops, such as cotton, fruits, and vegetables. Deng and his allies, moreover, encouraged light manufacturing in rural areas, a move so successful especially in the coastal provinces that 150,000,000 or so peasants are no longer engaged in agriculture. The gains of the early years persisted, and China's rural families are better off than they had been under the communes. Wages in rural manufacturing, though, are still below those paid in urban areas.

Change in the cities was more difficult than in the countryside. The government's first reform was to permit small private commercial businesses, most of which competed quite successfully against corresponding state-owned small enterprises.

To increase China's gross domestic product (GDP) substantially, Deng and his liberal cohorts needed to reform China's large enterprises. Factory workers had jobs for life with many subsidies and benefits–food, rent, education, health care, etc.–a socialist system known as the "iron rice bowl." Efficiency suffered because the iron rice bowl was suffused with the free rider problem. Although up to 20 percent of workers were unneeded, factory managers could not lay them off. Central planning also lowered efficiency. Managers received commands from remote bureaucrats often ignorant of local conditions concerning what products should be produced, in what quantities, and how they should be priced. Managers were also not required to show profits or be shut down, another hindrance to efficiency.

Premier Zhao Ziyang began to reform the large enterprises in 1984. Much planning was shifted to the provincial level, and managers gained a limited ability to select products, establish prices, and keep a percentage of revenues to buy new machinery, provide worker housing, etc. Ending the socialist system of equal pay for everyone, managers were also allowed to give raises and bonuses to the most productive workers–material incentives lacking in the Mao Zedong era. Managers, though, still could not lay off or fire lazy or incompetent workers.

Although these reforms, euphemistically called "socialism with Chinese characteristics" by the liberals, moved China closer to a free market economy, Deng Xiaoping knew that China needed substantial foreign investment to develop rapidly. In 1979, the government established the first of four Special Economic Zones (SEZs) permitting joint ventures between Chinese and foreign companies producing goods for export. These businesses operated on free market principles. The initial flood of foreign capital came mostly from Chinese in Hong Kong, Singapore, and Taiwan and from Japan. Soon other SEZs appeared along China's entire coast.

The restructuring of China's economy led to a degree of social instability. The SEZs contributed greatly to the growth of GDP but created social tensions by widening the gap between the prosperity of the coastal and the inland provinces. The higher wages paid in China's new private sector than in the state-owned industries (SOEs) compounded the social tension. A third source of tension came from inflation born of the new managerial discretion as to prices. Finally, there was discontent regarding corruption. The sons and daughters ("princelings") of many high officials peddled their influence as go-betweens in arranging business deals with foreign investors. Factory managers often purchased materials at a low price from the State, sold them in the open market and pocketed the profits. With the acquisition of money rising in importance in a land previously pursuing communitarian goals in the Maoist era, prostitution and drug trafficking also reappeared.

Concerned with rising social instability, Deng Xiaoping ordered Zhao Ziyang to appoint a new, mostly liberal commission in 1986 to study governmental reform. Not content to await the commission's recommendations, tens of thousands of students all over China demonstrated for democracy and freedom of expression. Party Chairman Hu Yaobang's toleration of the demonstrations infuriated political hard-liners in the leadership, and they successfully pressured Deng to dismiss him. Deng reversed course and condemned the demonstrations. To prevent the hard-liners, though, from taking over the government and stopping the move toward freer markets, Deng appointed Zhao Ziyang, his other liberal protégé, Party Chairman. To counter Zhao's appointment, the hard-liners secured the post of Premier for one of their own, Li Peng. The turmoil soon ceased after police arrested 30 students in Tiananmen Square.

Social instability continued to increase. Zhao's reform allowing factory managers to lay off unneeded workers and reduce the wages of unproductive ones led to social tensions. Especially hard hit were women, usually laid off in disproportionate numbers compared to men. By 1988, some 500,000 workers had lost their iron rice bowls and were jobless. Zhao's popularity also plummeted when he proposed to privatize housing and decontrol rents. At the same time, the growth of the agricultural economy having leveled off, tens of millions of peasants were flooding into the cities looking for work–with little choice but to accept foul and filthy living conditions in now-overcrowded cities.

In that year rumors–probably spread by hard-liners to discredit Zhao–predicted that all prices would soon be decontrolled. An orgy of buying by consumers fearful of more inflation fulfilled their fears as prices spiked upwards. Inflation raged, and Deng, torn as usual between liberal leanings and an authoritarian inclination to prevent social disturbances at all costs, began to lose confidence in Zhao.

Events came to a head in the spring of 1989 after an unexpected event, the death of Hu Yaobang. Tens of thousands of university students demonstrated in Tiananmen Square. Their stated demand was for a restoration of Hu's good name; their real demand was for greater democracy, a goal with which Hu had sympathized. By mid-May, ignoring a warning from Deng Xiaoping, a million students, workers, intellectuals, and ordinary citizens were demonstrating day after day in Tiananmen Square. Citizens in 23 other cities supported their cause.

Zhao Ziyang, who sought a peaceful outcome, was, like Hu Yaobang, sympathetic to the students. Political hard-liners, though, were fiercely opposed. Many of them were veterans of the Long March, men whose political views had been formed by decades of war and class struggle, men who thought that giving an inch could result in the overthrow of socialism. They plotted to use the demonstrations to discredit Zhao and persuade Deng to dismiss him.

Mikhail Gorbachev was shortly expected to arrive in Beijing. Aware that foreign television coverage would be extensive for his visit, some 500 students began a hunger strike in Tiananmen Square on May 13. Five days later Premier Li Peng visited Tiananmen Square to urge the students to stop their hunger strike but with no intention to accede to student demands. The student leaders treated him insolently on national television, and he left determined to crack down.

On May 19, Zhao Ziyang visited the students, tearfully apologizing for letting them down. An enraged Deng Xiaoping stripped him of his authority as Party Chairman and authorized Li Peng to declare martial law. Zhao spent the next 16 years until his death under mild house arrest.

The following day, as thousands of PLA troops entered Beijing to enforce martial law, tens of thousands of civilians blocked their trucks on the main roads leading to Tiananmen Square. In the remaining days of May, some 300 demonstrations broke out all over China involving more than 10,000,000 citizens.

The government broke the stalemate on June 3. The PLA began firing at the students and at civilians blocking the PLA's path to Tiananmen Square. Dead and wounded civilians totaled several thousand, and the latest chapter–and last chapter up to now–in the Democracy Movement ended.

The so-called Velvet Revolution in which Eastern European nations threw off the yoke of domination by the U.S.S.R. later that year resolved Deng's ambivalent feelings about political reform. Too rapid political reform was a threat to any Communist party and to the creation of a socialist society. He became a strong advocate of the political status quo–unquestioned and absolute leadership by the CCP.

Deng remained a liberal in the economic sphere. He saw no necessary contradiction between market reforms and creation of a socialist society. The hard-liners' political triumph, though, temporarily left him isolated in the face of opposition to his economic reforms. Before the crackdown at Tiananmen Square, he was easily able to overcome resistance to his plans. Afterwards with the liberal wing of the CCP in disarray, Deng faced a serious challenge from Party hard-liners concerned that the scope and pace of his economic reforms were too great a threat to socialism. They were willing to tolerate some market reforms but not too much and not as fast as Deng wanted. To preserve his cherished market reforms, Deng again sought to balance the growing power of the hard-liners by appointing Jiang Zemin, a centrist, General Secretary of the Communist Party.

By late 1991, the elderly Deng had developed Parkinson's disease, and the hard-liners pushed to roll back his market reforms. Party journals began to write favorably about the Great Leap Forward and class struggle and to refer to Deng's reforms as "capitalistic." Jiang Zemin, well aware that the last three of his predecessors as head of the CCP, Hua Guo Feng, Hu Yaobang, and Zhao Ziyang, had been dismissed from office tried to placate both Deng and the hard-liners–an unsuccessful balancing act.

Early in 1992, Deng, convinced that he risked losing the battle to make China more of a market economy, mustered his remaining strength and toured the prosperous Special Economic Zones of the southeast coast for five weeks. His speeches stressed the prosperity that his listeners were experiencing. He declared that the collapse of communism in the Soviet Union and Eastern Europe was not from too much economic reform but from too little. Over and over, he preached his message while the official press in Beijing remained silent. Finally, liberal supporters spoke out. Li Peng and the hard-liners reluctantly fell in line. Jiang Zemin ceased his balancing act and swung sharply to Deng's side.

Deng Xiaoping

Deng had won. He stripped Li Peng of his responsibilities for economic policy and gave them to Vice-Premier Zhu Rongji. Deng thereafter participated less and less in affairs of government until his death in 1997 from a lung infection and Parkinson's disease.

What was Deng Xiaoping's legacy? Deng's goals for China recall those of the late Qing reformers Li Hongzhang of the Self-Strengthening movement and Kang Youwei of the Hundred Days, but Deng succeeded where they failed in creating a modern China. In the economic sphere, Deng deserves high praise. That China is an economic power today is largely attributable to his unwavering support of market reforms. Thanks to him, hundreds of millions of Chinese have moved out of poverty. China has regained some of the national dignity it lost in the 19$^{th}$ century.

Politically, Deng's legacy is ambiguous. His major achievement was to institute a practice of filling high government posts with engineers and technocrats instead of ideologues. As concerns democracy, the questions arise: Were the students at Tiananmen Square right in demanding democracy? Or was Deng Xiaoping right in believing that the Chinese people would not be ready for political reform until the standard of living was substantially raised and better education was universal? Democracy in the West, after all, had a centuries-long incubation period. As concerns socialism, the questions arise: Is it really possible to create an equalitarian society, as Deng believed, once education and the standard of living improve? Or was he simply leading China down the "capitalist road" to its very end? We may know in another half century.

Deng also launched China on three decades of the fastest growth of any large country in world history. Unfortunately, economic growth at all costs was the goal. Little attention was paid to creating a balanced economy in which production for consumption by the people plays a major role. GDP increased mostly by capital investment and production for export. The full-speed-ahead growth has led to many "bridges to nowhere." China is full of massive apartment complexes that are empty and has many factories that stand idle because of insufficient demand for their products, including, for example, steel, cement, and shipbuilding facilities. Some of China's growth has been *unneeded* growth. The CCP today faces very difficult problems in rebalancing the economy.

The massacre at Tiananmen Square in 1989 will always remain a blot on Deng's reputation, though he was much less willing to sacrifice human life for his goals than Mao Zedong. Several thousand student and citizen deaths at Tiananmen Square do not begin to compare to the 18 to 42 million peasants who succumbed to starvation and disease as Mao cavalierly ignored the consequences of the Great Leap Forward in 1960-61.

# *10. Deng Xiaoping's Successors*

# (mid-1990s to 2014)

## A. Political Events

Zhu Rongji's reforms in the 1990s were extensive, including less central control over business decisions by state-owned enterprises (SOEs), privatization of the housing market, loosening of regulations on foreign investment, elimination of special prices for purchases by SOEs, and clarification of the circumstances in which inefficient or debt-ridden SOEs could be required to declare bankruptcy. More than half of those enterprises were inefficient and unprofitable.

The next several years witnessed rapid growth of the Chinese economy. When it reached 25 per cent annually, Zhu realized that his reforms were creating an inflationary bubble. To cool the overheated economy, he took further measures. His reform of the banking system stopped the practice of making loans without collateral to highly risky enterprises. His organization of a national tax system increased central and decreased local revenues, giving the government more leverage to block investment in speculative projects by provincial authorities. China experienced a soft landing that kept social tensions in check.

Existing social tensions continued apace–widening gaps in prosperity between the coastal and inland provinces, between workers in state-owned and private enterprises, between men and women, corruption, prostitution, and drug trafficking. Young people, once inspired idealistically by Mao's fanatic vision of an egalitarian society, became increasingly alienated under Deng Xiaoping, Jiang Zemin, and Zhu Rongji.

Zhu's elimination of guarantees of lifetime employment and other aspects of the iron rice bowl added a new social tension as 35 million workers in state-owned enterprises lost their jobs between 1998 and 2002, a problem gradually alleviated by increased hiring in the private sector.

Zhu Rongji became Premier in 1998 under Party General Secretary Jiang Zemin after Deng's death, as the so-called Third Generation of leaders took command. With the passing of the revolutionary veterans of the Long March, the Third Generation consisted almost entirely of men trained in science and technology. Zhu's gaining China's entry into the World Trade Organization in 2001 was the capstone of his talented economic management. Afterwards, China became an economic powerhouse and in 2010 the second largest economy in the world after the United States.

Jiang Zemin went beyond Deng's theory of "socialism with Chinese characteristics." After consolidating his position by cultivating the military, the ultimate arbiter in China since the Cultural Revolution, Jiang announced his Theory of the Three Represents. The CCP represented advanced productivity, advanced culture, and the fundamental interests of the majority. One of the periodic revisions of the CCP's constitution added The Three

Represents to Marxism-Leninism, the Thought of Mao Zedong and Deng Xiaoping Theory as the guiding principles of the party–a meaningless hodgepodge of conflicting ideas. In 2002, because capitalists were the driving force behind China's advance in productivity, Jiang permitted entrepreneurs and businessmen to join the Chinese Communist Party. Some 5,000,000 "red" capitalists, once enemies of the people, are now members.

Hu Jintao became General Secretary of the CCP after Jiang finished his ten-year term in that office. The Third Generation gave way to the so-called Fourth Generation of leaders without vigorous party infighting, a sign of increased political maturity. Jiang retained his office as Chair of the Central Military Commission, though, for two more years and continued to maintain a strong influence on the government. Six of the nine members of the ruling Standing Committee were Jiang's protégés. Within a few years, some of those six retired, and Hu gained in authority. The rivalry between Jiang and Hu reflected the division of leadership between officials who were children of the revolutionaries of the pre-1950 era (Jiang) and officials who had come up through the ranks of the Communist Youth League (Hu).

Hu and his prime minister, Wen Jiabao, modified the government's direction during their ten-year terms. One innovation was the establishment of 282 Confucian study centers overseas and a renewed study of Confucianism in Chinese schools. The CCP has even erected a statue to the once-despised Confucius in Tiananmen Square.

Chinese intellectuals are reevaluating their past, and some are reaching conclusions much like the Self-Strengthening movement of the late Qing dynasty: "Chinese learning for the fundamental principles, Western learning for the practical application." The approach of the Self-Strengtheners may well triumph over the approach of the intellectuals of the May 4th Movement who were open to the idea of Western learning for fundamental principles, especially liberal democracy.

Many aspects of Confucianism will infuse any new synthesis of China's fundamental principles. Fortunately, Confucianism, though authoritarian, valued highly social harmony, benevolent rule, and self-cultivation of leaders in morality. Hu spoke publically about China's "peaceful rise," a goal consonant with China's age-old practice of unaggressive behavior toward unthreatening neighbors.

Seeking to create a "Harmonious Society," a Confucian concept, Hu and Wen gave greater priority than Jiang to reducing the inequalities in Chinese society. They eliminated the agricultural tax and tuition for rural students in the first nine grades. They sought with only modest success to give peasants greater protection from expropriation of their land by corrupt local cadres favoring developers.

Hu and Wen attempted to develop China's interior provinces and close the economic gap with the coastal provinces. They also endeavored to strengthen the SOEs, where wages had fallen below those in the private sector. They greatly increased spending on education, particularly at the university level; none of China's universities, though, are yet at world-class level. They also increased spending on research to move China beyond low-tech manufacturing, At present only 5 per cent of China's research is in basic science compared to 19 per cent in the United States. Finally, they began a shift from export to domestic consumption as the driving force of the Chinese economy. Their ability to reallocate resources was facilitated by the continued growth of private sector employment and a relatively low inflation rate, but their success in their undertakings was modest.

Their favoritism toward SOEs, often at the expense of multinational corporations, has provoked anger in the developed world and fueled corruption. The 70 richest members of the National People's Congress have ten times more wealth than the 660 top officials of the United States.

The longstanding undervaluing of China's currency–once estimated at 30 to 40 percent has also provoked anger, especially among American labor unions and their political supporters as well as much of the press. China's consequent ability to export goods at very cheap prices may have cost many Americans their jobs. On the other hand, 300 million Americans have been able to stretch their budgets further by purchasing those undervalued goods made by Chinese workers. Cheap imports from China have also helped keep American inflation at bay.

The problem for the U.S. has diminished as Hu and Wen tolerated a 31 per cent rise in the value of China's currency on foreign exchange markets since 2005, and China's trade surplus has narrowed. Though the government retains the ability to manipulate the currency, the undervaluation of the currency is now reduced.

Under Hu and Wen, the Chinese economic "miracle" continued. Gross domestic product (GDP) rose at about the same average 10 per cent annual rate as in the 23 preceding years under Deng Xiaoping and Jiang Zemin–a huge advance over the 4 per cent annual growth rate under Mao Zedong. Per capita GDP in 2013 was 6,747 in U.S. dollars, an amount that could purchase half again as much in China as in the United States due to the lower cost of goods and services in China. Nonetheless, only about half of all Chinese previously living in poverty–less than $2.00 a day–have moved up the economic ladder. Hundreds of millions have escaped poverty, but a large number still remain destitute. Per capita income, even on a purchasing parity basis, is far less than that in the United States. China still has a long way to go to become a "middle-class nation." Only about 300 million or so Chinese out of more than 1,300 million are now middle class–less than 25 per cent.

In 2012, the Hu-Wen era ended, and the CCP chose Xi Jinping as president and Li Keqiang as premier for 10-year terms. Five of the seven members of the Standing Committee are protégés of the aged former president Jiang Zemin. All five are expected to retire by 2017 when Hu's protégés on the 25-member Central Committee may well move up and tip the balance on the Standing Committee to the Communist-Youth-League faction. That Jiang and Hu can wield power even after leaving office is another illustration of the lingering Confucian deference to elders. Conservatives outnumber political reformers on the Standing Committee

## B. Challenges Still Abound

### 1. Slowing Growth Rate

Hu Jintao stated in 2007 that China needed to grow at 8 per cent annually for the foreseeable future. Such a rate seems necessary for CCP to accomplish its goals of creating a modern balanced economy, lifting the great majority of its people out of poverty, and, incidentally, legitimating the authoritarian rule of the CCP. Premier Li Keqiang refined the goal in 2013 stating that China still needs over 7 per cent annual growth.

Such growth would lead almost to a quadrupling of the economy in just 20 years–a feat without precedent for an economy of its present size. While China grew at an average of about 10 per cent annually from the beginning of the Deng Xiaoping era to the present, the growth started from a much lower base, and China did not face some of the obstacles it faces today.

One challenge for China's new leaders is to reform state-owned enterprises (SOEs) that show a profit only because of government subsidies. Both Chinese and foreign economists urge greater reliance on the private sector for necessary growth. The CCP members who run these SOEs and have enriched themselves are expected, however, to resist reform fiercely.

China must also wrestle with total domestic debt at over 200 per cent of GDP and corporate debt at an estimated 128 per cent of GDP. Profligate lending and borrowing are particularly acute at local levels where most of the 100,000 or so SOEs are controlled. Loans from state banks to the SOEs are too often made on the basis of political connections rather than on an analysis of creditworthiness and efficient use of resources. Such practices have led to over-capacity and over-investment in shipbuilding, steel, cement, construction and infrastructure, to fragmented industries, to sharply rising real estate prices, and to shaky bank balance sheets. With its debt burden China has lost some fiscal flexibility and risks future financial instability. One source of worry is that the People's Bank of China has a shorter history and less experience than financial regulators in the developed nations. Provincial and local banks have been adept at getting around lending limits and making risky loans.

The growth rate is already down to less than 8 per cent. Furthermore, as the economy expands, growth from the resultant larger base will inevitably diminish: such has been the experience of South Korea and Taiwan, which have had their own earlier "economic miracles." China has a slim margin of safety in fending off social unrest while rebalancing its economy away from exports to a modern consumer-driven one.

## 2. Competition by Lower-Wage Countries

China is losing its edge as the preferred low-wage nation. Thanks to the one-child policy, fewer young workers are entering the urban labor force than are retiring from it, and wages are rising (20 per cent a year from 2005 to 2011). The number of working-age Chinese has dropped by almost 6 million in the last two years. Economists at Citigroup estimate a reduction of more than 3 per cent in China's growth rate from the one-child policy in the next 15 years.

Recent changes in the policy allow a second child if either spouse is an only child; previously only couples both of whom were only children qualified for a second child. The new policy will have little effect on dampening wage demands for 15 to 20 years until the hoped-for larger crop of babies grows up. Meanwhile, the labor force will continue to shrink and wages to rise.

The new policy may even immediately increase the shrinkage of the labor force as urban parents and grandparents reduce their hours of work to care for more children. On the other hand, money spent on a second child will modestly contribute to the shift of the economy toward consumption–a small plus and a small minus.

Some businesses in China are moving to lower-wage countries elsewhere. New foreign direct investment (FDI) has also begun to shift to lower-wage countries. Indonesia, for instance, is now almost as favored a site for FDI as China. Much investment, even by Chinese enterprises, is also flowing to Africa.

Higher wages, moreover, are causing China to lose customers as well as FDI. Chinese exports will trend down. On the other hand, there are two positive offsets to competition from lower-wage countries for foreign investment and for exports. First, there are still hundreds of millions of people in China who consume very little, and higher wages will increase their purchases. As increased internal demand for goods and services rises, China's economy may continue to grow even as some corporations and FDI move to lower wage countries and as exports taper off. Second, some businesses in China are moving from the coastal provinces to the lower-wage interior provinces rather than to other countries, a trend that will help to close the economic gap between the coast and the interior.

### 3. Shifting to domestic consumption

Achievement of a better-balanced economy is still many years in the future. Domestic consumption in China's *developing* economy is presently only about 45 percent of GDP, far below that of a middle-class *developed* economy–70 per cent in the United States. The rest of China's GDP has consisted of investment and exports. Too much of GDP depends on heavy industry and construction. Yet there is still great need for more infrastructure. Subways, for instance, are needed to reduce traffic congestion in China's cities–often half again as clogged as New York City–and to reduce severe air pollution. Proposed movement of some 10 million rural folk to cities will also require continued heavy expenditure on infrastructure.

Presumably increased wages, as noted above, will lead to more consumption but at the same time reduce exports as production shifts to lower-wage competitors. Shifting to a middle-class *developed* economy will be a difficult task. The economic decisions facing China's leaders are far more complicated than those facing the world's developed nations.

### 4. Economic problems of China's customers

China is also affected by the present economic problems of its export customers, especially the United States and the European Union, both of which have experienced slow growth and/or recession in the last six years. It may be difficult to maintain the 8 per cent growth rate for the foreseeable future deemed necessary by Hu Jintao in 2007 when major customers are retrenching their own economies.

### 5. Unavailability of foreign currency reserves

A corollary economic problem is the unavailability of $1.2 trillion lent by China to the United States government to help finance its deficit. If China asked for repayment to invest in its own economy, the U.S. would be forced into borrowing funds from other sources to repay China. The rise in interest rates to borrow such a large sum would almost certainly cause a recession in the United States, and Americans would then buy fewer Chinese goods–perhaps even causing a recession in China.

China cannot, therefore, ask for repayment of its loans to the United States. In short, a huge sum of money is essentially locked up and unavailable to China for solving its domestic social problems, such as the inadequacy of pensions and health care. There is little reason to believe that China will not have to continue lending money to the United States to help cover its deficit for the foreseeable future; it has, in fact, accelerated its purchases of U.S.

Treasury bonds in 2014. There is one good result of this strange "marriage." The economic dependency of the two on each other reduces the possibility of armed conflict between them.

## 6. Pensions and health care

Another economic problem stems from the inadequacy of public funds for meaningful pensions and health care for China's 185 million elderly citizens who comprised 11 percent of the population in 2010, a proportion expected to rise to over 400 million or 30 percent by 2050. Pensions at present are quite inadequate. Rural pensions, for instance, average a meager $100 a year, and some 42 million elderly are estimated to subsist on about $500 a year.

As in the Confucian era, most Chinese are dependent on their children–often one child–for most support in their old age, a situation aggravated by the breaking of the iron rice bowl in state-owned enterprises and the failure of private companies to take up the slack. With the population now aging, provision of adequate retirement funds for all will either severely strain public finances or family finances.

Some additional funds would be available if significant social security taxes were charged against increasing wages. An increase in public financing of retirement would allow Chinese of all ages to save less and consume more, thus helping to rebalance the economy. Adequate funds are not likely to be available, though, for the next 20 years or so until the working-class cohort starts increasing as fast as senior citizens. As matters stand, fear of poverty in old age causes many to save rather than to consume, impeding a shift of the economy toward greater consumption and continued growth.

## 7. Military Expenditures

The PLA has been the ultimate arbiter of Chinese policy ever since Mao Zedong ordered it in 1968 to stop the chaos of the Cultural Revolution. Its relation to the government has generally been one in which it stays out of politics so long as the government continuously increases military budgets. These annual increases of about 10 per cent compete with other needs, such as pensions, and put a further strain on the national budget.

## 8. Emigration of Talent and Money

An economic problem that has recently developed is emigration by many entrepreneurs and skilled professionals because of the persistence of corruption, possible threats by the CCP to continued economic freedom, political uncertainties, and polluted air to breathe.

Money and talent needed for tasks in modernizing China are leaving the country. An estimated $600 billion in capital left the country illegally in 2011. The "brain drain" is also substantial. Some 150,000 Chinese obtained permanent foreign residency in 2011 including 80,000 who obtained United States green cards. This emigration of talent is not being offset by immigration of foreign talent. China's total population of foreign-born residents of *all levels of education* is only about 800,000. The number of foreign-born residents of the United States with at least a bachelor's degree in science and engineering is over 4,000,000. A large outflow of skills and small inflow–mostly from Chinese returning home–poses problems for China.

## 9. Air pollution and other environmental problems

China has paid an enormous environmental price for its creation of an embryonic middle class. The Air Quality Index, for instance, on January 14, 2013, registered 755, well beyond "Hazardous," in Beijing and a mere 13 in New York City. China now uses almost as much coal as the rest of the world combined. Solving the air quality problems in the major cities will be costly and make China less competitive, another economic challenge. The government faces a dilemma: grow the economy rapidly even with its already abundant challenges or make the quality and length of life better for the people–and for the warming world as well. Promotions of regional leaders until recently had been judged above all on their contributions to the growth of GDP.

Wind and solar energy will not eliminate the dilemma until they become cost effective, still many years in the future. Probably even further in the future is a solution based on underwater tide-driven turbines that are presently even less cost effective.

According to the U.S. Energy Information Agency, China has possibly the largest recoverable shale-gas resources in the world, an energy source much cleaner than coal. Geological factors and lack of sufficient water, though, make shale-gas development difficult. Very frequent peasant protests in densely populated rural areas compound the difficulties. The likelihood of rapid development of shale-gas production to benefit the world along with China is slim, though Shell Oil has announced a joint venture to begin the work in Sichuan Province.

Loss of arable land is a serious challenge for a country with 20 percent of world population but less than 10 percent of the world's arable land. Losses stem from urbanization, contamination of rice supplies from deposits of toxic heavy metals on farm land, creeping desertification of western provinces; water pollution from industrial dumping, and rapidly falling water tables. Water shortages are particularly acute in North China where almost 30 per cent of China's population depends on only 7 per cent of China's surface water. All these problems run counter to the Daoist aspect of China's traditional culture–respect for nature–which will generate strong public demands for environmental solutions.

China's environmental problems also extend beyond its borders. The desire of China's newly wealthy for high-end furniture is contributing to the destruction of rain forests in New Guinea, for traditional ivory carvings to the illegal massacre of elephants in Africa, and for shark fin soup to the annual slaughter of millions of sharks, including endangered species.

## 10. Inequalities

Despite some attention by Hu and Wen during their ten-year terms to inequalities in Chinese society, large gaps remain between the coast and the interior, between workers in the private sector and the state sector, and between the cities and the countryside. One advance was initiation of a rudimentary health care insurance plan for rural citizens.

Some steps have also benefited the 250 million or so rural Chinese who have flooded into the cities looking for better-paid work. Migrant workers can now have labor representation. The government has also relaxed the *hukou* system binding peasants to their rural localities. Migrant workers without the proper papers are no longer "deported" to their home localities; but these "illegal immigrants" receive no benefits, often live in crowded, squalid conditions, and earn less than their established urban counterparts.

The effect of *hukou* is different for unmarried workers and for married workers with children. Unmarried workers often return to their rural villages when it comes time to raise a family, thus depriving the urban industrial hubs of their labor and their acquired skills. Married workers with children faced with tuition charges for educating their children in the cities tend to leave their families in the countryside where education is free up to ninth grade. Because they do not own their land, only lease it, they cannot sell their land and obtain the means to pay for educating their children in a city. This separation of millions of families is a daunting social problem for China, but a complex one, for migration to the cities supplies the labor needed in China's industrial centers and at the same time reduces the labor supply back home and raises rural wages.

The government also faces an investment dilemma concerning migration to the cities. Some 36 per cent of Chinese still earn a living from agriculture–compared to 1 per cent in the United States. Labor shortages aggravated by the one-child policy make rural migration necessary but require rapid improvements in urban housing and infrastructure to prevent creation of slums like those surrounding Rio de Janeiro. Just the right amount of migration at just the right time rather than too much too soon is a tricky problem.

Continuing discouragement of mobility by discrimination against migrants seems likely to persist, though Hu and Wen began to ease the problem by permitting "long-term" migrants who had worked in cities for a certain number of years to become permanent residents. They can now find "legal" jobs, receive some benefits, bring their families, and educate their children at state expense.

Two effects of this change are that these new permanent residents will earn more and spend more, helping to shift China from an export-driven economy to a consumer-driven one–but at the same time aggravating China's loss of its edge as the preferred low-wage nation.

A cultural offset to the many economic problems discussed in the last several pages is a legacy from the Confucian past. When the government finally succeeds in establishing world-class research universities to help upgrade the Chinese economy from low tech to high tech, the lingering heritage of Confucian devotion to scholarship will play a major role in solving economic problems, as will Confucian dedication to hard work and self-cultivation. Even here, though, there are obstacles. Despite the CCP's simplification of written Chinese characters and the earlier campaign by Hu Shi and others to write in the vernacular, it is still a time-consuming task in the lower grades to learn to write well. Moreover, too much education is still mere learning by rote, hardly a way to encourage innovative thinking.

## 11. Widespread Corruption

Controlling corruption is a political problem for the government and an economic problem for its victims–especially peasants, estimated at some 40 to 50 million to date, whose *lease* of farm land was terminated for inadequate compensation by local cadres to sell to developers. Peasants are often compensated for expropriated land at its value for agricultural use rather than its value for development, which is as much as 50 to 70 times greater. Local cadres have deprived some 40 million peasants of all or part of their land since 1990. Promotion of local cadres to higher offices long depended simply on the full-speed-ahead urban growth furnished by developers, a corrupt crony capitalism. Left without a livelihood, cheated peasants often have no choice but to migrate to a city in violation of the *hukou* system and to work at whatever wages are offered. Since the 1989 crushing of the pro-democracy movement in Tiananmen Square, public protests have centered on land confiscation–estimated at 65 per cent of all of the *hundreds of thousands* of public protests each year.

Other protests decry corrupt accumulations of wealth, often by children of high officials. Nepotism is a problem carried over from the imperial era. Unfortunately, the PRC has not adopted such imperial safeguards as rotation of officials every three years and never appointing officials to posts in their native provinces. The CCP needs to combat corruption successfully in order to retain its legitimacy. Recent prosecutions of a general and of people surrounding a former member of the Standing Committee indicate that Xi Jinping is serious about rooting out corruption.

The great growth of the economy and the enhanced material well-being of hundreds of millions have temporarily dampened demands for democracy. China with the exception of a few years under Sun Yatsen has had an authoritarian government for millennia. Under Confucian doctrine, such a government was the natural form of government, provided that the ruler governed benevolently. If an emperor governed oppressively, Heaven would transfer its Mandate to the founder of a new dynasty. The gist of this doctrine remains embedded in Chinese culture. Confucius and Mencius still speak through the ages in the culturally formed assumptions of many Chinese. A democracy movement may once again challenge the CCP if it fails to make progress against corruption.

# *11. China and the United States*

In four decades from the 1980s to the 2010s, the PRC changed from a revolutionary state under Mao Zedong to a status-quo state seeking safety and stability under Hu Jintao. The PRC generally remained at peace with other countries, a continuation of China's historical peaceful behavior. Not since the Sui dynasty 1,500 years ago have the Chinese sought permanent occupation of other lands for any purposes other than to secure their borders or to reassert sovereignty over areas they considered to have always been a part of China. The nearest exception was the annexation of Tibet in 1950, but that is ambiguous, for Tibet was nominally a part of China from 1724 to 1912.

Imperial China had a tributary system, especially during the Ming and Qing dynasties at the end of the Imperial era. Surrounding states periodically came to the Chinese capital, offered modest gifts as tribute–often matched by Chinese gifts–and recognized a vague suzerainty over them by the emperor. Tribute missions were often just trading missions and did not imply any real political control over the tribute bearers by the emperor. China sought recognition of its importance in Asia but rarely interfered in other countries except to protect an ally.

China's record in world affairs since the end of the Mao Zedong era, to the limited extent it has participated, has been positive. China has participated responsibly in the World Trade Organization, the World Bank, and the International Monetary Fund. China has supplied ground troops thirteen times to United Nations peacekeeping forces and naval forces to combat Somali pirates. It has settled some border disputes peacefully by negotiation. China has also abandoned the Marxist revolutionary ideology of the Maoist era.

Until recently, the Chinese have viewed themselves as a poor nation too weak to take on major international responsibilities. Not once has China taken the lead to solve a major global problem and produce results. China's leaders have instead concentrated on economic growth without much concern for its effect on other nations or on climate change. They have generally deferred to the United States in world affairs in fighting terrorism, in maintaining peace in the Middle East, in promoting nuclear nonproliferation, in providing leadership on international trade, and in maintaining maritime security.

China may have changed under the new leadership of Xi Jinping. Chinese economic success has recently changed their view of themselves. The goal of the Self-Strengthening movement of the late 19th century to adopt Western technology to protect China from foreign aggression has been achieved. The Fifth Generation of leaders now sees China–accurately–-as a major player in world affairs and has become more assertive. Several factors contribute to this shift in addition to the American "pivot" toward the Pacific. Psychologically, China has regained some sense of being, once again, the Middle Kingdom, as it was for 2,000 years, a center of world civilization. China also still harbors deep resentment of its never-forgotten 19th century humiliation by the Western powers. Some extreme nationalists in China believe that the West will always remain a threat to China with a goal unchanged since the 19th century of "commerce at bayonet point" and that war can be averted, if at all, only by superior Chinese military strength.

## A. The United States Pivot to Asia

Unfortunately, the Obama administration's unnecessary announcement of a "pivot," military as well as political and economic, from the Atlantic to the Pacific can only fuel China's historic resentments and raise Chinese suspicions that the United States wants to "contain" China. Pivots can only fuel extremist thinking.

Militarily, the United States has announced that it will maintain 60 percent of its naval strength in the Pacific region, up from a previous 50 percent. With a navy already much larger than that of China, the previous 50 per cent was surely adequate for any purpose of the United States except to send a message to China--a message sure to stir up latent resentments. Are the Chinese really naive enough to think the United States is trying to do anything other than keeping the military strength to prevent China from having much say in Asian affairs, anything other than keeping the United States' position as world hegemon?

## B. Hot Spots

The possibility of war between the United States and China can no longer be discounted. China asserts sovereignty over Taiwan and islands in the East and South China Seas. The situation in the South China Sea, where China is presently making aggressive moves, is by far the most fraught with danger.

## 1. Taiwan

Taiwan, which became a refuge for the defeated Nationalists in 1949, is traditionally part of China. Hu Jintao offered peace talks with Taiwan provided the island first recognize that it is still a part of China. Taiwan's government has not yet responded to the offer of talks.

The PRC seeks to reunite with Taiwan under a concept advanced by Deng Xiaoping: "one country, two systems," an arrangement whereby Taiwan would retain its existing capitalist economic and democratic political organization. China had already reunited with Hong Kong and Macau in the 1990s under that concept, and the PRC long respected this arrangement that may some day resolve the Taiwan issue. A recent attempt by Beijing to require advance approval of candidates of all parties in a Hong Kong election brought hundreds of thousands of citizens to the streets in protest. It remains to be seen whether Beijing will back down and the formula can some day serve to unite Taiwan with the mainland.

The overriding political issue on the island is whether Taiwan is a part of China or an independent nation. The Pan-Blue political coalition, presently in power, argues quixotically that not only is Taiwan a part of China but also that the Taiwanese government is the only legitimate government of all China. The Pan-Green coalition favors independence from China. Should Taiwan declare its independence, the PRC may well use military force to reunite the island with the mainland perhaps dragging the United States into the conflict on Taiwan's side. Fortunately, both political coalitions in Taiwan are cautious in public pronouncements and in their approach to the PRC, which, in turn, tolerates the present status quo.

Substantial investment in the PRC by the more prosperous and technologically advanced Taiwanese has already brought the two economically closer together, a significant step toward a peaceful resolution of the Taiwan issue. Still, the possibility of war, though desired by neither Taiwan nor the PRC, cannot be entirely discounted. Such a war would not, on the one hand, automatically involve the United States. President Jimmy Carter unilaterally abrogated the mutual defense treaty with Taiwan in 1980, one year after the U.S. recognition of the PRC. The PRC, on the other hand, cannot be sure that the United States would not defend Taiwan from attack. When the PRC threatened Taiwan and fired missiles into its territorial waters in 1995-6, the U.S. sent two aircraft carrier battle groups toward the Taiwan Strait.

Any attack by the PRC on Taiwan seems highly unlikely, in any event, because Taiwan has considerable military strength, and an amphibious invasion would be costly. Similarly, destruction of Taiwan's economy by the thousands of missiles along China's coast would hardly benefit China; only peaceful incorporation of Taiwan's vibrant technologically advanced economy would be a gain for the PRC. The present status quo is likely to endure for a long time. One key to a negotiated solution would be adoption of a more democratic form of government by China once the middle class is large enough to bring pressure on the CCP to give up its monopoly of power. The Internet makes such pressure possible, if not easy. Both Taiwan and South Korea shifted to democracy from authoritarianism when the majority of citizens reached middle-class status. Once China reaches a higher economic level, it too may escape the authoritarian aspect of Confucianism. One may note also that no one-party regime in modern history has lasted more than 75 years. If history repeats itself, the CCP will lose power in the next 10 to 15 years.

## 2. North Korea

Another source of tension between the United States and China exists if North Korea, should take some unexpected action such as an invasion of South Korea or firing a nuclear missile on Japan.

The Six-Party Talks over North Korea's violation of the Nuclear Nonproliferation Treaty began in 2003. The talks have had a stop-and-go character over the years. By 2013, North Korea had missiles capable of reaching Japan and possibly an atomic warhead sufficiently small to attach to a missile. Although China would prefer a non-nuclear North Korea, it has generally opposed strong sanctions against the rogue regime. China could easily bring about the collapse of North Korea's regime, which has been dominated by three generations of the Kim family. Cutting off exports of food and fuel to North Korea would accomplish that but with grave consequences for China itself. Millions of Korean refugees might flood across the eight-hundred-mile border into northern China in search of food, an outcome the Chinese are eager to avoid. In early 2013, the Chinese did back extended sanctions on North Korea, but China still prefers the status quo to a collapse of the Kim regime. The United States fears that unless the North Koreans abandon their nuclear ambitions and destroy their arsenal, a nuclear arms race may begin in East Asia as Japan and South Korea seek to produce their own atomic weapons. Such an arms race would create dangers for China, including a possible rapprochement between Japan and South Korea. Those two well-armed nations at present have strained relations because Japan forced Korean women to provide sex for Japanese soldiers in World War II, but the Chinese currently seem to fear a flood of refugees even more than cooperation between Japan and South Korea. The United States has long been reluctant simply to neutralize the North Korean atomic facilities because the PLA, in particular, still considers North Korea an ally. That mind-set is an echo of the PLA's attitude in the Korean War from 1950-53. Moreover, North Korea has thousands of artillery pieces along the border with South Korea, some of which can fire on Seoul. North Korea is, nonetheless, unlikely to start a war it cannot win.

### 3. The East China Sea

Both Japan and China assert sovereignty over some islands in the East China Sea–called Senkaku in Japanese and Diaoyu in Chinese. The United States has a mutual defense treaty with Japan and has reassured Japan that it will honor the treaty. The likelihood of major armed conflict between China and the United States seems remote. Public opinion, however, can influence the formulation of foreign policy, and strong Chinese resentment of Japan's aggression and atrocities in World War II, added to its strong resentment of its 19th century humiliation, is a complicating factor.

### 4. The South China Sea

China, Vietnam, Malaysia, Brunei, Indonesia, and the Philippines all claim islands in the South China Sea–the Paracel islands off the coast of Vietnam in the northern part of the Sea and the Spratly Islands in the middle of the Sea. Some islands have multiple claimants. A map drawn by the Nationalist government under Chiang Kai-shek has a so-called "Nine-Dash Line," a vague hand-drawn map showing Chinese sovereignty over 90 per cent of the South China Sea.

At stake are potential undersea petroleum deposits estimated by the United States at 11 billion barrels of oil, a quantity large enough to supply China's needs for a mere three years. The amount involved would be long dissipated, and China would be still the second largest importer of oil in the world, if not the first, by the time it would be militarily strong enough to challenge the United States–probably no sooner than sometime in the 2030s. Furthermore, the quantity of oil involved seems hardly enough to warrant the damage to China's international reputation if China unilaterally seizes the islands in dispute. China would become a pariah in Asia and would hasten the efforts of some Asian nations to prevent Chinese domination of the continent some time in the next few decades. Japan and India, for instance, are becoming closer and are now participating in joint naval exercises with the United States. The Philippines filed a legal challenge to China's claims with the United Nations tribunal in The Hague in March 2014 to which China has not responded. China has felt compelled, though, to send a document to the U.N. setting forth its position. Vietnam is also considering filing a legal challenge to China's claim to the Paracel islands near Vietnam. The attitude of China's neighbors is constantly hardening even though their close economic ties with China complicate unified action. At present, China's only allies in Asia are North Korea and Cambodia and perhaps Malaysia.

Any Chinese invasion of one of its neighbors, *other than one of the disputed islands*, is highly unlikely because they are major trading partners of the PRC. The economic consequences to both would be severe. Besides, such an invasion might further formation of a coalition to oppose aggression. Conceivably China might have to oppose Japan, South Korea, Vietnam, India, the Philippines, Indonesia, and Myanmar–and perhaps Australia and New

Zealand–simultaneously. Defense of China's enormously long border with ground troops is practically impossible.

An attack by China on Philippine forces beyond mere skirmishing would involve the United States, which has a mutual defense treaty with the Philippines. The possible costs to both the United States and China are likely to deter any attack by the Chinese on the Philippines.

An attack by China on Malaysia or Vietnam is similarly improbable. Malaysia is already a large producer of oil and seems willing to cooperate with China, perhaps hoping to keep all or part of its oil by such cooperation. Vietnam fought both the United States and China to a draw in the 1970's. Its military capabilities are significant; its active duty forces are about 500,000, sufficient *on defense* to confront a much larger Chinese offense.

Furthermore, these countries have been cultivating good relations with the United States, and China cannot know if an attack directly on them (other than just an occupation of the disputed islands) would bring an American response despite the absence of any "entangling alliances." Chinese aggressiveness would also likely spur military cooperation among the other claimants to the islands, countries not without modern military strength/ experience in guerrilla warfare, especially Vietnam. On the other hand, it is unlikely that the United States would react militarily to Chinese attacks limited to the disputed islands themselves. The United States has not taken any position as to which countries own any islands in dispute. *The fate of these small, sparsely inhabited islands is hardly a major concern of the United States.*

## C. The United States: World Hegemon?

Another risk of war between China and the United States involves an academic theory about causes of war between a hegemon (or dominant super power) and a rising super power: the power-transition theory. According to the theory when a hegemon, the nation that unilaterally sets the rules for international relations and seeks to maintain the status quo, is faced with another rapidly growing power, there is a significant danger of war between the two just before or just after the challenger surpasses the hegemon in power (a ill-defined term including military, economic, and all other types of power). The theory has become a new paradigm that both China and the United States are taking seriously. Secretary of State John Kerry noted that such a clash is not an inevitability but a choice. According to the theory, the aggressor is normally the rising power. The United States should treat China in a way that will discourage that choice.

At present the United States is the world hegemon, and a look at how it achieved that position is instructive about China's chance to achieve a similar domination. The United States became world hegemon because it was the only developed nation that ended World War II with its industrial base intact. It then produced about 50 per cent of the world's goods, a share that has dwindled to less than 25 per cent as the other developed nations recovered over the last 60-odd years. With the newly developing countries also becoming stronger economically and militarily in a global economy, it is likely that by the 2050s there will be no hegemon. No nation, including the United States will be powerful enough to impose its own rules unilaterally on the rest of the world. The world order is already changing. Five nations–Brazil, Russia, India, China, and

South Africa–are considering alternatives to the World Bank and International Monetary Fund, organizations whose U.S.-backed financial rules have controlled world finance for decades.

China will be unable to become the new hegemon. First, while China has been increasing its military spending at about 10 per cent a year, the United States, according to a Pentagon estimate (adjusted for purchasing power parity) spends at least four to six times as much on its military annually. Because pay scales in the U.S. military are higher, moreover, the gap between Chinese and American expenditures on more military equipment is surely even less than four to six times. Offsetting China's ability to spend more on equipment than is apparent from the Pentagon estimate is the far greater stock of weapons already possessed by the United States. China will have to play "catch up" for many years to rival the U. S. China has too many serious economic, social, and political problems to solve without attacking the United States' armed forces.

China borders 14 other nations, many of which have significant economic and military strength. The United States need not fear domination by China and must realize that *it is soon to lose its own position as world hegemon.* The world in the future will eventually be multipolar, not bipolar or monopolar. In a multipolar world, cooperation among nations to compromise and to maintain peaceful international relations is more likely than in the present prospective brief bipolar situation.

Both China and the United States each possess weapons of mass destruction. These include not only atomic weapons but soon may include cyber warfare, a possible way to paralyze a nation's electrical grid and its financial, communications, and transportation systems and achieve victory before a single shot is fired–a modern application of the military strategy of Sun Wu from the 6th century, B.C.E. Such a paralysis of the electrical grid could lead to mass starvation if long continued. Both nations are working on capabilities and defenses in cyber warfare. Fortunately, mutual destruction should not appeal to either China or the United States.

The United States is entitled to protect and promote its own national interests, such as seeking solutions to terrorism and unrest in the Middle East, insisting on rights of free navigation in international waters, protection of our allies in Europe, Japan, South Korea, and the Philippines under our treaty obligations, and perhaps even enforcement of the Monroe Doctrine if a nation in the New World requests help. It should be willing to participate in internationally authorized actions. In a multipolar world, however, the United States cannot deter or defeat any action no matter where in the world. It is time for the United States to take a first step of withdrawal from its present role of world hegemon, a sign that the United States is not a threat to China. Future steps at appropriate times and intervals will encourage China to cooperate in keeping the peace. Facing future reality is not a sign of weakness but of wisdom.

For the last three decades China and the United States have enjoyed mostly friendly relations. The United States would make a great mistake if it sought to "contain" China. There is no need to create a new Cold War.

There will be disputes between the two countries as each has different particular interests. For the United States, issues of intellectual property rights, China's appetite for raw materials, manipulation of the value of China's currency, discrimination against American firms in China, North Korean misbehavior, and, especially, cyber security will be the most important. Human rights may also be an occasional issue. Some issues they will resolve in whole, some in part, and sometimes they will simply agree to disagree. Both nations should make clear to each other in what areas they have strong disagreements and in what areas they can cooperate more fully on the world stage. Among the latter are, for instance, mutual economic interests, threats to both from terrorism, now increasing in the Uighur regions of western China, climate change, and, of course, the maintenance of peace.

More important than specific disputes, though, is the basic attitude that each will take to the other. The harder task psychologically will be that of the United States, which is still the world's hegemon (or dominant super power). Accepting a change from a monopolar world to a bipolar or multipolar one will not be easy. The world is changing, however, and sometime in the 21st century there will probably be at least 4 super powers: the United States, China, India, the European Union and, maybe, Russia.

Wisdom dictates that the United States now should accept China as a future great power–something inevitable anyway–and seek Chinese cooperation in maintaining a stable, peaceful world. There is no reason for the United States to oppose China's rise in power. China is a commercial competitor of the United States, not an ideological competitor, as was the case with the Soviet Union. Since the death of Mao Zedong, China has never expressed any desire to impose its ideology on the United States. With its mixture of free enterprise and state capitalism, China may not even have an ideology.

Americans will also need to react less negatively to much of the nationalistic rhetoric that can be expected from China in the near and medium terms as that nation slowly consolidates a more internationalist outlook less influenced by its humiliation in the 19th century and the quasi-destruction of its remarkable agricultural civilization. Not all nationalist rhetoric should be taken at face value. Politically, the leaders of the PRC can find an aggressive tone useful to deflect public opinion away from the multiple problems that China presently faces, a technique of deflecting internal unrest as old as civilization itself. Moderate Chinese leaders can also ward off internal criticism from extreme nationalists still incensed by the humiliations of the 19th century by co-opting their rhetoric.

Americans will also need to realize that China is not destined to become a democracy in the near future. Hectoring China's leaders about democracy will only raise their suspicion that the United States is seeking regime change and lessen chances for mutual cooperation. China's leaders have made clear their view that loss of power by the CCP now would result in internal chaos. Whatever society China develops over coming decades, it will have a large Confucian component probably including some degree of authoritarianism and respect for Confucian morality and the Mandate of Heaven. Confucian values are already reemerging in Chinese life.

In the meantime, both nations must bear in mind that each possesses weapons of mass destruction.

Consultations between Chinese and American political and military leaders should be frequent and according to a fixed schedule. Periodic conferences on Asian issues should include leaders of Japan, Russia, Vietnam, South Korea, Malaysia, the Philippines, Australia, Laos, Cambodia, Thailand, Myanmar, Indonesia, India, and others, for these Asian nations together potentially dwarf both China and the United States in economic and military power. India's economy, alone, is predicted by some to become larger than China's before the end of the present century. India's demography is now far more favorable to development than

China's. Young people entering the work force will continue to exceed the number of people retiring for decades to come. India will be the new land of cheap labor.

The nations of the North Atlantic have reached what seems to be a permanent peace with each other. The border between Canada and the United States, for instance, is by far the longest unsecured border in the world, and European nations appear to have given up their centuries-old habit of regularly attacking each other. Despite greater internal cultural differences, Asia can emulate the North Atlantic. China and the United States, though, will have to show leadership to achieve such a result.

# *About the Author*

George Du Bois has been an avid student of history for the past 50 years, both professionally and for personal pleasure. He grew up in Chevy Chase, Maryland. He received his B.A. from Cornell University, where he first studied Chinese history. He obtained the degree of Doctor of Jurisprudence in 1957 from the University of Virginia, where he taught a course on labor law. His first book was *Cross-Class Alliances and the Birth of Modern Liberalism: Maryland's Workers, 1865-1916.* He also taught in independent schools for many years, including courses on Chinese history. He obtained his Ph.D. in history from the University of Maryland in 1995. The present volume is the product of eight years of research and writing. The author of several articles on historical topics in *The Torch* magazine, Du Bois lives with his wife in Frederick, Maryland.